Right Moves

Right Moves

The Conservative Think Tank in
American Political Culture since 1945

Jason Stahl

The University of North Carolina Press *Chapel Hill*

This book was published with the assistance of the
Thornton H. Brooks Fund of the University of North Carolina Press.

© 2016 The University of North Carolina Press
All rights reserved
Set in Espinosa Nova and Alegreya Sans by Westchester Publishing Services
Manufactured in the United States of America

The paper in this book meets the guidelines for permanence and durability
of the Committee on Production Guidelines for Book Longevity of the
Council on Library Resources. The University of North Carolina Press
has been a member of the Green Press Initiative since 2003.

Library of Congress Cataloging-in-Publication Data
Stahl, Jason, author.
Right moves : the conservative think tank in American political culture
since 1945 / Jason Stahl.
pages cm
Includes bibliographical references and index.
ISBN 978-1-4696-2786-1 (cloth : alk. paper)
ISBN 978-1-4696-4635-0 (pbk. : alk. paper)
ISBN 978-1-4696-2787-8 (ebook)
1. Conservatism—United States—History—20th century. 2. Conservatism—
United States—History—21st century. 3. Research institutes—United States—
History. 4. Political culture—United States. 5. United States—Politics and
government—1945-1989. 6. United States—Politics and government—1989-
I. Title.
JC573.2.U6S73 2016
320.520973—dc23
2015028433

For Elliot and Corinne

Contents

Acknowledgments

I am honored to publish this book with the University of North Carolina Press and am particularly thankful to my editor, Joe Parsons. Joe took a chance on this project and convinced the press to award an advance contract when even I was not fully convinced it deserved one. Joe has since been a tireless advocate for the project every step of the way. He and the entire press have been supportive of the vision I had for the book throughout the process. Joe also secured two fantastic readers for my manuscript: Alice O'Connor and Andrew Hartman. Both Professor O'Connor and Professor Hartman offered the right mix of praise and trenchant criticism. This book is immensely better because of their readings. I offer additional thanks to Professor Hartman, whose 2012 offer of a guest post at the U.S. Intellectual History Blog led to my eventual book contract with UNC Press.

I have been at the University of Minnesota for the last fifteen years, first as a graduate student and now as a teacher. In my time here, I have made friends across the university who have supported the creation of this book in ways both large and small. First, to Ryan Murphy—a true friend if there ever was one. You have supported my personal and intellectual growth unlike anyone I have ever known, and this book is better for having known you. To Lary May and Elaine Tyler May for being the best advisers and friends anyone could ask for. Your unwavering support has sustained me over the past seven years. Thanks to Sarah Crabtree for your friendship, wit, and intelligence, and thanks to Kevin Murphy for your friendship and support when I needed it most. Thank you to Jeff Manuel for your friendship and your ability to get me to think about my work in new ways. Thank you to Pam Butler and Mark Soderstrom for your support and friendship. Thank you to Melissa Williams, Megan Feeney, Danny LaChance, and others from the May House Reading Group. You all asked the right questions about this project when it was still in its infancy. Thank you to other mentors and committee members I had while a graduate student at the U of M, including J. B. Shank, Karen Ho, Keith Mayes, Timothy Brennan, and Lisa Norling. Special thanks to Barbara Welke—another mentor and committee member who was particularly supportive during my time as a graduate student. I am grateful to everyone I met and became friends with on the 2004–5 campaign to unionize the graduate students at the U of M. Although we lost, I met individuals from across the university I never would have known otherwise—many of whom prodded me to think in new ways, which are reflected in this book. Additionally, I am grateful to those in the Department of Postsecondary Teaching and Learning (PSTL) who were supportive while I taught there from 2010 through 2015. In particular, I am extremely grateful for the friendship of Kris Cory, Rashne Jehangir, K. C. Harrison, Tabitha Grier-Reed, Margaret Kelly, Bob Poch, and Mike Stebleton. Thanks to Rebecca Ropers-Huilman in the Department of Organizational Leadership and Policy Development for helping me secure my newest faculty home at Minnesota. Finally, thank you to Dean Na'im Madyun for your unwavering support and trust over the years.

I'm extremely grateful for the external financial support this book received as well. Thanks to the Gerald Ford Foundation for a travel grant. Additionally, I owe an enormous debt of gratitude to the American Historical Association and the Library of Congress for their J. Franklin Jameson Fellowship. The Jameson Fellowship was the only time I had during the entire researching and writing of this book where I could devote all of my mental energies to the book itself. The fellowship allowed for two months of research and writing in the John W. Kluge Center at the Library of Congress in Washington, D.C. It was during these two months that the central arguments in this book took shape as I was able to immerse myself in the archives and within the scholarly community at the Kluge Center. The librarians and archivists at the library ensured that I made the best use of my entire time there, and the other scholars at the Kluge Center, particularly Johanna Bockman, pushed me to think more deeply about my subject.

Numerous other archivists and librarians have assisted in the research for this book, including those at the Hoover Institution, the Gerald R. Ford Presidential Library, the William J. Clinton Presidential Library, and the Arizona Historical Foundation. I want, in particular, to single out Linda Whitaker at the Arizona Historical Foundation who saved me a trip to Tempe by mailing me files after doing photocopying work herself. Without all of these librarians and archivists, all historians would be lost.

I have been very fortunate to publish work related to this book in online forums at the U.S. Intellectual History Blog and Salon.com. I am enormously grateful to both forums for these opportunities. In publishing at both of these places, I reached a readership I would not have otherwise. These readers pushed me to clarify my arguments, and the editors at these sites pushed me to write for a wide audience. Additionally, these readers and editors continue to be invested in the promotion of my work, and I cannot thank them enough for this. In this regard, I'd like to single out Mike Konczal, Ben Alpers, Robert Greene, L. D. Burnett, Tim Lacy, Blake Zeff, Alex Halperin, and Jane Mayer.

Thank you to my high school English teacher Barbara Funke, who taught me how to write and convinced me I might be able to write well enough that others would want to read what I wrote. Thanks to Professor Jim Madison and Andy Evans for making me want to be a historian. Thank you to Regan Ryan for your friendship and for always prodding me to consider conservative arguments that are heartfelt and well articulated. Thank you to my parents for your love and support and for convincing me to pursue my education to the fullest. Thank you to my siblings, Jeff, Mandy, and Mark. I love you all. Thanks especially to Mark for your friendship and for taking interest in this book over the years. Thank you to my in-laws Tim Connolly and Nancy Connolly for always taking a legitimate interest in what I do for a living.

Throughout the entire writing of this book, I have been immersed in a heavy teaching load. While the demands of my teaching have sometimes inhibited the research and writing of this book, I am nevertheless grateful to the hundreds of University of Minnesota undergraduates who have kept me grounded throughout this process. Through my teaching, I feel socially connected in a way I otherwise would not. Doing all of this teaching, research, and writing would not have been possible without enormous support structures in place. In this regard, I want to thank all of my teaching assistants over the last six years, as well as the research assistants who helped with the work of this book—Rose Miron, Makiki Reuvers, and Lauren Rosenberg. Most important, I want to thank all the child care workers at the University of Minnesota Child Development Center as well as Carol Sexton for caring for my two children. It was nice knowing they were in good hands when I could not be there with them myself.

Finally, thanks to my wife, Katie Connolly, and our children. Katie, after seventeen years together, only you know all it took to complete this project. Without you, this book would obviously not exist. You supported me when I didn't support myself, and you kept me focused on this project's completion when I wanted to give up. I owe you everything. To Elliot and Corinne, your births and young childhoods have undoubtedly made the writing of this book a greater challenge than it otherwise would have been. But what you have brought to my life was worth it all. You have given this book new purpose, and you have brought intense periods of joy to my daily existence. I love you both and dedicate this book to you.

Right Moves

Introduction

In November 1962, William J. Baroody Sr., the recently anointed president of the American Enterprise Institute (AEI), a small "research institute" in Washington, D.C., wrote one of his newly hired research assistants a letter explaining his duties in AEI's "Special Projects" program. The recipient was thirty-nine-year-old Karl Hess. Although Baroody was only seven years Hess's senior, the letter was written as if from a father to his son. Baroody offered friendly but stern warnings to his new employee with whom he was also a friend. As with Baroody, Hess was a committed conservative and both men would go on, only a year and a half later, to work on Barry Goldwater's 1964 campaign for the presidency. Hess undoubtedly came to Baroody's AEI given that, in Washington, it was viewed as a "business-friendly" research institute—especially when contrasted to the more reliably liberal Brookings Institution. Hess came to AEI to turn his personal conservatism into political action. In his letter to Hess, Baroody gave his friend a rude awakening in this regard, writing that in Hess's job "the 'don'ts' are every bit as significant in this respect as the 'do's.' The Institute does *not* press any particular policy position or even attempt to form, suggest, or support any particular policy position. The Institute *does* attempt to provide the research assistance which will bring to bear upon any policy consideration the most pertinent facts available and the most knowledgeable considerations by acknowledged authorities in the field. By thus informing policy considerations, at the request of policymakers, we can make our only and best contribution to the educative support of policy discussions. We serve, in this respect, as a research adjunct to the staffs of all policymakers who request our assistance. It is they, regardless of their political positions, who must form the actual policy. We can provide only such research background and assistance as they request."[1] In essence, Baroody was telling Hess to check his conservatism at the door when working on AEI's "Special Projects." In his job, Hess was only to serve as a "research adjunct" to Congress and provide "pertinent facts," not policy advocacy.

Almost exactly ten years later, in October 1972, the same William Baroody, still as president of AEI, rose before a group of corporate leaders in Hot Springs, Virginia, to deliver a speech entitled "The Corporate Role in the Decade Ahead." In the speech, Baroody took a starkly different view of public policy formation than he had in the letter to Hess. Gone were paeans to objectivity and disinterestedness. In their place were metaphors of war, competition, and the marketing of pro-business public policy. Borrowing a line from renowned public intellectual Daniel Bell, Baroody argued that there had been an "abdication of the corporate class" when it came to advocating business-friendly policies in a "marketplace of ideas." As such, Baroody argued that within the public policy community, there now existed "a monopoly hostile to business." Baroody argued that "to break this monopoly requires a calculated, positive, major commitment—one which will insure that the views of other competent [business-friendly] intellectuals are given the opportunity to contend effectively in the mainstream of our country's intellectual activity. There are such people. They can be encouraged and mobilized. Their numbers can increase. But, that can hardly happen without reordering priorities in the support patterns of corporations and foundations—at least by those corporations and foundations concerned with preserving the basic values of this free society and its free institutions."[2] Baroody was telling these corporate leaders to get involved in public policy formation, lest they, their agendas, and the values they hold dear be swallowed up by a liberal intellectual monolith.

For those in the present day who have any conception of AEI and what it is, Baroody's 1972 speech, as opposed to his 1962 letter, contains much more familiar rhetoric. Today, to the extent that Americans consider the conservative think tank—that is, to the extent they consider institutions like AEI, the Heritage Foundation, or the Cato Institute—Baroody's 1972 speech seems more in sync with dominant conceptions. In the present day, a conservative think tank president like Baroody exhorting corporate CEOs to financially support AEI seems so utterly commonplace as to be unremarkable. In the present, we think of conservative think tanks as research and public relations institutions, populated by conservative policymakers with the sole intention of making, promoting, and marketing conservatism and conservative policies. However, as we see with Baroody's 1962 letter, such was not always the case. In 1962, while still personally conservative, Baroody set strict limitations for his think tank in regard to its advocacy for conservative causes and policies. Why did Baroody set such limitations? What changed in those intervening years to make him alter AEI's institutional mission? How did such change, furthered by him and other think tank leaders, forever alter American political culture in a more conservative direction? Answering these questions is the central project of this book. *Right Moves: The Conservative Think Tank in American Political Culture since 1945* investigates the rise and historical development of the think tank as an institution of political and cultural power within the United States. In particular, this book focuses on how the think tank as an institutional apparatus has been particularly conducive for conservative political organizing and creating a more conservative American political culture. What we know now as conservative think tanks—research and public relations institutions, populated by conservative intellectuals and policymakers—were developed over the postwar period as sites designed for theorizing and selling conservative public policies and ideologies to both lawmakers and the public at large. In this book, I argue that such a development was instrumental in the rise of a broad postwar conservative movement and in the turn away from New Deal liberalism—both its policy recommendations and its way of debating public policy.

In drawing off think tank archival records, presidential archival records, think tank public papers, and a variety of media sources, I argue that there were three stages in the development of the think tank as a site of conservative political and cultural power. First, from the end of World War II to the late 1960s, conservative think tanks like AEI largely had to figure out ways to remain relevant during a time when the policymaking apparatus of the federal government tended toward a liberal technocratic orientation. As we see in Baroody's 1962 letter, this often meant denying that think tanks like AEI advocated anything resembling conservatism—that instead it was firmly committed to a "just the facts" approach to policymaking and research. At other times, though, this meant experimentation with different ways of promoting conservatism. For instance, young conservative activists would have their identities as conservatives formed within think tanks like AEI. Or think tank heads like Baroody would experiment with more activist conservative think-tank-like projects outside AEI.

Such a period of experimentation came to an end in the late 1960s as those who ran conservative think tanks became bolder in their institutional agendas and less reticent to speak plainly as conservative institutions. Such a change was emboldened by the various crises of American liberalism and liberal government during this same period. These two dynamics gave rise to the second stage in the development of the think tank as a site of conservative political power. During this stage, conservatives within think tanks were able to situate themselves as favorable policymaking alternatives to liberally oriented institutions. The decade of the 1970s was pivotal in this stage of development as think tanks like AEI, and others such as the Heritage Foundation, were not shy about asking elite conservative individuals and institutions for new monies in the way we see in Baroody's 1972 speech. Such requests led to drastically increased funding and, more important, to the high-profile promotion of a new model of public policy argumentation that greatly benefited conservatism. Such a model, which I, and some conservatives at the time, characterize as the "marketplace of ideas," placed ideological differences and "balancing" these differences in a public policy "marketplace" as the highest value of all when debating policy. Throughout the 1970s, with conservative think tanks as the main promoter, the marketplace of ideas came to replace the liberal technocratic postwar model of policymaking argumentation. With the replacement complete by the end of the 1970s, a massive shift to a new language of public policy argumentation had taken place. This shift would greatly aid in shifting ideological and policy discussions to the right in that the "marketplace of ideas" model would allow conservatives entrance into public policy debates by sheer virtue of their identity as "conservative" rather than on the merits of their beliefs, per se.[3] Such a way of debating policy, which we are still living under today, means that a policy's identity as a conservative one that "balances" a liberal one is the only thing required for it to be heard. Such a model does not foreclose the idea that liberal and/or conservative policies could be founded on analytical rigor, but it also does not require it.

With this new model of public policy argumentation in place, the conservative think tank was able to advance to its final stage of development as a site of political and cultural power—policymaking and ideological promotion on a wide scale inside and outside the state. Although AEI continued to retain significance in such a project, by the 1980s the Heritage Foundation had moved to the forefront in the conservative think tank world. As a fast-acting think tank that prized the speed, production, and promotion of policy and ideology, Heritage was particularly well suited to the marketplace of ideas. Conservative elites, recognizing this, funded Heritage's rise in the 1980s as it pushed the Reagan administration to the most conservative position possible, helped write its policy, and helped keep Republican congressmen committed to the conservative agenda. Outside the state, Heritage was constantly in the news media as the go-to conservative voice in the marketplace of ideas. In this way, the public was widely exposed to its policies as well as its ideological promotion—the latter of which tended to focus on fusing the sometimes fractured impulses of the postwar conservative movement. Such promotion of policy and ideology continued into the 1990s, with Heritage leading the way in terms of promoting a forthrightly conservative agenda. Additionally, in the 1990s, new think tanks like the Progressive Policy Institute, which was under the umbrella of the Democratic Leadership Council, gave ideological and policy form to a Democratic conservative position within the marketplace of ideas. This new development showcased the power of the marketplace of ideas to shift the parameters of policy debate rightward at the end of the twentieth century.

Despite the plethora of recent studies examining conservative and right-wing political movements in U.S. history, to date there has been no full-length historical study of one of the central institutions of conservative political organizing: the think tank.[4] Given the central importance that think tanks have played in the rise of postwar conservatism, and given their power to influence media and public opinion, this omission is striking. Such an omission is in large part due to the way in which historians have written the history of American conservatism over the past twenty-five years. For much of the 1990s and early 2000s, the field of the history of American conservatism was dominated by grassroots social histories of the American Right.[5] Although this trend yielded rich new insights, more recent histories are now beginning to broaden this grassroots focus through a focus on the individuals, institutions, and ideas of elite conservatives.[6] *Right Moves* adds significantly to this body of research given that very little of these elite-focused studies of conservatism address the centrality of think tanks and, when done, only do so as one part of a broader study of elite conservative organizing in the postwar period.[7] However, even though this book is certainly concerned with "studying up" and examining the elite realms of the postwar conservative movement, I also seek to practice what historian Kim Phillips-Fein calls the "new intellectual history of conservatism," which focuses on "treating conservative intellectuals as part of a social movement, looking at how their ideas contributed to activism and vice versa, at the political and institutional context for conservative ideas, and at conservatives' attempts to build an alternative intellectual infrastructure."[8] In practicing such a project, *Right Moves* seeks to blur the lines between what is ultimately a false binary of "elite" and grassroots conservatism. Think tanks and the conservative intellectuals who inhabited them were important only when they could connect—through various mechanisms—to a broader conservative social movement. They were important only when they helped build meaning for elite and ordinary Americans alike of what it meant to be a "conservative," a "libertarian," or a "neoconservative." They were, and continue to be, important because they helped create coherent political identities that conservative activists and ordinary Americans alike could access.[9] And it is this project with which *Right Moves* is ultimately concerned: how, when, and why the think tank as an institution became so useful to conservatives in forwarding their ideologies, policies, and coherent political identities. It is to this story that we now turn.

1

The Think Tank in an Era of Liberal Consensus

Before turning to the question of the post–World War II conservative think tank and its usefulness as an institutional basis for conservative organizing, the pre–World War II think tank must be considered. Although the term "think tank" did not come into wide circulation until the 1960s, there most certainly existed such structures before World War II. Before the war, the Brookings Institution, still the largest think tank in existence, provided the preeminent institutional model. While in the postwar period, especially by the late 1960s and early 1970s, Brookings came to occupy a position as the bête noire of conservatives, in the prewar period it ironically had much in common with its still-unformed conservative counterparts.

The Brookings Institution was named after Robert S. Brookings, a successful Saint Louis businessman who organized and funded the think tank in the 1910s and 1920s. The Brookings Institution as we now know it was actually the product of two think tanks—the Institute for Governmental Research (founded in 1916) and the Institute of Economics (founded in 1922). The two were merged into the Brookings Institution in 1927. Given the dates of its emergence, it is possible at first glance to see Brookings as an institution of progressive political reform—that is, as part of a series of technocratic institutions that emerged at the same time and were committed to an ideology of progressive "new liberalism." Historian Alice O'Connor, in her history of one such institution, the Russell Sage Foundation, describes this "new liberalism" of the period as an ideology that attempted to occupy "the vast space between laissez-faire and socialist extremes."[1] Progressive "new liberal" institutions like Russell Sage were the first to articulate what we now recognize as a modern, liberal political economy. Such institutions promoted an ideology that was distinct from the laissez-faire liberalism of the nineteenth century in its commitment to reform the worst ills of industrial corporate capitalism through "rational empirical investigation" by technocratic experts.[2] This reformist capitalism was a compromise of sorts whereby corporations and their leaders accepted, and sometimes willingly welcomed, government intervention in exchange for order. Such ameliorative measures were seen as vastly preferable to the alternatives, namely, various forms of radicalism and party politics, the latter of which was seen as hopelessly corrupt.

When the first two institutions that would come to encompass Brookings were founded in 1916 and 1922, they were being born in an America in which many elites accepted such a new liberalism as consensus. Given such a consensus, it would only be natural to assume that the Brookings Institution itself would be part of this emerging order. In some ways this assumption was validated by the very rhetoric employed by those at the institution to explain what it was and what it did. As historian Donald Critchlow has shown in his history of the early years of Brookings, the institution was fundamentally dedicated to the idea of "nonpartisan" technocratic expertise whereby "the main purpose of the institution is to stand above specific economic, political, or class interests and to speak for the general welfare of society" through "scientific" policy implementation.[3] Critchlow argues that it was a quintessentially Progressive institution in that it emerged at a time when "America was undergoing an organizational revolution that demanded technical expertise in corporate business and in state and federal government." However, Critchlow also argues that Brookings was participating in a uniquely American phenomenon in that "other industrialized nations did not turn to independent, nonpartisan research institutes to meet this need for technical expertise." As with other Progressive Era institutions, many of which operated outside government, Brookings had a deep suspicion of party politics and the ability of elected party officials to create "rational" policies. As a result, Brookings worked to develop "nonpartisanship" as an explicit political strategy that would be counterposed to radical social movements and, especially, unruly party politics. Through Brookings an elite group of social scientists, especially economists, would then come together with businessmen to develop "nonpartisan" policy free from the corruption of parties and the "special interests" they brought with them. As a collective, these elite actors desired a technocracy, one in which a "self-designated 'better element'" would decide, quite simply, what was best for American society above the supposed biased and unenlightened self-interest of the people, their parties, and their representatives.[4] Critchlow aptly and succinctly describes this as the "ideal of a natural aristocracy" being replaced "by the ideal of the nonpartisan expert."[5]

Economists were very often the social scientists at the center of the "nonpartisan" think tank model. This is unsurprising given the state of the discipline at the time. Economist and historian Michael Bernstein, in his history of the discipline, argues that economists in the early twentieth century were heavily influenced by, and exercised their influence within, progressive thought. The main professional body of economists, the American Economic Association (AEA), was founded in 1885. However, according to Bernstein, "by 1905, in the wake of what had been a two-decade struggle over the roles of 'advocacy and objectivity' in modern social science, the AEA (not unlike several other social science societies) set course toward the realization of a more 'scientistic' and seemingly dispassionate set of professional ideals."[6] Such an impetus, while clearly internalized and accepted by economists at the time, also had the benefit of shifting the terms of economic practice from fuzzier notions of political economy to "objective science." Bernstein argues that such a move allowed economists to position themselves as the discipline that could and would "remove the last vestiges of unprincipled and thoughtless passion from politics and replace them with the cool reason of logic and tested performance."[7] The question that plagued these economists, however, was *how* to do this given the lack of venues from which to do so. Bernstein focuses on the development of Brookings as one of the solutions to such a problem—a privately funded institution that cultivated direct ties to state power and authority.[8]

Despite the similarity to Progressive "new liberal" thought in their invocations of nonpartisanship, efficiency, and objectivity, the economists at Brookings in the pre–World War II years departed from this same ideology in important ways. More often than not, those who subscribed to such invocations were inclined to advocate expansion of the welfare state as an ameliorative for the downsides of corporate industrial capitalism. However, the economists at Brookings had a strong "antistatist bias," which advocated managerial expertise in an era of corporate capitalism but, somewhat paradoxically, "called for minimal state intervention in the economy."[9] What this ideology meant in practice was that those at Brookings contributed "to the establishment of a modern budget system in the United States, the reorganization of the Bureau of Indian Affairs in the 1920s, the drafting of The National Industrial Recovery Act, and the founding of the United Nations at the end of World War II" while at the same time opposing "the National Industrial Recovery Administration, Keynesian economics, and Truman's proposals for national health insurance and for the extension of social security benefit payments."[10] Among the professional economic voices in the 1930s and 1940s, no institutional voice was louder than Brookings in opposing large swaths of Roosevelt's New Deal and Truman's Fair Deal. In seeking to explain this institutional "antistatist" view, Critchlow argues that it "was a peculiar result of the institution's perceived obligation to stand for the public interest of society against partisan political forces that seemed to subvert the free workings of the marketplace."[11] In other words, the economists at Brookings felt that endorsing new expansions of the welfare state would go against their mission of government intervening for the favor of a particular group over the whole—the whole being "the market" itself.

This combination of nonpartisanship and antistatism meant that Brookings, in the 1930s and 1940s, was often on the outside of power looking in. In a time when many, though not all, businessmen were making peace with progressive new liberalism and the welfare state, Brookings and its economists seemed behind the times—particularly as Keynesian thought came to dominate the economics profession in the same period. Ironically, by the time Brookings president Harold Moulton stepped down in 1952, the institution was perceived as anything but free from special interests. By the post–World War II period, Brookings had "gained a reputation, especially among liberals, as a spokesman for 'big business'" as "their critical studies of the New Deal and Fair Deal programs found a receptive audience among the most conservative elements in the country."[12] Such a reputation would begin to change as the 1950s progressed.

THE SIMPLEST EXPLANATION of the shift in Brookings's orientation in the post–World War II period was that it changed its staff makeup, bringing in more Keynesian-oriented economists. In 1952, when Harold Moulton retired, he and his staff were replaced by economists who "maintained a belief in a capitalist society, but they rejected past notions of a self-adjusting economy. Not to accept fiscal planning, they claimed, was to deny the advance of economics as a science. The trustees of the institution deliberately sought to reintegrate the institution into the mainstream of current economic thought."[13] Such a reorientation can be viewed simply as a tactical maneuver—Brookings lacked influence in policy because of the institution's anachronistic economic views, thus trustees shifted course in an effort to change that.

And while certainly true, this explanation neglects larger trends in American political culture in the postwar period and particularly the shifts in political culture related to the Cold War. The reorientation of Brookings needs to be seen as part of a larger trend of dominant, elite institutions during the Cold War toward what historians have termed a "liberal consensus" ideology. While much of this book is dedicated to the idea, enumerated by many historians of postwar conservatism, that the liberal consensus was never as powerful or monolithic as it appeared, it would be an overstatement to suggest that it lacked coherency or enormous power over the minds and actions of elites from World War II until the late 1960s. In essence, such an ideology is best seen as an updated version of progressive, new liberal political thought applied in a Cold War context. My understanding of such a postwar liberal consensus is guided by historian Godfrey Hodgson's still relevant understanding of the phrase. Hodgson's understanding of the term essentially gives scholars the following definition of the beliefs that constituted the liberal consensus: First, American free enterprise is now different from older forms of capitalism as it has revolutionary potential for social justice. Second, tenet one is true because the federal government has found a way to sustain unending economic growth, so no class conflict over resources will ever be needed again. Third, the United States is moving toward social equality and abolishing social classes, as all workers are becoming middle class and business is controlled by enlightened management. Fourth, social scientists and politicians within the government are capable of defining social problems and then coming up with solutions to those problems. Fifth, communism, in the context of the Cold War, is the main threat to this American system just described, so the United States will have to engage in a prolonged struggle against communism at home and abroad.[14]

By its very nature, such an ideology saw politics and political life as essentially an elite endeavor—one that would reward and place at its pinnacle elite institutions that accepted such a worldview. This is not to suggest that Brookings trustees brought in economists who accepted such a worldview as a ploy. It is more accurate to say that their own views had reoriented to the liberal consensus ideology as had most other dominant institutions in American society. Among academic disciplines that shift was most profound. Economics moved toward a Keynesian worldview that synced with the technocratic sensibilities of the liberal consensus. Political science de-emphasized theory in favor of seeing itself as a quantitative, truly scientific endeavor. Psychology was popularized and encouraged Americans to depoliticize their problems and focus on individual "scientific" behavioral changes instead of collective political action.[15] Although much of this liberal consensus academic thought achieved power from traditional institutions of higher education, think tanks like Brookings were also integral, especially when it came to direct policymaking power. They served as an institutional bridge to the state in a way that most universities could not match. In addition to Brookings, other historians have shown how newly emergent think tanks were able to explicitly position themselves as "objective" Cold War foreign policy think tanks, especially in the 1950s and 1960s.[16] Foundations also proved integral in securing this ideological consensus as well, given that foundations like Russell Sage and, more important, the Ford Foundation, had resources that could fund research that synced with the consensus. Taken together, all these institutions worked to solidify their worldview as the uncontestable, apolitical, nonideological norm. In such a dominant worldview, both the Right and the Social Democratic Left were seen as anachronistic, ideological, irrational, and irrelevant. In this way, these institutions used "the theoretical, methodological, and technical tools at hand to give liberalism and its core ideas the aura of an applied social science and an objective, nonideological body of knowledge. Thus neutralized by the alchemy of social science, the liberal consensus became the program of the growing philanthropic establishment and the constitutive center, as it were, of the postwar construction of neutrality in social scientific research."[17]

Brookings, after its Keynesian reorientation in 1952, was clearly one of the institutions that propagated such a worldview and sought to actively police its consensus position. By the end of the Eisenhower administration in 1960, Brookings had so thoroughly positioned itself at the center of this consensus that it was the go-to institution for experts in both the Kennedy and Johnson administrations from 1961 to 1968. This involvement in the federal government led President Johnson, in 1966 at Brookings's fiftieth anniversary, to declare, "You are a national institution, so important to, at least, the Executive branch—and I think the Congress and the country—that if you did not exist we would have to ask someone to create you."[18] By the late 1960s, through institutions like Brookings, liberals were able to secure their consensus and their institutional role in propagating and planning such a consensus. And it was against this consensus that postwar conservatives, through their own think tanks, would battle. The central problem postwar conservative think tanks would encounter was how to make their institutions relevant in a world where their own politics was immediately seen as outside the realm of respectability—biased, irrational, and anachronistic as opposed to the liberal worldview, which was now thoroughly constructed as rational, objective, modern, and nonideological.

CONSERVATIVE THINK TANKS in the 1950s and early to mid-1960s operated within a policymaking apparatus increasingly committed to the Cold War technocratic liberal consensus; hence, historians have tended to dismiss their significance during this period. Even those historians that do note that there were conservative think tanks during this period tend to downplay their significance and influence given that generally they operated outside policymaking power. Writing about AEA—the precursor to AEI founded in 1938 and incorporated in 1943—James Smith writes that "during the late 1940s and early 1950s, the American Enterprise Association remained an unobtrusive and obscure organization." Repeating the criticism of the time that the "organization was nothing but 'a high-level luncheon club,'" Smith argues that the AEA "was largely ineffective, both as a business-propaganda organization and as a center of policy research."[19] More recent work by Thomas Medvetz largely accepts this view of AEA in its early years, arguing that the think tank "generally occupied a marginalized position in the nascent technoscientific establishment."[20] Only Kim Phillips-Fein's work on the organization of elite businessmen against the New Deal has accorded any real significance to AEA's early years. Phillips-Fein argues that, while obscure in Washington power circles, AEA was nevertheless a key component of an emerging power network of conservative elites in the postwar period. Phillips-Fein and other historians like Angus Burgin have to date been the most attuned to the elite conservative institutions of the immediate postwar period that were instrumental in the pushback against the postwar liberal consensus. In this sense, think tanks like AEA and AEI in the 1940s and 1950s always need to be situated within the nascent conservative institutional movement of that same period. As Phillips-Fein, Burgin, and others have shown, these nascent conservative think tanks were one of many sites—including business associations, academic networks like the Mont Pèlerin Society, and others—that sought to organize long-term resistance against the emerging liberal consensus.[21] Such institutions also should not be severed from other highly popular critiques of the liberal welfare state written in the early postwar period by the likes of Friedrich von Hayek, Ludwig von Mises, and Ayn Rand.

Taken together, all of these institutions and writings gave conservatives solid foundations for a critique of the liberal consensus from its very beginning.

However, even in these new histories that take early conservative think tanks into account, AEA as an institution is only briefly dealt with in the mid- to late 1940s and the early 1950s—the years before the arrival of William Baroody as the head of the organization. And while it is true that the arrival of Baroody led to the full flowering of the think tank and its potential, this does not mean that there was nothing of significance going on at AEA before these years. AEA, between its incorporation in 1943 and the arrival of Baroody in 1954, was the first organization to fit the modern-day parameters of what it means to be a "conservative think tank." The organization sought to influence policy in Washington in a more conservative direction and sought to persuade more and more Americans, elite and otherwise, to accept the identity "conservative." This differentiates it from other conservative political organizations at the time, such as the Foundation for Economic Education and the Mont Pèlerin Society, that were largely concerned with identity formation in the long term.

When AEA formed in 1938 in New York City, there was no doubt why it was forming—to combat New Deal liberalism with a conservative anti–welfare state position similar to the Brookings position of the same period. This similarity was so profound that in AEA's early years, before Brookings's reorientation as a liberal technocratic institution, several Brookings scholars were approached to write AEA's economic studies.[22] The onset of World War II led to the brief disbanding of AEA, but it was revived and incorporated in Washington, D.C., in 1943. The original articles of incorporation for the association show the first glimmers of tension regarding how it would position itself within a world increasingly dedicated to liberal social-scientific expertise at the federal level. The statement at once declared that AEA would "function on a purely educational basis and it [would] not engage in political or legislative activities of any nature whatsoever," while at the same time forthrightly stating that the institution would seek to convince legislators and the public at large as to "the social and economic advantages accruing to the American people through the maintenance of the system of free, competitive enterprise."[23] Such a position of "apolitical politics" was familiar to the time. AEA was merely seeking to mimic the rhetorical strategies of New Deal liberalism that often sought to cloak a bias toward an expanded welfare state in the garb of objectivity. The original articles of incorporation seek to use the same formulation, but this time in the service of a supposedly value-free dedication to the advantages of "free, competitive enterprise." AEA was also mimicking the early rhetorical position of Brookings in the 1930s by arguing that an antistatist economic orientation was the only truly "nonpartisan" formulation in that no group or interest would be favored over another in a society where the state left "free, competitive enterprise" alone to its own devices. The use of the rhetoric of "free enterprise" in 1943 also suggests that the founders of AEA were familiar with newly emergent conservative rhetoric of the time that sought to add the concept to Franklin Roosevelt's more liberally minded "Four Freedoms." Such an addition would be important for conservatives in the postwar period as a bludgeon against communism at home and abroad.[24] Finally, there was another more practical reason for adopting such rhetoric. At the time of incorporation, AEA used a section of the IRS code (section 101, subsection 6) that designated the institution as a "nonpartisan, nonprofit educational organization" not subject to taxation or to regulation under the Federal Regulation of Lobbying Act.[25] The pretense of nonpartisanship was not only a rhetorical strategy but also a practical necessity for the enormous taxation benefits it would bring. All think tanks still operate under such tax-exempt status—only today under the 501(c)(3) portion of the IRS code.

AEA's first chairman, Lewis H. Brown, articulated such a position of "nonpartisan" free enterprise promotion better than anyone. It is unsurprising that Brown himself would have accepted such a worldview given his background. At the young age of thirty-five, he became chairman of the Johns Manville Corporation and instituted an eight-hour workday and collective bargaining rights before they were required by law.[26] To his mind, the involvement of government in business affairs was unneeded and counterproductive as more and more business owners were now supposedly becoming benevolent. In a speech Brown gave around the time of AEA's incorporation, and one that in part was meant to sell the relevance of "private business agencies to achieve public goals," Brown assured his listeners that he and his fellow business owners had "no desire to go back to the good old days of the twenties." However, at the same time he argued that he did not "want to live over again the depression and experimentation era of the thirties." Instead, he would "rejoice when we have behind us the first half of the forties—these days of a bureaucratically controlled economy made necessary by war."[27] Later in the speech this seeming middle ground gave way to a clearer articulation of Brown's conservative position as he argued that New Dealers took the belief "that the state was all-important; that the state could bring to pass the millennium," whereas he and his brethren were "men who undertook risks to better the lot of man in return for rewards."[28] Finally, as with other conservatives of his day, Brown could not resist ending the speech with an equation of liberalism to Marxism and totalitarianism, arguing that "we should never again, as we did in the thirties, try to put totalitarian water in the freedom gasoline and expect the enterprise machine to work properly."[29]

Given Brown's clearly expressed antistatist philosophy, it should come as no surprise that AEA would be institutionally committed to such views. The problem still remained that his new think tank would be working against the emerging liberal technocratic headwinds of the period. The question at the outset of the association became how to advance their position in such a world. In developing a "plan of action" for the association, in many ways Brown developed the three foundations of the modern conservative think tank that exist in the present: First, AEA hired young staffers looking for experience in one of the few conservative outlets in Washington. By doing this, within the think tank itself formed and/or solidified conservative identities of impressionable young Americans. Second, AEA hired conservative writers in their New York City office to produce longer-form pamphlets focusing on broadly defined economic issues and worldviews. Such documents were sent to lawmakers but, more importantly, were also produced for a wider public audience, including businessmen and academics. Through this practice AEA sought to influence American institutions and the individuals who made up those institutions in a more conservative direction. Finally, AEA's Washington-based writers also produced legislative analyses of pending legislation almost exclusively targeted at congresspeople. Such analyses gestured toward the idea of presenting "both sides" of an ongoing policy dispute but, as will soon be seen, were most definitely designed to influence legislators in a conservative direction.

The first of these conservative think tank projects—forming or solidifying the conservative identities of young staffers—was the easiest to accomplish in that all it required were impressionable young Americans. These young staffers could then be inculcated with the antistatist values of AEA within the think tank itself. For historians, this first project of the conservative think tank is the hardest to recover in the historical record because the young staffers at the time left little written evidence of their identity formation. However, it is worth exploring what we do know about this conservative think tank project since it is often the most widely ignored by historians because of its archival inaccessibility. During the early period of AEA, these young Americans were often of two types—those already committed to the "conservative cause" and those who were actually formed into conservatives in the think tank itself. Today, almost all young recruits come from the former category, especially given that the present-day think tank is seen as a perfect entrance point into the conservative movement. However, in the early postwar period, no one really knew what a "conservative think tank" was, and young recruits were more likely to come from the latter category.

It would be hard to find a more perfect example of such a figure as Phyllis Stewart, known today as Phyllis Schlafly, who came to Washington, D.C., in 1945 as a twenty-one-year-old AEA recruit. As Donald Critchlow argues in his biography of Schlafly, it was AEA that literally formed her into the conservative she eventually became. Critchlow argues that before entering the AEA, she had "not been particularly political in high-school or college."[30] If anything, her politics were that of a moderate Republican. In her year working at AEA, however, she was introduced to the uncompromising vision of postwar conservatism and "when the year was over she emerged as a conservative."[31] Here, then, we have the literal creation of a key postwar conservative subject within the think tank itself—not simply from reading think tank publications but from being surrounded by a new burgeoning culture of conservatism. As we learn from Critchlow, this experience would be integral in Schlafly's coming role within the postwar conservative movement because she "learned from her work experience at AEA how to articulate complex issues and arguments into a simplified form easily understood by an average reader."[32] This experience led to her unique positioning throughout the entirety of postwar conservatism: "Phyllis Schlafly's importance in grassroots conservatism came because she helped translate the ideas of intellectuals and anticommunist authors to the grassroots, while at the same time providing leadership to activists who eventually came to identify themselves as conservatives. With her background at the American Enterprise Association ... Schlafly acted a conduit linking this intellectual movement and grassroots anticommunism. Her importance came because she helped evangelize the ideas of intellectuals and anticommunist authors to grassroots conservatives."[33] This interpretation by Critchlow correctly identifies the first key role of think tanks during this period—namely, propagating a conservative identity within the think tank itself for young postwar Americans to latch on to. Schlafly learned this skill early in her activist career, enabling her to "carry it forward" and make other conservatives in her future public work.

Beyond this identity formation of young staffers, the other two projects of AEA in its early years were much more challenging given the emerging liberal headwinds of the late 1940s and early 1950s. Whereas the training, mentoring, and identity formation of young staffers was easy to accomplish, directly challenging the welfare state through widely disseminated public writings was a much more challenging prospect, especially since AEA's tax-exempt status limited it to "nonprofit, nonpartisan, and educational" activities only. Any writings the organization produced would have to be positioned within such a framework. To establish their writing projects, AEA assembled an advisory board that would dictate the course of the think tank's intellectual work. The board was made up of many prominent conservative intellectuals of the postwar period, including the economic journalist Henry Hazlitt and Roscoe Pound of Harvard Law School. Sometimes these board members did the writing themselves, but more often than not they contracted out the work. As was previously stated, the writing was divided between the New York City and Washington offices. Within the New York offices, pamphlets were produced that primarily targeted interested members of the public, including businessmen and academics. These pamphlets took on various forms. Most were longer-form analyses of public policy issues; others were critical exegeses of the political-economic worldview of AEA itself. Both are interesting in their attempts to develop an anti–welfare state conservative framework within the seeming constraints of a nonpartisan, tax-exempt institution. At the very beginning of all their publications, AEA wrote the disclaimer that "as an educational and nonpartisan body, the Association endeavors to be completely impartial and objective in its work. The Association takes no stand either in favor of or against any proposed legislative measures."

This disclaimer was a constraint for AEA's writers to square with their own antistatist leanings. In AEA's longer-form analyses of certain policies out of the New York City office, this often meant posing an examination of a policy as a question or merely as an analysis. Pamphlets were produced with such representative titles as *The Full Employment Bill: An Analysis, Should State Unemployment Insurance Be Federalized?*, and *The National Health Program Scheme: An Analysis of the Wagner-Murray Health Bill*.[34] Whatever the title, all of these pamphlets arrived at the "objective" conclusion of less governmental intervention in economic affairs and argued against any large expansion of the welfare state. Nowhere was this clearer than in AEA's writings on labor. In a pamphlet produced by the New York office by John V. Van Sickle that examines whether unions should be able to collectively bargain for an "industrywide" workforce, as opposed to within individual shops or companies, Van Sickle presents a half-page "case for industry-wide collective bargaining" before presenting seven full pages regarding "how industry-wide collective bargaining really works" that focuses on the "facts" that "it reduces wages as a whole and increases wage inequalities; it destroys purchasing power; it hurts small business and discourages the starting of new business; it promotes monopoly; and it promotes cartelization."[35] While this imbalance in presentation seemed to undermine the claim that "the Association takes no stand either in favor of or against any proposed legislative measures," what is most interesting is the way in which Van Sickle works in the introduction to the pamphlet at presenting a solution to this problem. Namely, he employs a rhetorical strategy that defines "the public interest" in the following way: "Presumably the American people are in substantial agreement that it is in the public interest to keep our democratic form of government and our competitive 'individual enterprise system.' These are the assumptions underlying this article." Here Van Sickle argues for what is essentially a "natural" definition of the "public interest" grounded in a supposedly uncontested nationalist tradition. In doing so, Van Sickle, and AEA more generally in its early writings, argues that he would apply this "objective" definition of the public interest "to the issue of industry-wide collective bargaining this question: Will it strengthen or weaken the individual enterprise system?"[36] With such definitions and such a question in place, the rational, objective answer is that industrywide collective bargaining is not in the public interest.

Writings that situated the antistatist politics of AEA as quintessentially American, and thus above reproach, were common among the think tank in its early period. However, other strategies were employed as well in order to keep AEA's tax-exempt status and to enter into the emerging liberal consensus of the late 1940s. One such strategy was that AEA worked to make "nonpartisan" synonymous with "bipartisan" in their writings. A 1950 AEA pamphlet by Joseph Ball illustrates this point well. In *Where Does Statism Begin?* Ball works to frame "statism" and the "welfare state" in the most negative terms, arguing that the term "statism" itself should be used as it is "more unpleasant" than "welfare state." Statism, in Ball's writing, is synonymous with socialism and is defined as "the concentration of more and more power in government which results from its efforts to substitute government planning of production, distribution and pricing of goods for the free market mechanism of capitalism, in order to fulfill its welfare promises to the people."[37] According to Ball, Truman's Fair Deal program—an extension of Franklin Roosevelt's New Deal welfare state—was the primary example of such statism in the United States. The rest of the pamphlet details how such statism is a threat to the United States and not merely a "scare word." Given the obvious political position being taken by Ball and AEA in this pamphlet, they would need to employ rhetoric that situated such a position as educational and nonpartisan only. To do so, Ball argued that opposition to such statism was bipartisan and thus nonpartisan: "Origin of the present political use of the terms [statism and welfare state] is not partisan. Republicans and some Democrats have been describing such proposals as compulsory health insurance and subsidized housing as socialistic for years." Conceding that "although in the main Republicans will oppose statism and Democrats will support the welfare state," Ball nevertheless argued for the importance of the fact that "a vociferous minority of Republicans support the so-called Fair Deal ardently and a minority of Democrats, mostly Southerners, oppose it just as bitterly."[38] In this way, such bipartisanship made Ball's work easier in that "bipartisan" could now become synonymous with "nonpartisan" in his pamphlet.

In addition to these longer-form writings published out of New York City for a wider public, AEA's Washington office worked to target policymakers more directly through shorter analyses of pending legislation in Congress. In the late 1940s, such analyses could have significant impact because no equivalent of the modern Congressional Research Service existed for congresspeople to turn to in order to understand pending legislation. The services of a private organization such as AEA were invaluable to members of Congress for this reason. By 1947, 235 congressional offices had asked for this service, and AEA was given its own congressional mailbox so the association could receive pending legislation as soon as it was printed.[39] These early years also produced influential contacts with legislators who loved the service. For instance,

Representative Gerald Ford of Michigan, who would eventually rise to the presidency of the United States, wrote the association in 1950 indicating that the legislative analyses have "been excellent in all respects, and I want you to know that I deeply appreciate" them.[40] Ford would from this point forward have a lifelong connection to AEA/AEI including after his presidency when he was employed by the organization as a distinguished fellow.

In many ways, those historians who have addressed these legislative analyses of AEA's early years have taken them too much at face value. The association argued that the purpose of these analyses was to take "no stand either in favor of or against any proposed legislative measures" and that "all analyses are prepared by the American Enterprise Association with special reference to the following: (a) How these measures affect the public interest; (b) how they affect the broad general interests of the free competitive enterprise system; (c) possible financial effect on Government and on industry."[41] This shows that the association was making the case for the relevance of its legislative analyses within the emerging dominant public policy paradigm of the liberal consensus—objectively and impartially weighing the effect of pending legislation on "the public interest." However, historians have been too quick to accept this rhetoric at face value and ignore the way such analyses, in their defense of supposedly apolitical values such as "the public interest" in maintaining a "free competitive enterprise system," were hardly value-free and instead led to legislative analyses that skewed toward the association's conservative views.[42]

It was exactly this type of skewing that led to an investigation of AEA, and other tax-exempt "educational organizations," by the House Select Committee on Lobbying Activities in late 1950. The AEA investigation was part of a series of investigations of various organizations examining "all lobbying activities intended to influence, encourage, promote, or retard legislation."[43] The House report is worth examining in-depth not only for the wealth of information it contains regarding AEA's activities in the late 1940s but also because of what it says about how successful, or unsuccessful, AEA had been in inserting its intellectual work into a government that was increasingly dedicated to a liberal consensus worldview. It was this worldview that the liberal members of the committee held—thus, the report is interesting in the way it reveals this worldview and its usefulness in marginalizing an institution like AEA. From the outset of the report, liberal legislators on the committee target AEA because of its seeming bias toward business interests. Some legislators argue that this bias disqualified the think tank from tax exemption and from opting out of filing requirements under the Federal Regulation of Lobbying Act. With these disqualifications as its goal, the report begins with an exhaustive analysis of AEA's finances—the first of its kind available in the historical record. While noting the average annual budget of AEA from 1947 to 1949 was a modest $170,000, the committee explains that AEA "derives the major part of its income from a relatively small number of large contributions."[44] In 1949, the largest single donors were General Motors ($7,500), the Ford Motor Company ($5,000), and DuPont ($5,000). In total, nearly 78 percent of donations came from eighty-seven high donors (more than $500) with nearly every sector of American business on the list.[45] Such donations, the committee reports, were secured through "such familiar techniques as promotional dinners and luncheons, personal contacts, and direct-mail appeals." It was this big-business funding that the committee cites as its specific worry: "Since AEA does not file reports under the Lobbying Act, Members of Congress to whom the Association submitted studies have no way of knowing who these contributors are and to what extent they underwrite the association's work. These are facts which might have considerable weight in evaluating the association's reports on pending legislation."[46]

The committee presents an argument for the bias of AEA toward the agenda of its big-business underwriters. It argues that this bias should not only be taken into account when reading AEA's reports but also should fundamentally alter the way legislators and the public relate to the organization—not as a nonpartisan educational institution but as a lobby for big business. Not content to stop there, the committee examines much of AEA's work up until 1950—much of which has been examined in this chapter. The committee starts by undermining the nonpartisan positioning AEA had studiously worked to develop. It notes that the group's claims to speak for the "public interest" and the "broad general interest of free competitive enterprise" were hardly value-free and that these were "terms about which reasonable and intelligent men may have widely different opinions. Each of us views the world through a window of our own in articulate major premises."[47] After this, the committee then seeks to illuminate the conservative premises that underlay AEA's research, arguing that their conception of the "public interest" was only the specific one held by their "individual and industrial subscribers."[48] It should be noted as well that from this point forward in the report the committee begins referring to AEA's work as "research" (using quotation marks) so as to distinguish it from "impartial and objective research studies."[49] For example, "research" into deficit financing by the federal government is shown by the committee to have been produced by AEA in order to "counterblast" a report by "14 economists favoring deficit financing"; a study on "Expanding Welfare in a Free Economy" is only "devoted to a critical examination of current legislative proposals for public health and welfare"; and an examination of a minimum-wage bill only points to "AEA's view of its undesirable features."[50] The committee asserts that while AEA's claim of "impartiality and objectivity" is "laudable," "the general tone of AEA studies suggest either that the advisory board has been unsuccessful in finding qualified experts with views opposed to its own, or that it has simply not exerted any great effort in this direction."[51] The committee remarks that the group should not be allowed to hide behind "academic freedom" for what is a "one-sided pamphleteering endeavor" where "only one viewpoint is presented, and that is the viewpoint of the big-business supporters of AEA."[52]

AEA's attempt to insert its conservative worldview into institutions increasingly dedicated to the liberal consensus had proven problematic. Within this committee report, it is easy to see just how powerful liberal consensus rhetoric could be when used against conservative groups such as AEA. Not only did it situate such groups as biased and worth ignoring, it set the liberal policymaking endeavor as objective and value-free. The inquiry led to a self-disciplining by AEA rather than a disciplining by the committee itself. Legislators were told in testimony by AEA officials that "major changes" were in the works to their legislative analysis series that would "add short bibliographies and pro-and-con statements to each analysis." The committee recommended such changes as they "would undoubtedly enhance the value of the bill analyses" and "diminish or increase the possibilities of slanted analyses, depending on the selection of analysts."[53] Even more stringently, the committee recommended that AEA register under the Federal Lobbying Act because "there is no reason to accept its claims of objectivity and impartiality when every material circumstance points to a contrary conclusion."[54] Thankfully for the association, this recommendation was not taken up given that the group's tax-exempt status would have been revoked and its quasi-academic facade obliterated. Nevertheless, despite avoiding this harsh judgment, the congressional inquiry presented a blow to the organization just when it was trying to establish itself as a key postwar conservative institution. For many organizations, such a blow would have precipitated a tailspin into utter irrelevancy or oblivion, but AEA was able to recover and find new ways to make the organization relevant in the 1950s and, especially, the 1960s.

KNOWING THAT AEA was able to recover from this congressional inquiry should not minimize the immediate impact of it—particularly because the inquiry coincided with the death of Lewis Brown in 1951, precipitating a true crisis for the young think tank. AEA closed its Washington office temporarily in 1951 and 1952, leading many to assume the think tank would eventually close up shop for good. However, in January 1953, shortly before the inauguration of Dwight Eisenhower as president, "a small group of AEA's backers and friends including Representative Melvin Laird (R-WI) and economists Paul McCracken and Murray Weidenbaum decided to revive the organization using the existing structure of AEA."[55] The first step they took was hiring Allen D. Marshall, an officer of the General Electric Company, as president of AEA. Marshall had also been a trustee of AEA as well as a member of the Chamber of Commerce. All three of these appointments made him the perfect person to head up a think tank like AEA, which received the lion's share of its income from big business. Even more than this influence with the business community, Marshall made staff appointments that truly made the difference in reviving AEA. From the Chamber of Commerce he hired William J. Baroody Sr. and W. Glenn Campbell. Campbell had a Ph.D. in economics from Harvard and was hired to write and bring in new intellectual talent. But Baroody, with his strong interest in public policy, conservative politics, and organizational savvy, was truly the hire that would revive the organization. He would start as the think tank's executive vice president before quickly moving to the presidency.

Baroody was an outsider within the largely WASP power elite of official Washington. He was the son of a Lebanese immigrant stonecutter and a devout Melkite Catholic. His religion was reflected in his personal life as he married at age nineteen and had seven children. He would stay married to the same woman until his death in 1980. This personal conservatism undoubtedly influenced his politics, but so did his time working in government within the Veterans Administration. There he developed an "insider's skepticism about government programs," which then led him to seek out an appointment at the conservative Chamber of Commerce.[56] Although Marshall had been impressed with Baroody's work on the financing of Social Security and other social insurance programs while at the Chamber, Baroody's organizational skills when applied to the fledgling think tank precipitated the turnaround of AEA. Although it is easy to see now that Baroody's appointment at AEA led to the organization's turnaround, this is only in hindsight. When he arrived at the organization in 1954, it was still in trouble and he was taking an enormous personal risk leaving a secure job at the Chamber—especially with a large family to support. His new job of executive vice president of AEA sounded important, but it would have been largely viewed as inconsequential in an institutional Washington increasingly dedicated to technocratic liberalism. It became Baroody's job to guide the organization to relevancy within this world.

Working with Marshall, Baroody revived the think tank through increased funding and changes to its publications that were aimed at gaining more influence not only within official Washington but also among the wider public. As to fundraising, Baroody and Marshall embarked on an ambitious strategy in the late mid- to late 1950s and early 1960s, designed to make sure the think tank was on sound financial footing. Donations had been steadily falling since the congressional inquiry, so Baroody and Marshall sought to revive interest in the organization among those in the business world. AEA trustees such as B. Edwin Hutchinson were the first enlisted to raise funds, and particularly to raise funds from past donors who had lapsed. In a typical letter from April 1955, Marshall asks Hutchinson, then vice president of Chrysler, to help reorganize and "circularize" the "300 odd companies who had been affiliated with AEA during its early days." Marshall asks Hutchinson to sign a form fundraising letter that would be sent out in his name to these three hundred companies. Further, Marshall seeks his help at "a series of informal dinner meetings . . . to bring together selected congressional subscribers with trustees and prospective members of the Association."[57] Baroody and Marshall took to calling such donations "revivals," signaling the revival of memberships and, hopefully, the think tank itself. A year after Marshall's and Baroody's arrivals at AEA, a revival was definitely under way. Although the think tank's finances were well short of the average $170,000 annual income of the late 1940s, the $144,074 they took in for the fiscal year ending 30 June 1955 nevertheless showed a 31 percent gain in total receipts from the previous year. The sounder financial footing was immediately reported to all AEA trustees, who were then asked to expand on the new financial haul.[58] Baroody was deemed so successful in fund-raising that by November 1955 Marshall reported to the AEA executive committee that he was giving Baroody a $2,000 year-end bonus to his $18,000 salary. Marshall argued that Baroody had given AEA a "new lease on life."[59]

In the same letter Glenn Campbell was given a $1,500 bonus for his work overhauling AEA publications from his position as research direc-tor. After Baroody's and Campbell's arrivals, AEA shut down its New York office and consolidated all research efforts in the Washington of-fice. The move did not mean that the organization would solely target policymakers with their efforts. On the contrary, Campbell worked to develop wider dissemination of AEA's longer pamphlet studies through the mass media. What was also interesting about these revamped "longer-range" studies was that they were more moderate in their aims, tenor, and promotion. While they certainly promoted a conservative position they were at the same time not the antistatist diatribes that attracted con-gressional scrutiny in the late 1940s. This was no doubt intentional as AEA sought to moderate its image in the wake of the investigation. Whatever the personal politics of the men who ran the institution—and let there be no doubt that they identified with American postwar conservatism—they knew that in the mid-1950s they were likely to be dismissed outright if their work seemed too biased in this direction. So, an AEA study, "States' Rights and Labor Law," made a conservative case that more, though not all, labor regulation should be handled by the states. This report was then written up by conservative *Newsweek* col-umnist Henry Hazlitt but only to stress that the "statement of the case is moderate" and the "legislative recommendations are moderate."[60] Like-wise, a longer-range study by Roger Freeman entitled *Federal Aid to Education—Boon or Bane?* made the conservative case for less federal fund-ing to local schools by, at least in part, arguing that turning off the fed-eral spigot would increase the rapidity of school desegregation in the wake of *Brown v. Board of Education*. Freeman notes that "federal funds—unless conditioned—would help [Deep South states] resist [desegrega-tion] longer and more effectively."[61] This report too was actively promoted by AEA in the media and probably received the widest coverage of AEA longer-range studies to that date.

It was not just the longer-range studies that took somewhat more mod-erate positions; Campbell also revamped AEA's legislative analyses to incorporate the congressional committee's recommendation of having "pro" and "con" arguments for every piece of legislation analyzed. Additionally, AEA during this period also began offering "spot analyses" for congresspeople as a "special service." AEA stressed that such "special projects" would merely "lay out the facts" and not try to push a specific viewpoint. Members of Congress began to take notice of these services and quotes from both Republican and Democratic members were used in AEA's promotional materials with increasing frequency. Letters from lawmakers, particularly Republican lawmakers, were often sent to Baroody with thanks. Senator Barry Goldwater (R-Ariz.), with whom Baroody had developed a close friendship, was particularly effusive in an April 1955 letter: "My purpose in writing you goes beyond an expression of appreciation for a job well done. I want to say as emphatically as I can that there is a great need for objective, factual and penetrating analyses. The need I refer to is not a partisan one, but is recognized by all Members of Congress who are interested in obtaining the basic facts necessary for the intelligent appraisal of important legislative proposals and understanding their impact on the competitive enterprise system. AEA is doing a fine job to help fill this need, but I cannot overemphasize how much more of the same must be produced and effectively used if federal legislation is to be kept in line with basic American principles."[62] Likewise, Representative Thomas E. Martin (R-Iowa) wrote Baroody: "Proper evaluation of proposed legislation is a never ending study for all Members of Congress. So also is our effort to preserve the American principles of competitive enterprise and constitutional government. The program of the American Enterprise Association consisting of bill analysis, economic studies and information research is built on a high plane that has been very informative and useful."[63] These two letters are particularly revealing in that they had so thoroughly internalized AEA's rhetoric of nonpartisan antistatism grounded in an unobjectionable, apolitical American tradition of "competitive enterprise" and American "constitutional principles." Even though the research was seemingly coming more into line with liberal consensus modes of governance, conservative lawmakers were still getting the message that AEA was part of the nascent "conservative movement" of the period.

However, not all conservatives were so convinced that the conservative worldview was present in this new research. They worried that AEA was alienating its big-business backers by compromising too much with the liberal technocratic worldview. Trustee Hutchinson wrote Marshall in June 1955, expressing his concern in the following way: "If I may venture a gratuitous comment on the AEA's future, it is this: your long-term problem will be to preserve among the AEA trustees and in the staff the correct ideological bias. While the AEA avowedly is *not* an 'ivory tower' operation it is avowedly dedicated to dealing on a practical basis with current affairs, it is inevitable that as time goes on what it does and the way it does it will be interpreted within the framework of the ideological controversy that plagues these times." This language is stark, particularly Hutchinson's call for "the correct ideological bias." What was this correct bias? According to Hutchinson, AEA needed to represent "those who believe in a 'voluntary society' " against those who believe in "regulation" arguing that the "future growth and usefulness of the American Enterprise Association will be largely determined by the integrity within the scope of the practical limitations imposed upon its operations as it directs its influence in the direction of a 'voluntary society.' "[64] This letter shows the tension inherent in a conservative think tank like AEA at the time. The institution's conservative backers wanted a more forthright antistatist message, whereas Marshall, Baroody, and Campbell, while certainly sympathetic, felt that some compromise with the liberal policymaking worldview was necessary for relevancy and in order to maintain AEA's status as a tax-exempt, nonpartisan, educational institution. Marshall's response reflects this tension: "I'd like to assure you that I, and the staff, are in full agreement with your proposition that the AEA is dedicated to dealing on a practical basis with current affairs. We understand that, with this purpose and in a period such as this, it is a great deal easier to make enemies than to make friends. We are not afraid of this as long as we continue to deal *with facts* in the issue of a voluntary versus a regulated society, but we do hope that we continue to have the support of friends who feel as we do."[65] Despite the coded nature of Marshall's response, his worry is clear: if AEA does not submit at least implicitly to the liberal notions of objective policymaking (that is, "*with facts*"), the institution will never get a hearing for their own conservatism. To come out and openly assert their biases would only make it "easier to make enemies."

As AEA continued to grow in the late 1950s and early 1960s, the institution felt the tension of either coming in line with liberal consensus views of policymaking or, in the eyes of their conservative backers, "selling out" the nascent conservative movement of the period with a "watered-down" message. This tension often led to multiple institutional "faces" being presented to different publics throughout the late 1950s. For instance, in a fundraising letter to H. W. Prantis Jr., the chairman of the Armstrong Cork Company, Marshall invokes a liberal intellectual monolith, specifically unions and the group Americans for Democratic Action (ADA), that moved policymaking toward the "liberal program." Marshall tells Prantis that such groups advanced this program primarily through intense "issue analysis" before making the case for AEA: "Issue analysis is our job we want to make certain that the *facts and the implications of those issues* are brought out in *objective and nonpartisan* fashion and are disseminated as effectively as the propaganda which pours out in astonishing volume" from ADA and the unions.[66] This letter, in content and in tone, is interesting in several respects. It was one of the first used by AEA, when targeting big-business financial support, that situated an *enemy*—in this case, the liberal consensus group ADA and labor unions. Arguing that ADA and labor were engaged in a program designed to pass more liberal legislation, Marshall situates AEA as a counterweight to such a trend, deserving of big-business support. While still clearly highlighting the "objectivity" and "nonpartisanship" of AEA research, such rhetoric was for the first time situated as a conservative counterweight to the "propaganda" published by ADA and unions. Such rhetoric would become a tried-and-true staple of AEA's fundraising and rationale for existence in the future.

However, in the late 1950s, AEA still seemed uncomfortable with such rhetoric when presenting an institutional face to the wider public. In a 1956 pamphlet on AEA's "Current Operations," value-free technocratic activities are expressed above all. After highlighting the three activities of AEA—legislative analyses, spot research, and longer-range studies—the pamphlet stresses that "each of these programs has a common target—making clear through intensive research the implications of major issues of national importance. Each of these programs has a common purpose—providing maximum assistance on a nonpartisan basis to the policymakers upon whom arrest the responsibility of decision. Each of these programs rests on a common premise—that factual analysis, unbiased and understanding, offers the best means of ensuring sound national policy."[67] While interest in "competitive enterprise" and "constitutional government" is stressed, the "Current Operations" handbook primarily maintains fealty to liberal technocratic rhetoric and closes with Republican and Democratic congressmen singing the group's praises.

The research produced by AEA during the late 1950s also reflects this pull between being part of the postwar conservative movement and maintaining "objectivity and nonpartisanship" for relevance within the liberal consensus. On the one hand, increasingly well-known conservative intellectuals such as Milton Friedman were brought on to AEA's Academic Advisory Board, which set the research agenda of the institution.[68] Longer-range studies on labor poured forth that set forth a fairly monolithic conservative antilabor union message—namely, on the issue of involuntary membership in labor unions.[69] Likewise, a long-range study on health care argued against any national system to provide medical care for all and even against a program for old-age recipients only.[70] At the same time, two long-range studies focusing on national aid to higher education and federal antitrust laws were models of intellectual rigor as both issues were examined from multiple viewpoints and with interesting insights for the time.[71] On antitrust laws, AEA actually became widely acknowledged by legal academics as having produced judicious research in the area. In 1964 the think tank even "established an Antitrust Center that included a state-of-the-art data retrieval system with excerpts from and a digest of antitrust debates, significant litigation, and all consent decrees."[72]

Such a tension between being within or without the postwar conservative movement was also reflected in fundraising decisions. Although Baroody's entrance into the organization had solidified the think tank's financial standing, trustees like Hutchinson wanted to expand the think tank's base of support to more conservative-friendly companies and individuals. Baroody resisted, arguing, "While most Trustees of AEA would agree that some selective broadening of the Association's base of support is desirable, I think they would all feel that AEA ought not to become a mass-supported organization. It seems to me that the very nature of the job AEA does militates against a large membership numerically." He later continued, "Certainly as the Association continues to increase its effectiveness and do a better job, more and more companies will be encouraged to support its work. Realistically, however, the non-glamorous nature of AEA's function makes it virtually certain that this base of support will always be relatively small number within the total business community."[73] Here Baroody showed that he still saw AEA's work, at a fundamental level, as "nonglamorous" and technocratic—making it impossible to draw a large base of financial support. Hutchinson, once again seeing a larger role for the think tank within the conservative movement, disagrees and even argues that a larger base of support would enhance the think tank's "public relations position" as it would not seem so beholden to a few wealthy contributors.[74] In hindsight, there is no doubt that Hutchinson's position was stronger. His plan to broaden AEA's base of financial support would have not only made it more embedded in the postwar conservative movement but would have also enhanced the association's reputation among those who accepted the liberal consensus position. Baroody ultimately rejected this type of wide base broadening—one of the few tactical mistakes he made during his early tenure at AEA.

To most on the board of trustees Baroody's decision and the tension within the organization did not matter by the close of the 1950s given that the organization was experiencing unprecedented success. In the fiscal year ending in June 1959, the think tank had, for the first time, surpassed the $200,000 mark in total income. By this point, 85 percent of the Senate and 73 percent of the House of Representatives received AEA's legislative analyses with liberal Senator Hubert Humphrey (D-Minn.) commending their health care analyses and Richard Nixon writing in support of their " 'tough-minded' approach to foreign policy" and "true objectivity in presenting all the relevant facts and all the competing policy proposals."[75] When the board of trustees met in March 1960, Baroody's praises were sung once again and board members agreed to expand the impact of AEA long-range studies by sending them to university libraries and more "persons in the newspaper world, professors of political science, economics and related social science departments of colleges and universities."[76] Success continued in the following fiscal year as the think tank's income increased more than 27 percent to nearly $260,000, due in large part to the $49,000 AEA received from conservative foundations in support of their work—a trend that would continue over the next two decades as many in the conservative movement began exploring the use of foundations in support of conservative causes.[77] Baroody immediately recognized the usefulness of such conservative foundations as a counterweight to places like the Ford Foundation, which were seen as part of the liberal technocratic establishment. In 1963, the publisher of the conservative *National Review* wrote Baroody after the "rather long conversation we already had" on the "conservative foundation idea." The publisher argued that only one such foundation existed, the Relm Foundation, but that there were "considerable sums of money available from a number of foundations with this orientation, as well as from individuals, which could be channelized for this most important activity if there existed an operating foundation sufficiently financed and properly guided, and legally set up to make such grants."[78] The publisher and Baroody were clearly thinking of creating such a foundation during this period in support of conservative causes.

With these fundraising decisions and activities, it is clear that by the early 1960s Baroody was torn between making AEA a full-throated institution of the burgeoning conservative movement and retaining influence and respectability within the liberal technocratic establishment in Washington. Baroody's more personal writings in the late 1950s suggest that he definitely wanted a more conservative institution—one that could counter what he saw as a liberal intellectual monopoly in American life. One letter from 1959 Baroody wrote to a supporter and friend is worth examining in depth for its forthright expression of the man's long-term goals for AEI. The letter of 17 July to Harvey Peters stands out for two reasons. First, it is of a different tone and length than most of Baroody's letters. Whereas most of his other letters were short, to-the-point, and understated, this letter is a lengthy four-page, personal, and emotional expression of his own politics and how he saw those politics intersecting with his institution. Second, it is the clearest articulation in the archives up until this date of what conservative think tanks would become in the future—institutions of immense political power that heavily influenced American public policy debates. As we will see in chapter 2, in the 1970s, when conservative think tanks proliferated and gained enormous new political power, other individuals were often credited with truly creating and "thinking up" the idea of the modern conservative think tank. However, Baroody's letter to Peters shows that he was a man ahead of his time.

Baroody was responding to a letter written by Peters, which, although unavailable, clearly despaired over the state of the nation. Peters suggests that "the liberals" and "leftists" are destroying the country to such an extent that all good conservatives can do is wait around for total destruction and then try to pick up the pieces afterward. Baroody rejects such a nihilistic view, and much of the letter reads as a pep talk that encourages Peters to reject a view akin to "the Marxist concept of historical determinism." Baroody instead encourages Peters to accept the more "realistic approach that 'circumstances do not make men; it is *men* who make circumstances.'" While agreeing with Peters that the problem is a "more or less steady trend toward a controlled economy (and all that implies) and away from free, competitive enterprise," he disagrees that such a trend toward a "socialist society" is irreversible. Instead, Baroody argues that such a move occurred because intellectuals of the liberal/Left had "out organized" those of the Right and had effectively shut them out of the debate. Here Baroody is worth quoting at length: "There is sufficient evidence readily attainable toward the conclusion that the leftist movement derives a substantial portion of its strength from its virtual monopoly of the so-called intellectual segment of American society. It is our opinion that this has not resulted accidentally but has been brought about through systematic employment of techniques and devices designed to establish what might loosely be referred to as an intellectual reservoir of leftist ideology. The net effect of this development has been to cloak leftist ideology with an aura of respectability in the public view that increasingly cannot be matched by existing resources on the conservative side of the fence." It is important to note that when Baroody speaks of "leftist ideology" he means various strains of Marxism *and* Keynesian liberalism—as he makes clear later in his letter. With this quote, we see Baroody astutely noting how a liberal consensus had been formed and policed in order to marginalize conservative voices. While unduly hyperbolic given that those who enforced the liberal consensus also worked just as hard, if not harder, at marginalizing actually existing Left voices, Baroody was nevertheless accurate in his assessment.

Even more important was his diagnosis of the "techniques" through which such a consensus was continually solidified and reproduced. These included, "Systematic encouragement of young academics demonstrating a willingness to conform to leftist ideology (the opposite side of the same coin is the systematic discouragement of young academics demonstrating a leaning toward the conservative point of view and independent thinking)." Such "leftist encouragement" was done through "fellowships, scholarships, and opportunities for research, writing and publication always readily available to the 'chosen' group." Additionally, such intellectuals were always on "loan assignments to various components of government in the legislative, judicial and executive branches. Through this approach, the favorite professors are given leaves of absence from the faculty assignments and assigned to key staff positions carrying policy advisory functions which usually produce a favorable substantial of result from the leftist point of view as well as enhance the personal reputation of the chosen individuals." Finally, "popular acceptability for the professor" was always "engineered through carefully selected opportunities for his appearances on public forums, publication of his articles and journals of opinion, etc." As will be seen in chapter 2, this early diagnosis by Baroody would become a common staple in conservative rhetoric of the late 1960s and early 1970s as such an "intellectual monopoly" by liberals within American political life was situated as having created a whole host of problems that could only be remedied by allowing conservative voices into the debate. Such conservative voices, from Baroody's perspective, needed to be "supported, encouraged, and given, through the *intelligent* use of available resources, the kind of opportunities which the leftists give to their people." If this occurred, Baroody argues, "some extremely beneficial results will ensue." He closes the letter admitting that although such a project was "admittedly long range," such an approach would ultimately insert conservative voices "into the mainstream of the nation's intellectual life."[79] The only question in the future for men like Baroody would be how to break into this "mainstream," which had henceforth shut them out.

Despite such a clear personal conservatism, in the early 1960s such an "intellectual monopoly" would be hard to break. Baroody and AEA continued to feel a pull between his conservative institutional vision and the dominant liberal technocratic worldview of the time. Such a tension would be heightened even further in 1962 as Baroody became president of AEA. His first steps appeared to move decidedly in the direction of "respectability" within official Washington as he renamed the think tank the American Enterprise Institute (AEI) to give it more academic cache and distance the think tank from being dismissed as merely a "business association."[80] Moreover, Baroody's letters in this early period of his presidency show a decided shift toward the technocratic consensus. One such exchange was with AEI staffer Karl Hess in November 1962—the exchange that began this book. By this point Hess was part of the burgeoning conservative movement and saw AEI, like Phyllis Schlafly and others before him, as an institution where he could hone and develop his conservatism. Baroody quickly disabused him of such an idea, writing Hess a terse letter explaining that the purpose of the special projects program was not to move policymakers in a conservative direction. Baroody's letter is worth quoting again at length: "Our Special Projects program is responsive only to the direct request of policymakers, particularly Members of Congress. The program does not and should not *initiate* projects nor, under any circumstances, formulate or espouse policy positions. . . . The Institute has no position except to serve. You can anticipate that, as in the past, the originators of requests for Special Projects research will occupy positions all along the political spectrum. Our job is neither to form nor to change those positions but only to provide materials appropriate to them." He goes on later in the letter to further clarify the position: "The 'don'ts' are every bit as significant in this respect as the 'do's.' The Institute does *not* press any particular policy position or even attempt to form, suggest, or support any particular policy position. The Institute *does* attempt to provide the research assistance which will bring to bear upon any policy consideration the most pertinent facts available and the most knowledgeable considerations by acknowledged authorities in the field. By thus informing policy considerations, at the request of policymakers, we can make our only and best contribution to the educative support of policy discussions. We serve, in this respect, as a research adjunct to the staffs of all policymakers who request our assistance. It is they, regardless of their political positions, who must form the actual policy. We can provide only such research background and assistance as they request."[81] Taken together, these statements could not be a clearer explication of the liberal technocratic ideal of policymaking. There is no equivocation or attempt to offer support for even a nonpartisan antistatist position as AEA had done in the past. Rather, Baroody clearly and explicitly asserts that AEI, and its special projects program in particular, was not there to move legislators in a conservative policy direction. Without a doubt, such a position was as frustrating to Hess as it was to Baroody, but his new institute needed to walk a fine line in the early 1960s between garnering support from conservatives who were considered outside the mainstream of the liberal consensus and maintaining relevancy within the institutions of that same liberal consensus. Such a tightrope may have been too hard for some at AEI, including Baroody, to walk. In the mid-1960s he and others at the institute began looking for new ways to more forthrightly express their conservative politics.

FOR GLENN CAMPBELL, this initially meant taking over a think tank of his own. In 1960 Campbell gave up his position as research director of AEA and became director of the Hoover Institution on War, Revolution, and Peace—a position he occupied until 1989. The Hoover Institution in 1960, and even today, occupies a strange space within the wider constellation of conservative think tanks. Founded in 1919 by soon-to-be-president Herbert Hoover on the campus of Stanford University, it was, until Campbell's arrival, largely known as an institution dedicated to anticommunism. What this meant in practice was developing one of the largest archives dedicated to communist records in the noncommunist world. To this day, researchers still come to the institution in droves to examine these materials, as well as to examine the numerous files pertaining to conservatism in the United States. In 1960, former president Herbert Hoover wanted to expand the work of the institution. This included not only enlarging the archives but also other activities—namely, increased public policy research aimed at moving lawmakers and the public in the direction of "individual liberty here at home and throughout the world."[82] In other words, Hoover wanted his institution to do the same work as emerging conservative think tanks like AEI. The institution's connection with Stanford would be an asset in such a project as it lent academic respectability to Hoover's conservative project. Glenn Campbell seemed like the perfect person for the job given his years at AEA/AEI.

In Hoover's first stated goal of expanding the breadth and use of the institution archives, Campbell was enormously successful. Moreover, his success was in many ways attributed to foundational support of the kind Baroody had been interested in developing at AEI. In December 1962, Campbell received a grant of $50,000 from conservative financier Richard Mellon Scaife aimed at bringing in "scholars who can benefit greatly from spending some time at the Institution from either coming here or from staying as long as they should in order to gain maximum benefits."[83] Scaife, as will be seen later, would go on to develop his own foundation aimed at funding various conservative political projects. His grant to the Hoover Institution in 1962—and another of $750,000 in 1964—were the earliest ones he would make to a conservative think tank and would pale in comparison to the ones he would end up making in the 1970s.[84] In addition to conservative financiers, in 1963 the institution was also awarded $500,000 by the Ford Foundation to expand its physical resources into a new building on Stanford's campus.[85] This grant was far more surprising since conservatives were, by this point in time, increasingly seeing Ford as a foundation dedicated to the financing of only liberal projects. Once again, the location of the institution at Stanford undoubtedly played a role in garnering the think tank a measure of scholarly respectability, which helped in securing the grant. Along with funding from Stanford, the institution was expanded into a new building in the mid-1960s.

After this initial round of fundraising in Campbell's first three years, he felt comfortable moving on to his next project of expanding the institution's scholarly staff. This staff would then be dedicated to conservative foreign and domestic policy research of the type normally seen in conservative think tanks like AEI. In fact, Baroody and Campbell worked out a fundraising and research partnership between the two think tanks in 1963 designed to "expand scholarly research, both pure and applied, in examining the relationships of government to the individual citizen." A memo setting forth the partnership argues that the "research would seek to define more clearly how the structure of government can be made more efficient while, at the same time, preserving a free society in which individuals can function with maximum opportunity for self-betterment, thus, increasing the well-being of society as a whole." This seemingly generic language is nevertheless interesting in that it was clearly working through new language for describing a conservative political project within institutions still ostensibly dedicated to nonpartisan inquiry. A focus on the category of a "free society" became one of the primary ones in the mid-1960s through which conservative institutions and individuals sought to accomplish such a goal. In the end, the memo advocates the raising of $350,000 in new monies dedicated to both institutions' expansion of scholarly research into not only "foreign affairs and domestic economic affairs, but also elements of study involving the fields of political and social sciences as related to the whole process of government."[86]

However, by 1964, it was becoming clear that Campbell, Baroody, and other conservatives at AEI were growing tired of feeling constrained by the liberal technocratic worldview in their respective think tanks. These men craved expression of their own personal conservatism in a more forthright way. As with many conservative Americans in 1964, they found expression in Republican Barry Goldwater's presidential campaign as many at AEI and Hoover left to work directly for Goldwater. In Goldwater's campaign, Campbell, Baroody, Hess, and other AEI intellectuals such as Edward McCabe saw, as many other conservatives did, an outlet for their conservative politics that think tanks could not provide. Whereas at AEI and Hoover they were at some level always dedicated to the liberal technocratic ideal and to distancing themselves from the interests of their corporate and wealthy funders, in the Goldwater campaign they could embrace this same funding and forthrightly promote their own conservative politics through Goldwater. Their experience on the campaign provided the foundation for a new understanding of the conservative think tank after the campaign was over. In Goldwater's campaign Baroody and his AEI associates saw a perfect venue to insert a forthright conservatism into American politics. The most comprehensive source detailing this effort by AEI and Hoover associates is Stephen Shadegg's

1965 memoir *What Happened to Goldwater?*[87] Shadegg was a member of Goldwater's inner circle who had run his 1952 campaign for the Senate. He was an adviser on the 1964 campaign, but one who ultimately felt he was phased out for Goldwater's "brain trust" drawn largely from the two think tanks. While historians should view his memoir with some suspicion, given his jaded outlook, Shadegg's memoir is invaluable at providing insight into the role of AEI associates in the Goldwater campaign and the lessons they would draw from this experience for the overall project of political conservatism. While Shadegg's sometimes Rasputin-like portrayal of Baroody is undeniably hyperbolic, it is nevertheless clear that Baroody and at least six AEI "associates" played key roles in the Goldwater campaign's "brain trust." In fact, this is one of the first sources available in the postwar period that describes conservative activism of this type using the phrase "think tank." More important, Shadegg's portrayal, as we will see, is backed up by Goldwater's own autobiographies and archival material regarding the role of AEI associates on the campaign.[88]

Baroody, ever the entrepreneur, clearly understood the Goldwater campaign as a space he and other conservatives could advocate for conservatism in a way he thought impossible within AEI itself. From the beginning of the campaign, Baroody and his associates attempted to take over all aspects of campaign policymaking, speechwriting, and strategy. According to Goldwater, Baroody leaked an unflattering report to the *New York Times* that indicated the campaign was in the process of being taken over by "Far Right" intellectuals William F. Buckley Jr. and L. Brent Bozell of the *National Review*. In his 1988 autobiography, Goldwater asserts he was "now convinced that Baroody quickly slammed the door because he saw a possibility that he might have to share power with the two men, both of whom were highly intelligent and very political."[89] After this coup, Baroody and his associate Edward McCabe immediately began providing polling research for Goldwater. However, this was just a precursor to their main role as key advisers and speechwriters for the campaign. By 1964, Shadegg argues, Baroody was "dictating the content of the speeches."[90] In this role, Baroody, McCabe, and Hess were most interested in promoting the unabashed conservatism that they had curbed within AEI.

At the Republican nominating convention in 1964, Shadegg argues, Baroody, Campbell, McCabe, Hess, and three other AEI-affiliated individuals—Warren Nutter, Harry Jaffa, and Chuck Lichtenstein—

made up Goldwater's "brain trust." This group worked as a committee to come up with Goldwater's speech, including the widely quoted line, "Extremism in the defense of liberty is no vice, and moderation in the pursuit of justice is no virtue"—words, according to Shadegg, "which attracted national attention which added to the disunity in the party, and which were to be interpreted and explained in a dozen different ways." Shadegg bitterly asserts that "the manner in which the acceptance speech was written became the pattern for the Goldwater statements during the campaign—ideas and phrases gathered together under Baroody's supervision, edited by McCabe, Kitchel, and Hess, until all unity of thought and style was completely destroyed."[91] Goldwater's autobiographies back up this portrayal from the convention onward, asserting that Baroody wrote "our ideological speeches with the help of others. Hess wrote the daily material." Goldwater also asserts that after the convention speech, he, Baroody, and Goldwater's campaign manager, Denison Kitchel, alone decided the speech would mark the start of a campaign where "for better or worse, I would be myself—a straight-shooting, down-the-line conservative—for the entire campaign."[92] Baroody and his AEI associations now had the conservative ideological project they thought they could not have at the think tank itself.

After the convention, Baroody consolidated his power, brought in more of his AEI people, and took on more activities in the campaign. Baroody and his team took up the "third floor in an office reserved for the Senator and his brain trust, forty speech writers, stenographers, and clerks, all selected by Bill Baroody and who were busily framing major policy statements, planning the content of television presentations, and developing the over-all strategy." Now explicitly describing the group as a "think tank," Shadegg argues that they were "responsible for the preparation of speeches and statements to be released through the PR department and on nationwide television."[93] Goldwater agrees with this interpretation, arguing that after the nomination speech, "Baroody saw himself as the head of a new brain trust around me. He would gather the research, direct the speechwriters, and be our resident intellectual with a team of his own bright young assistants. Baroody was classicist, almost an ancient Greek or Roman. He was also a man who enjoyed power."[94]

In this role, the think tankers were instrumental in producing more ideologically conservative speeches like the nominating speech. Gone was any need to present "balanced" portrayals of issues like at AEI—on the campaign they could directly express conservatism to the masses.

For example, they wrote a speech on "checks and balances" that dogged Goldwater on the campaign trail after they inserted the line, "I weigh my words carefully when I say that—of all three branches of government—today's Supreme Court is the least faithful to the constitutional tradition of limited government, and to the principle of legitimacy in the exercise of power."[95] A common staple of conservative discourse today, at the time—in the context of Supreme Court decisions on school prayer and state legislature reapportionment—it was seen by many as too ideological for a presidential campaign. Likewise, toward the end of the campaign, Goldwater gave a televised address written by Baroody and his associates entitled "The Free Society," which spoke out against busing, "racial quotas," and government intervention to alleviate private sector discrimination. In this address, Goldwater also spoke out against street demonstrations for civil rights and conflated them with everyday street crime. He asserts, "Above all, no Administration should, as [Johnson's] has, call men into the streets to solve their problems. The leadership of this nation has a clear and immediate challenge to go to work effectively and go to work immediately to restore proper respect for law and order in this land—*and not just prior to election day either*!" This exhortation came directly after Goldwater maintained that "our wives, all women, feel unsafe on our streets. Crime grows faster than population, while those who *break* the law are accorded more consideration than those who try to *enforce* the law."[96] Shadegg writes that this second section of the speech was widely declared to be excessive and contributed to the perception that Goldwater was nothing but an authoritarian. He argues that in the end, the "conflict between the practical politicians on the second floor and the elite members of Bill Baroody's 'think tank' on the third floor" was too much for the campaign.[97] Goldwater himself agrees, stating in his first memoir, "My critics have remarked, and in retrospect I must agree with them, that my inner circle of advisers had very little experience in the politics of campaigning. Baroody, an intellectual, had devoted his career to dealing in abstracts," while "Hess was a good writer, a strongly conservative ideologue, but no politician."[98]

After the losing campaign, Baroody and his associates were despondent, but their experience on the campaign's "brain trust" was invigorating for their own personal conservatism. The question after the campaign became how they would channel these energies and whether such energies could be channeled into think tanks like AEI and Hoover. On a retreat to Jamaica after the campaign's end, Goldwater, Baroody, and other members of the campaign's AEI "brain trust" began discussing this dilemma.[99] Still convinced that AEI could not offer a proper place for conservative activism, the men conceived of an entirely new think tank—the Free Society Association (FSA). The FSA has never been fully examined by historians of American conservatism. This inattention is for good reason as the organization only existed for four years. Despite this short existence, the FSA was an important "working through" phase for those who sought to build institutions that could boldly and loudly express a conservative political ideology and policy.

Upon the incorporation of the FSA in May 1965, the organization used only vague conservative rhetoric when describing its mission. Its founders declared that the think tank's main goals would be to "assist in the enhancement of a broader public understanding" and "analyze the principal public policy issues" of the "Constitutional Republic of the United States and the free society of the United States."[100] Such rhetoric differentiated the think tank very little from others of the time. Despite this, the FSA sought to break free from the AEI think tank model in two key ways. First, Baroody and others like Denison Kitchel—Goldwater's campaign manager and the first president of the FSA—decided against tax-exempt status for the FSA. This decision meant that the think tank could be more openly conservative in a way that had proven problematic for places like AEI. In many ways, such a decision was necessary since Barry Goldwater was the honorary chairman of the FSA, thereby disabling any claim to institutional "nonpartisanship." The decision was a conscious one as well, however, and one that would allow the group to be forthright in its conservatism. The name of the organization was chosen to convey this conservatism in that it drew from Goldwater's "Free Society" campaign speech, which was meant as an antithesis to Lyndon Johnson's "Great Society" liberalism. In addition to this forthright conservative orientation, the second key way the FSA differed from AEI was that it actively sought a wide basis of support—one that would not be grounded in a small number of large donations from big businesses. Such a decision was interesting because Baroody had rejected such a wide basis of support for AEI. Once again, this decision was based, at least in part, on Goldwater's involvement in founding the organization. One of the key advantages the FSA had was access to Goldwater's campaign contributor list. Given this fact, the possibility of creating a mammoth membership base was too enticing for the founders to ignore. The FSA would seek to educate as big of an audience as possible in the political project of conservatism. Kitchel, Baroody, and others hoped that such a project would "introduce, to the most general public, the voices of responsible conservatism" through a publication style that would be "without condescension" and "readily comprehensible and of real interest in service to a maximum audience."[101]

It is also interesting to note that the authors chose the phrase "responsible conservatism" to describe the political identity the FSA promoted. For example, they argue that the group would "demonstrate the distinction between true conservatism and the pseudo-conservatism of the many existing organizations which have as their basic and laudable purpose the preaching of anti-communism but as their hallmark, resulting in strong public antipathy, irresponsible leadership and untenable positions." They argue that they hoped to "furnish a respectable and respected, non-partisan haven for all true conservatives, Republicans, Democrats and independents alike, who, failing the creation of such a haven, will either lose hope or misguidedly channel their interests and energies into the pseudo-conservative organizations which are now aggressively seeking new members."[102] Such rhetoric of "respectability" mimicked the myriad ways in which AEI sought to position itself within the liberal consensus. However, such rhetoric when employed by the FSA, took on entirely different connotations as the organization was setting itself up as a counterweight to the John Birch Society (JBS)—the conservative anticommunist organization that had attracted millions of Americans as members by this point in time. Founded in 1958 by candy manufacturer Robert H. W. Welch Jr., the organization had become something of an albatross for the Republican Party by 1965. While it provided much-needed grassroots conservative activists, it was used repeatedly in the mass media to tar the entire postwar conservative movement as extremist.[103]

No one understood this dynamic better than Barry Goldwater, who in his run for the presidency depended on many JBS members for his "ground troops," all the while being hounded by such associations in the press. The FSA was clearly designed by Goldwater, Kitchel, Baroody, and others on the Goldwater campaign to provide an organizational counterweight to the JBS. In his announcement of the new organization, Goldwater himself echoed this theme of "responsible conservatism," arguing that "we as conservatives serve no good by being negative" and must instead be "soundly positive" in our solutions—all a clear allusion to the anticommunism of the JBS.[104] However, in Goldwater's speech there was no direct reference to the JBS, showing how he and the FSA would have to tread lightly in order to gain a wide base of support. At least initially, it did not appear that such a wide base of support for the FSA would be a problem. Goldwater's personal appeal to the 27 million Americans who had voted for him was a powerful force for increasing the membership ranks of the FSA. By October 1965, more than 10,000 new people became subscribers to FSA publications and by the end of 1965 the group had more than 30,000 members. The swelled membership ranks seemed to prove that a grassroots-supported think tank was possible.[105]

Despite such growth, in 1965 Goldwater worried that the public had "no idea what the Association stands for because they have never been told."[106] Much of this problem was due to understaffing at the think tank, but another factor at play was the FSA's broad membership model. By the end of 1965, the only political identity the think tank seemed to be promoting was that of "responsible conservatism" that was counterposed to the JBS brand of conservatism. The problem with this promotion was that much of the membership of the FSA also supported the JBS. Denison Kitchel exacerbated this problem even further when he told the *New York Times* in 1965 that JBS produced "the type of irresponsible, sensational writing which is best designed to undermine and destroy the very institutions which the John Birch Society was ostensibly designed to preserve."[107] Letters poured into Kitchel after the news broke expressing dismay with him and the FSA. One castigated him for "being on the defensive" with the liberal *New York Times* and asked, "Why can't we conservatives carry the fight to the liberals instead of letting them bring the fight to us then reacting in a defensive manner?"[108] Another argued that the FSA under Kitchel was administered "with greed, jealousy, shortsightedness, stupidity, back-biting and disruption, leaving the conservative mass hopelessly divided and innocuous—an enormous chaos in which the Red thrives."[109]

Such a dynamic showed the problem inherent in a wide membership base drawn from conservative activists who were clearly not interested in undermining JBS. By early 1966 finances began to suffer from this problem. To begin the year, the FSA had a net deficit of $24,000 and only added around 1,000 members in the first two months of the year.[110] The organization's small staff could not do the work of adding new members and producing written work for the existing ones. The only literature it produced in 1966 with any depth, or that received any attention, were two studies that delineated the "threats posed" by the New Left and Black

Power movements.[111] Such forces put Denison Kitchel in a bind as he advocated a new round of fundraising and membership drive to Goldwater in February 1966. Goldwater disagreed, noting, "I have been anticipating need for additional funds for some time but while I certainly don't want to discourage this effort, I might suggest that we would be wise in recognizing that we just about hit our potential . . . I think it would be very wise to service [existing members] in such an excellent manner that additional membership would come in without solicitation."[112] Another problem with a wide base of membership is highlighted here. AEI's dependence on large donations from corporations and individuals meant that intellectual production could take precedence above all. At the FSA, Kitchel had no such luxury and no staff to keep up with servicing the membership base.

From 1966 to 1969, several efforts were made to get the new think tank back on track. In May 1966, the FSA held a "regional meeting" in Chicago with Goldwater headlining the event, but the event actually left the FSA further in debt. By 1967, the organization sought tax-exempt status in order to get big money donations from individuals and conservatively oriented foundations and corporations.[113] Despite such a move, the group continued to hemorrhage money through 1967 and 1968. Goldwater became concerned about the money he had committed to the organization as well as the fallout for his 1968 Senate campaign if the organization failed.[114] Goldwater wrote Baroody letters to this effect, going so far as to advocate AEI rescuing the FSA financially.[115] As a favor to Goldwater, Baroody and Kitchel kept its doors open until after he won his campaign—a process helped along by acquiring tax-exempt status in December 1967. But through the end of 1967 until it closed up shop in June 1969, the organization did little for its dwindling membership.[116] Despite this inauspicious ending, it would be a mistake to describe the FSA model as a wholesale failure for the overall project of the conservative think tank. While it was unsuccessful as a whole, it nevertheless provided an experiment in how conservative think tanks could more forthrightly express their views and, more important, how they might reach out to a broader audience to bridge the elite and grassroots bases of the emerging postwar conservative movement. Eschewing tax exemption was shown to be a problematic proposition for these goals. Conservative think tanks would clearly have to figure out a way to keep tax-exempt status while still expressing their institutional conservatism. As to the broader base of "grassroots" financial support, the FSA showed (albeit for a brief period) that this could be done—even if it also showed the perils of such a project. Such lessons would not soon be forgotten by AEI and other conservative think tanks after the demise of the FSA.

THE EXPERIENCE OF BAROODY, Campbell, Kitchel, and others with projects such as the Goldwater campaign and the FSA undoubtedly convinced them that they would have to make their conservatism "work" through their existing think tanks at AEI and Hoover. In the aftermath of such failures, and at a time in 1965 and 1966 where American liberalism seemed to be triumphant, it was unclear how such a goal was possible. Adding further complications for Baroody at AEI was his participation in the Goldwater campaign and the implications of such participation on the nonpartisan, tax-exempt status of AEI. Immediately after the 1964 campaign ended, Baroody had to account for his activities at the AEI board of trustees meeting. Baroody produced a letter from the chairman of the trustees at the meeting that was written to him in July 1964. The letter states, "I concur in your view that the resources and facilities of the American Enterprise Institute should not become involved in any way in any partisan effort. I feel also that your first duty is to the Institute and that in the event your personal activities require time normally devoted to your duties as President of American Enterprise Institute, such time will be charged annual leaves." Moreover, Baroody asserts, "The Institute was in no way involved in the presidential campaign" and "that the Chairman of the Brookings Institution (a tax-exempt organization) participated as an individual in the Johnson campaign and that his support, and his affiliation with Brookings, was widely publicized."[117] By organizing his defense of his campaign activities in such a manner, Baroody engaged in what would become a tried-and-true conservative strategy in the late 1960s and 1970s—namely, that the activities of the Brookings Institution were never recognized as politically partisan because they were in the service of the liberal technocratic consensus.

It is undeniable that Baroody had a point. Brookings men were involved in Johnson's campaign and were intensely involved in writing the legislation for Johnson's Great Society agenda in 1965 and 1966. This fact is what led Johnson to declare in 1966 when speaking of Brookings, "You are a national institution, so important to, at least, the Executive branch—and I think the Congress and the country—that if you did not exist we would have to ask someone to create you." Despite Brookings's support to Johnson, his campaign, and his agenda, the liberal think tank's tax-exempt status was left unchallenged. Such a courtesy was not extended to Baroody and AEI, especially after a 1965 *St. Louis Dispatch* report revealed that despite working eighteen-hour days on the Goldwater campaign, Baroody continued to take his salary from AEI. An examination of AEI's financials filed with the IRS showed that Baroody was given a raise in 1964 from $35,000 to $39,167. As the *Post* report drily noted, the institute's IRS 990-A form asked the question, "Have you during the year participated in, or intervened in (including the publishing or distributing of statements) any political campaign on behalf of any candidate for public office?" To this question, "The institute answered, 'No.'"[118] When combined with Stephen Shadegg's 1965 portrait of Goldwater's campaign, there was now damning evidence against Baroody that could be used to revoke the tax-exempt status of AEI. Thus, in 1965 a House select committee began an inquiry into "whether the involvement of AEI's staff in the campaign violated the institute's tax-exempt status." The committee "subpoenaed its financial records, prompting a two-year investigation by the Internal Revenue Service."[119] Ultimately, because Baroody and his associates had taken official leave of AEI, the investigation resulted in no punishment, but Baroody was chastened by this new run-in with the IRS and would never directly participate in a political campaign again.

AEI and Baroody took many lessons from this new run-in with the IRS—many of them positive. First and foremost, the IRS probe showed Baroody that tax exemption for AEI was here to stay. If his activities on Goldwater's campaign had not led to revocation, what would? The episode convinced Baroody that a more forthrightly conservative think tank was possible without disrupting tax exemption. The question still remained as to how AEI would be able to insert such a voice within the "intellectual monopoly" of the liberal consensus. As 1968 approached, what Baroody and others in conservative think tanks began to realize is that to truly break this "monopoly" what was needed was an entirely new way to debate public policy—one that would be more amenable to conservative voices and policy alternatives and that represented a clear break from the postwar liberal technocratic consensus. As we will see in chapter 2, such a break was helped along by the unraveling of this consensus in 1968.

2

Think Tanks in a Marketplace of Ideas

In 1967–68, it was initially unclear how elite conservatives in think tanks and elsewhere would ultimately undermine the liberal technocratic consensus. With a way of debating and creating policy so firmly entrenched, it was hard to imagine how something so powerful could be undermined and replaced. Was there even a way of debating and creating policy that would be more amenable to conservative policy aims? Glenn Campbell at Hoover and, even more important, William Baroody at AEI were at the forefront in trying to answer this question. In 1967–68, both men began to grapple with new ways of debating policy that would be more amenable to their points of view. While during this period both men still stressed their institutions' supposed neutrality and objectivity, they were nevertheless becoming more comfortable with the idea of forthrightly asserting their long-standing biases toward conservatism and big business. Even more significant, they began to argue that such biases were *positive* attributes that were *more important* than "neutrality" or "objectivity" in that they would balance a marketplace of ideas that had been dominated by liberals and their ideas.

Whether they knew it or not at the time, both men were in the process of creating the very idea of a "marketplace of ideas" as a way of debating policy. Although such a term had been employed in the past, elite conservatives, and especially those in think tanks, began to employ the term as a way to undermine the liberal technocratic consensus. Such a framework elevated values such as balance and openness to a higher plane than those of nonpartisanship, neutrality, and objectivity. In the promotion of the marketplace of ideas, elite conservatives created much needed intellectual space for their own ideas. In a 1967 *New York Times* profile of Hoover, its staff articulated such a conception in response to claims that the institution had "moved beyond objective research into the realm of politics." While many Hoover employees in the article still primarily relied on claims to "objectivity" to defend the institution, a visiting fellow at Hoover takes a different route—arguing that the institution faculty is Republican-oriented and that this is a good thing given that "this may be the nation's only academic body viewed as Republican, and we need more like it to establish an equilibrium."[1] Balance and equilibrium above objectivity and neutrality—such tropes became essential to conservatives seeking to be heard in policymaking debates. Beyond the obvious value shift such a way of thinking produces, it is also important to note the way it explicitly situates liberal institutions, in this case academia, as fundamentally nonobjective—biased toward the liberalism of the Democratic Party and in need of the "balance" provided by those at Hoover.

Baroody at AEI also intuitively understood these newly emergent conservative tropes and their usefulness in both entering policy debates and fundraising from like-minded donors. As to the latter, Baroody's 1968 fundraising appeals for his institution show a marked shift toward the marketplace of ideas. While still making appeals to the "objective, nonpartisan" research done at AEI, Baroody nevertheless situated academia, and its liberal leanings, as the paramount problem that institutions like AEI needed to overcome. Baroody describes the problem in this way: "Much of our thinking at AEI is conditioned by a conviction that the intellectual community plays an increasingly major role in the formulation of public policy—in short the conviction that most governmental programs, for example, enacted in the last 30 years did not originate either in the mind of a politician or from the overwhelming demand of the people or from the planks of the party platform, they were born in and can trace their origins through the thought and writings of an academician or a group of academicians whose views concerning the organization of society may not necessarily coincide with yours or mine." In particular, Baroody notes the way in which "50 to 75 percent of the bold new programs developed by the Johnson Administration during the last two years were generated outside the government . . . in fact the President uses a catalog of ideas gathered from 115 of the nation's greatest intellects situated on university campuses from Berkeley to Boston." In the same way as the senior fellow at Hoover, Baroody relies on the trope of a liberally biased academia to argue for funding a conservatively biased think tank. Baroody even takes such an argument one step further when he argues that this liberal bias in policymaking created a whole host of problems for the nation in 1968, including, "the problem of the cities, of school disorders and riots, the fiscal and monetary situation, balance of payments, the whole range of foreign-policy issues, etc."[2] Only through a balancing of the policy marketplace, with conservative institutions and ideas to balance liberal ones, could such national and international problems be remedied.

With the election of Republican Richard Nixon to the presidency in 1968, there was at least some hope among conservatives that their ideas would enter into policy debates through the presidency. Although he was often distrusted by the conservative grass roots at the time, there was nevertheless a feeling that conservatives could inject their own policies through the presidency under Nixon. Baroody clearly felt this way as shortly after Nixon's election he received a letter from the president-elect requesting "evaluative studies of significant government programs to be done immediately." Baroody eagerly replies, "Pursuant to your request, we have started to set up our plans and procedures for the program. We are consulting with the Chairman and several members of our Academic Advisory Board in an attempt to launch the project as quickly as possible."[3]

Despite such initial excitement, throughout 1969 there existed a palpable frustration among members the Nixon administration itself and among conservative activists in think tanks that they could never get their legislation off the ground in a Congress still dedicated to a liberal technocratic worldview. Such a sentiment existed in large measure because both houses of Congress were controlled by the Democratic Party. However, both Nixon and elite conservative activists like Baroody saw something more sinister at play—a liberal legislative monolith that, when combined with Democratic majorities, was immensely powerful in proposing, passing, and promoting liberal legislation. While a liberal/left-leaning academia was seen as part of this monolith, other institutional sources were situated as equally, if not more important, in upholding the liberal technocratic consensus. By 1969, Nixon, his aides, and Baroody himself began to focus on the Brookings Institution as the linchpin in a powerful institutional liberalism. Such a view of the importance of Brookings undeniably contained more than a kernel of truth. As suggested in chapter 1, by the mid-1960s Brookings was seen throughout Washington as a reliable supporter of the Democratic Party. It helped write and promote much of Johnson's Great Society initiatives and provided the staffing for Democrats in Congress and the presidency. Given that mid-1960s policy debates were reliant upon liberal technocratic expertise, Brookings and its staff could often cloak their ideology within a technoscientific aura that obscured its liberal Democratic leanings. Nixon chief of staff H. R. Haldeman was the first Nixon aide to recognize the power Brookings held over many in the federal government, including members of Nixon's White House staff. Recognizing this, Haldeman noted in a memo to Kenneth Cole, who worked as an assistant to the president for domestic affairs, that "the President wants to issue an order to all White House staff people (I will have to do this verbally) as well as to Cabinet people (also have to be done verbally) that they are not to use Brookings Institution."[4]

Although this particular memo from Haldeman does not specifically explain why there existed animosity toward Brookings, it can be gleaned from other correspondence at the time that conservative policymakers saw Brookings as a think tank that wielded entirely too much power in official Washington. Around the same time as Haldeman's memo, the *Washington Post* ran a column that, in a small way, describes the power the Institution wielded. Entitled "Congressmen Seek Experts' Advice as Self-Improvement Becomes a Fad," the writers of the piece correctly describe the problem encountered by many congressman—they had too much to learn and neither the staff nor the time to learn it. The column by Richard Harwood and Laurence Stern focuses in particular on defense policy, noting that many legislators were trying "to find money for domestic needs by taking it away from the swollen military bureaucracy." To do so, congresspeople had to understand the military budget first. The column notes, "The Brookings Institution at the behest of 25 Congressmen, is offering instruction on the ins and outs of the DOD budget" and that the only truly left think tank, the Institute for Policy Studies, was conducting a "Bi-Monthly Defense Spending Seminar."[5] Such instruction was providing legislators with the intellectual ammunition they needed to restructure the military budget if they so desired. Conservatives within and without the administration took note of this influence. Bill Baroody forwarded the column to Nixon counselor Arthur Burns, noting, "It is not my intent to add to your burdens by deluging you with a mass of written materials. However, in view of our conversation the other evening, the enclosed marked clip of a column in today's *Washington Post* is quite pertinent."[6] Burns immediately responded, thanking Baroody for the article and noting that he had "put it to good use."[7]

As the 1960s turned into the 1970s, such a critique of Brookings ramped up further. However, conservatives within and without the Nixon administration began to diverge in the political usefulness of the institution. On the one hand, Nixon and his associates came to see Brookings as a political enemy—one that needed to be fought in multiple ways—

both legal and illegal. For Bill Baroody at AEI, however, the institution proved useful as it offered a foil and provided the necessary counterposition for a shift to a "marketplace of ideas" and away from the liberal technocratic consensus. As to the former, 1970 saw a flurry of memos within the Nixon administration regarding Brookings that can only be described as increasing in their paranoia. No longer content to see Brookings as a reliable producer and promoter of liberal Democratic legislation, Nixon staffers saw something much more nefarious. Noting the *Washington Post* report regarding Brookings and Institute for Policy Studies seminars on defense spending, Haldeman assistant Lawrence Higby wrote to White House Aide Thomas Huston that we "should go after Brookings and the Institute for Policy Studies" and "have the Internal Revenue make some discreet inquiries" into them. Huston, author of the notorious "Huston Plan," which came to light during the Watergate hearings, agreed to this and other domestic surveillance activities targeted at liberal/left political movements and institutions.[8] Haldeman disagreed with the IRS plan, arguing that "making sensitive political inquiries at the IRS is about as safe a procedure as trusting a whore." Instead, he argued that various avenues, both legal and illegal, should be pursued against Brookings. As to the latter, he argued, "If we reach the point that we really want to start playing the game tough, you might wish to consider my suggestion of some months ago that we consider going into Brookings after the classified material which they have stashed over there. There are a number of ways we could handle this. There are risks in all of them, of course; but there are also risks in allowing this government-in-exile to grow increasingly arrogant and powerful as each day goes by." Such a focus on supposed "classified materials" held at Brookings reached a fever pitch in 1971 when "there was even talk of firebombing the institution on the assumption that Daniel Ellsberg's Pentagon Papers were being held there."[9] However, in his 1970 memo, Haldeman leans toward legal avenues, arguing that "it would be both very valuable and quite feasible to set up an operation which would enable us to get our point of view across to the Congressional staff members whose principles are generally sympathetic to the Administration."[10] He told Huston that Nixon aide Pat Buchanan was researching such a possibility.

Bill Baroody, of course, was already seeking to position AEI as the "operation" Haldeman and Buchanan desired. Whereas Nixon and his advisers saw Brookings primarily as a political enemy to be demolished by any means necessary, Baroody saw it as a place that could be used to increase the power, prestige, and finances of AEI. Baroody's positioning of AEI as the necessary "balance" to Brookings was particularly appealing to donors who wished to advance conservative legislation and ideas. By the early 1970s these donors began to establish their own foundations to advance such causes. Given that Baroody had long thought of foundations as being the key to his think tank's success, he was better positioned than anyone in the early 1970s to reap the rewards of these new institutions. Headed by conservative families and individuals, the foundation—as opposed to, say, corporations, small businesses, and wealthy individuals—had several advantages. First and foremost, whatever the political orientation of their founders, foundations imparted a scholarly and detached aura. Grants could be made with less suspicion that they were merely in the service of big business or "the rich" more generally. Second, foundations provided yet another institutional base from which conservatives could "make their voices heard" in the marketplace of ideas. To do so, these new conservative foundations very often counterposed themselves to the Ford Foundation—which they saw as the primary liberal funder of Brookings. When taken together, Brookings, Ford, and academia more generally, were increasingly positioned by conservatives as the key components of a liberally biased intellectual monolith—one in need of "balance" by conservative think tanks, conservative foundations, and conservative intellectuals. So, even if conservative foundations and think tanks were positioned as being conservatively biased, the emerging rhetoric of the policy marketplace made such charges increasingly irrelevant. In fact, such "conservative bias" was increasingly sought after in policy debates to "balance" the voices of institutional liberalism.

Baroody was one of the first conservatives to realize the significance of this rhetorical shift in policy debates and use it to his advantage. Brookings and its power were extremely useful as Baroody increasingly sought the support of conservative foundations in the early 1970s. Writing one such foundation, the Earhart Foundation, in March 1970 Baroody immediately counterpositioned AEI to Brookings, noting, "Compared to other institutions in the public policy research area, the total resources available to AEI have been modest. Its annual budget is perhaps one seventh that of the Brookings Institution." Specifically noting that AEI already had new foundation support from the conservative Relm Foundation, Baroody argued that even more would be needed in order to match Brookings in the marketplace of ideas: "As you know, Brookings has been built up very markedly over the last several years and now operates with assets of some $50 million. In some Washington circles, Brookings currently is considered to be the 'government in exile.' The present status of Brookings was accomplished largely by major infusions of financial resources from one foundation. Some of the projects which Brookings has recently mounted and which will be financed by additional grants principally from the foundation referred to above will, I can assure you, make a major impact on the future shape of public policy in an area of vital to the interests of the United States."[11] Such rhetoric became common as Baroody sought foundation support for AEI throughout the 1970s. Brookings is positioned as all-powerful liberal "government-in-exile" in possession of an endless cash flow from the Ford Foundation (Baroody's "one foundation") that it used to plan liberal public policy "vital to the interests of the United States." Such rhetoric played on the fears of wealthy conservatives and urged them to get involved in the "major league competition" by funding AEI. Another AEI internal memo often sent to conservative foundations to detail the activities of Brookings goes even further in endorsing the idea that Brookings was "one of a number of tax-exempt organizations that have launched an 'assault on the political, economic and social structure of the country.'"[12] Such rhetoric yielded immediate results from conservative foundations like Earhart, Relm, and one of the biggest conservative players of the early 1970s—the Lilly Foundation, which in October 1970 awarded AEI $750,000 for its new "Center for Evaluative Research."[13]

Sensing AEI's rhetoric, members of the Nixon administration saw a kindred institutional spirit and directly aligned itself with Baroody's think tank in a fundraising effort. Such a partnership was helped along by the fact that Baroody's son, William Baroody Jr., was an aide to Nixon secretary of defense Melvin Laird. As such, Baroody Sr. wrote Laird directly in early 1971 asking for his help holding fundraising meetings with prospective contributors at the Pentagon.[14] The relationship was announced publicly during August of the same year as a *Washington Daily News* story noted that Laird, "with Pres. Nixon's blessing," would head up a $25 million fundraising drive for AEI in order to expand it "into a potential haven for top GOP officials when the Republicans no longer control the administration." The story helpfully adopted Baroody's anti-Brookings rationale as the reason for the new fundraising drive, noting, "Informed sources said today the goal of the fund-raising is to bring AEI up to equal footing with the Brookings Institution, a noted Washington research center which has served as a haven for out-of-office Democrats.

They noted that when a Democratic administration leaves office, many of its experts in appointed jobs find posts at Brookings, the Ford Foundation and similar organizations where they can keep abreast of affairs in Washington and be ready to move back into power with the next Democratic administration."[15]

Despite the usefulness of "Brookings as foil" for fundraising purposes, it would be a mistake to interpret Baroody's efforts as merely financially motivated. All the evidence suggests that he saw Brookings, Ford, and academia as useful for shifting the way official Washington, and quite possibly the American public at large, debated policy. If it could become "common sense" that such institutions were liberally biased and in need of balancing in a marketplace of ideas, the financial rewards for AEI would be dwarfed by the increase in influence it would see as a result. The earliest evidence of Baroody's awareness of such a fact can be found in a November 1971 memo outlining AEI's importance for prospective donors. In that memo, Baroody argues that while Brookings "projects the public image of partisan disinterest and ideological objectivity," it was actually "quite partisan and ideologically oriented" toward liberalism and liberal public policy. He argued that Americans needed to be made aware of such a bias if conservatives were ever to dislodge Brookings from its "dominant competitive position" in the marketplace of ideas. AEI would be the institution to "right the imbalance . . . on public opinion formation in public policy determination." Unlike Nixon, Baroody stresses that righting the imbalance should not be done by taking "any action against such existing centers." Rather, he argues, "It can only be achieved by assuring similar resources to institutions and centers not similarly oriented. *The goal of such an effort would be to make certain that the American people are exposed to varying points of view on public policy issues. It is essential that fair competition exists in the arena of idea formation.*" Such would become the crux of the new marketplace rhetoric of policy debate. "Balance," "competition," and "varying points of view" were all integral to the shift as AEI would now be "selling" its bias as opposed to any pretense toward objectivity. The institution would now exist to balance a marketplace where an "intellectual monopoly" had occurred because of the actions of liberal academics, Brookings and the Ford Foundation—all of which, Baroody asserts, denied their own liberal bias. Unsurprisingly, Baroody then goes on to assert that only AEI "uniquely provides [the] base" from which to counter Brookings with a conservative public policy program. Finally, it is important to note how, under this new marketplace rhetoric, the bias of conservative and corporate funders—who are being targeted with this memo—is no longer a problem to explain away, but rather a *solution* that is needed to balance what is seen as a monolithic liberal establishment. Moreover, this particular discursive formation actually presents corporate and wealthy interests as fundamentally *powerless*—as the "little guys" struggling to make their voices heard above that of the all-powerful Brookings.[16]

New conservative foundations and financiers took notice and sought Baroody out to not only fund AEI but also to understand the problem he was describing. The earliest, surprisingly, was beer magnate Joseph Coors. Coors, as will be seen, would become the primary funder of the Heritage Foundation when it emerged on the conservative think tank scene in 1973. He was driven by his own personal conservatism to use his fortune in support of conservative causes. Although his support of Heritage was a blow to Baroody later on, it was nevertheless Baroody who helped him understand how conservative think tanks could be integral in a "marketplace of ideas."[17] With his new sales pitch that wealthy conservatives should add their voices to the marketplace of ideas, Baroody was able to secure new funding from other new wealthy conservative interests. One stands out in this regard: Richard Mellon Scaife. Scaife was the principal heir to the Mellon oil and banking fortune, who, in the 1970s, began using this fortune to support his conservative politics. AEI seemed like a natural outlet for his support. In the early 1970s, his Scaife Family Charitable Trust gave massive amounts of money to AEI. In each of the four fiscal years from 1972 to 1975, the trust allocated $1 million to AEI. This was far and away the largest grant AEI had ever received. It was so large that in 1974 AEI had to get the donations classified as "excludable unusual grants" in order to maintain its tax-exempt status.[18]

Such donations also set off a pattern for AEI as it launched Baroody's long-sought-after goal of moving from individual and corporate support to support primarily via foundations. Such a shift had two tangible benefits. First, it offered a new avenue through which wealthy conservatives could better allocate their money to conservative causes given that foundation expenditures were far better in terms of scrutiny and taxation benefits than corporate expenditures. Moreover, unlike corporate expenditures, they required only the approval of a small group of people as opposed to shareholders or corporate boards. Secondly, foundations were inherently thought of as more respectable, and thus less open to charges of corporate or wealthy bias. Despite the fact that such charges of bias were increasingly seen as being irrelevant within a marketplace of ideas interested in balancing various points of view, foundations nevertheless were further useful in conveying an aura of academic respectability, and even humanitarianism, for those who set them up. The pace of AEI's shift to such support was swift. In the fiscal year from July 1971 to June 1972, AEI took in total revenues of just under $2.3 million, a full 81 percent of which came from foundations or trusts. The largest in this regard were nearly a quarter million dollars from the Earhart Foundation, exactly that amount from the Lilly Endowment, and the same from the Pew Memorial Trust. And, as previously discussed, AEI received a mammoth $1 million from the Scaife Family Charitable Trust in the same fiscal year.[19]

However, a much smaller foundation grant stands out in this same fiscal year because of its importance for furthering the new conservative marketplace policy rhetoric. During this same fiscal year, AEI received the first $50,000 of a $300,000 total grant from the Ford Foundation—despite, or more accurately because of, its status as the primary foundation supporter of Brookings. Such a grant, despite its modest size when compared with other AEI contributions, was a coup for Baroody, who had worked to secure the support of Ford for some time. After news broke of AEI receiving the grant, a friend wrote Baroody, declaring, "That was quite the heist you pulled on the Ford Foundation, Congratulations!"[20] Baroody replied, "At this stage of development, the 'heist' to which you refer is a token—but a good one."[21] To understand why it was a good one for both Baroody and Ford, one need only look at the way the Ford Foundation publicized the grant. In their *Ford Foundation Newsletter*, they situated the grant in the following way: "Although scholarly research on the American economic system has become increasingly scientific in the last few decades, particularly in mathematical analysis, it is far from free of ideology. Reasonable scholars may differ, and economic analysis is carried on by a range of research centers. Among the largest is the Brookings Institution. A smaller institution also of high professional repute is the American Enterprise Institute for Public Policy Research, which has just received a $300,000 Foundation grant. The two centers plow much of the same territory, but their different locations along the spectrum may be indicated by the fact that a chairman of the President's Council of Economic Advisers in the Johnson Administration (Arthur Okun) is a senior fellow of Brookings, and the chairman during most of the Nixon Administration (Prof. Paul McCracken) is head of the American Enterprise Institute's academic advisory board."

What is interesting here is the way in which the Ford Foundation, one of the premier institutions of the liberal consensus along with Brookings, was now internalizing the new marketplace policy rhetoric Baroody and others were promoting. AEI was seen as the proper balance to Brookings given its differing economic ideology and "high professional repute." Here "scientific" means and "mathematical analysis" are subsumed as values to ideological balance and differing viewpoints. So, at base, the grant represents an *intellectual* coup, more than a monetary one, since Ford had clearly internalized conservative policy-debating rhetoric. The same article goes on to note: "Once dependent entirely on business support, [AEI] is now assisted by several private foundations as well."[22] Baroody's shift to foundation support was paying dividends as it convinced a premier liberal institution of AEI's academic respectability and had Ford willingly presenting such a view itself.

As the emerging marketplace rhetoric of policy debate and formation began to take hold, it begs the question as to what AEI actually did with the new monies they received. In the early 1970s, the money was used primarily to build up the institute's ability to produce new conservative policy work. Along these lines, and arguably "the most consequential event at AEI in the early 1970s," was to establish a "resident scholars program" at the institute. As the institutional history of AEI notes, "For all its growing repute in academic circles, AEI was basically a specialty publisher and intellectual broker. It mainly organized conferences and lectures and edited publications by university-based scholars. In contrast to Brookings and RAND, its small staff did little research of its own. The resident scholars program signaled a change of approach that was recognized far more quickly in the academic world than elsewhere."[23] Additionally in 1972 AEI also established an adjunct scholars program of conservative intellectuals who were affiliated with the academic institution but not in residence at AEI. By 1974, the institute had forty-five to fifty resident scholars and twenty-four adjuncts.[24] As the appointment titles indicate, AEI was in many ways becoming more like a university—with in-house scholars dedicated to academic study of conservative positions on policy issues. The new funds AEI was receiving during this period went to these salaries and, as will be seen later in this chapter and the next, various "centers" dedicated to the study of particular issues. This switch to a university-like setup also conveyed academic respectability and situated AEI as a true balance to a liberally dominated academia. Such influence enabled AEI to host more events and publish more studies that would attract the attention of greater Washington and public at large.

The new funding sources for AEI also had a more insidious side to them as many conservative financiers wanted their donations to directly dictate which ideas would enter the marketplace. One such funder was John Merrill Olin, a wealthy conservative businessman in the chemicals and munitions industries. In the early 1970s, Olin became interested in what his personal wealth could do for conservative causes. He and Baroody knew each other well, and Baroody taught him about the policy world and how funding AEI would help him promote conservative causes. Olin's donations to AEI in the early 1970s were modest as it was not until the late 1970s that he reoriented the foundation in his name toward more explicitly political causes.[25] Despite this modesty, Olin clearly wanted intellectual returns on his money. He wrote Baroody in April 1972 after reading a story in the *Wall Street Journal* that suggested that new tax legislation was being produced that would adversely affect corporations and wealthy individuals. Olin wrote, "I, of course, am particularly concerned with the possible revamping of the present estate and gift tax regulations and most alarming is the proposed requirement to extract capital gain payments upon the difference between the book value and market value of securities constituting the estate of a deceased before distribution to the beneficiaries."[26] Baroody replied noting that AEI had six separate studies in the works, but "we have not released any of these studies as yet, and plan not to do so until the appropriate time."[27] Olin tersely replied, "So far as I'm concerned the appropriate time is now at least for the purpose of my reading what you have prepared."[28] Baroody then sped up the studies, produced them for Olin, and spent several letters over the course of the 1970s having Olin press him on the issue. This exchange, while anomalously blatant in its literal buying of ideas, is nevertheless instructive as to the world Baroody was now opening up with his attempt to shift policy debates to his marketplace ideal. Such a shift made the literal buying of idea production acceptable and even welcome. More often than not, such purchasing was not needed, in that conservative think tanks would increasingly have such policy production sped up and supported by identically thinking scholars. However, the new world Baroody was helping create would make such purchasing possible.

In 1972, other already existing conservative think tanks also wanted to amplify their voice in the newly emergent policy marketplace. Hoover, in July 1972, expanded their policy production to the domestic sphere and also started beefing up their in-house scholars in the same way AEI had. In announcing that the institution would now study domestic affairs as well as international, Hoover senior fellow Martin Anderson argued that some at Hoover "feel that we are at a point where it is just as important to understand the background and causes of social and political changes taking place in this country as it is to understand those taking place in other countries around the world."[29] Such a shift allowed Hoover new access to the same sources of funding Baroody was accessing at AEI. Given the long-term relationship between Baroody and Glenn Campbell, Hoover also partnered with AEI in a joint "Policy Studies Series" for which Campbell solicited new monies from Richard Scaife. In writing Scaife in August 1972, a request for $2 million over three years was made and eventually received.[30]

In the fall of 1972, it appeared as if AEI and Hoover were well on their way to monetarily and intellectually capitalizing on the marketplace of ideas. Wealthy conservatives were obviously convinced of their new way of discussing policy and were also convinced that AEI and Hoover were well positioned to allow conservative voices to enter the marketplace in the name of balancing a perceived liberal monolith. On 28 September 1972, however, a momentous event would occur that brought this new way of discussing policy into a much larger public sphere. On this day, a columnist for the *Washington Post*, Jack Anderson, brought to light the existence of a Chamber of Commerce internal memo that had been written in August 1971 for that organization. Authored by newly minted Supreme Court Justice Lewis F. Powell Jr., the so-called Powell Memo sought to delineate, as the memo's title suggests, that there existed in the United States an "Attack on [the] American Free Enterprise System." Until Anderson's column, the existence of the memo was only read by a handful of individuals within the Chamber—which existed, as it still does today, to lobby for business interests among lawmakers. With Anderson's column, the memo achieved wide notoriety. For his part, Anderson highlighted in his initial column the small sections of the thirty-three-page memo that focused on Powell's using the courts as a "'social, economic and political' instrument" through which to defend capitalism. Anderson, in particular, suggested in this column and another the following day that the FBI was at fault for not bringing this document to light during Powell's confirmation hearings so that senators could ask him "whether he might use his position on the Supreme Court to put his ideas into practice to influence the court in behalf of business interests."[31]

The Powell Memo has been enshrined and mythologized in conservative history and historiography since its publication. Such mythologizing has obscured more than it has revealed. For liberals, it is a "road map" of sorts to elite conservative organizing in the four decades since. Conservatives, for their part, tend to downplay its significance, noting that other figures and documents were much more significant. The debate surrounding the memo has made it the single most requested document in the archives of the Powell papers. For the purposes of this study, then, it is most important to try and reconstruct what the memo actually advocated and then to reconstruct how conservative elites, especially in think tanks, responded to its publication. Only through this double reconstruction can we gauge its true impact on the conservative movement in 1972–73. In this regard, the memo was important, just not in the way liberals and conservatives might expect.

The memo itself was written at the request of Powell's friend, Eugene B. Sydnor Jr., who in 1971 was the chair of the education committee for the Chamber. From the delivery of the memo on 23 August 1971 to its discussion by Anderson in his columns it was only viewed by a select few people within the Chamber. After Anderson brought the memo to light, the Chamber made it available to anyone who asked for a copy, leading to its wide circulation.[32] What did the thirty-three-page document actually advocate? First and foremost, as the title suggests, Powell argues that capitalism in the United States is under attack, but that the attack "varies in scope, intensity, and the techniques employed, and in the level of visibility." Powell describes the variety as follows: "There always have been some who oppose the American system, and preferred socialism or some form of statism (communism or fascism). Also, there always have been critics of the system, whose criticism has been wholesome and constructive so long as the objective was to improve rather than subvert or destroy. But what now concerns us is quite new in the history of America. We are not dealing with sporadic or isolated attacks from a relatively few extremists or even from the minority socialist cadre. Rather, the assault on the enterprise system is broadly based and consistently pursued. It is gaining momentum and converts." Such an attack, Powell argues, came from "perfectly respectable elements of society," including "the college campus, the pulpit, the media, the intellectual and literary journals, the arts and sciences, and from politicians."

What is surprising, given the memo's canonical status, is how little of this rhetoric was new. Conservatives, as was seen in chapter 1, had been employing the rhetoric of "capitalism under assault" domestically for quite some time. Moreover, Powell's focus on the sources of such criticism was not new either. The media and academia, in particular, had been beaten up by conservatives as biased in this manner by many conservatives in the late 1960s and 1970s—and even before that.

What was new about the memo, at least to the general public, and even to many conservative elites, was its focus on what businesses needed to do in response. Powell argues that "one of the bewildering paradoxes of our time is the extent to which the enterprise system tolerates, if not participates in, its own destruction" through "appeasement, ineptitude and ignoring the problem." Powell argues that businessmen needed to "confront this problem as a primary responsibility of corporate management." He argues that such action should not be taken independently and in an uncoordinated way. Instead, "Strength lies in organization, in careful long-range planning and implementation, in consistency of action over an indefinite period of years, in the scale of financing available only through joint effort, and in the political power available only through united action and national organizations." Given whom Powell was authoring the memo for, he obviously felt that the Chamber of Commerce was uniquely situated for such an effort. However, as has been seen in this chapter, men like Baroody were already positioning conservative think tanks to take up such an effort.

Powell also employs the newly emergent rhetoric of balancing the marketplace, specifically in regard to academia: "Social science faculties (the political scientists, economists, sociologists and many of the historians) tend to be liberally oriented, even when leftists are not present. This is not a criticism per se, as the need for liberal thought is essential to a balanced viewpoint. The difficulty is that 'balance' is conspicuous by its absence on many campuses, with relatively few members being of conservative or moderate persuasion and even the relatively few often being less articulate and aggressive than their crusading colleagues." Moreover, the students who studied under the liberal faculty "seek opportunities to change a system which they have been taught to distrust—if not, indeed 'despise'—they seek employment in the centers of the real power and influence in our country, namely: (i) with the news media, especially television; (ii) in government, as 'staffers' and consultants at various levels; (iii) in elective politics; (iv) as lecturers and writers, and

(v) on the faculties at various levels of education." Once again, if one were to add institutions like Brookings, much of this was rhetoric Baroody and others were already developing in order to make their own institutions more powerful and influential. Even many of Powell's solutions for what businessmen could do with their coordinated action echo Baroody and AEI. Like Baroody, Powell recommends a generally more aggressive attitude that did not neglect the political arena; a blitz of media in order to more aggressively present the conservative case through television, scholarly journals, books, paperbacks, and pamphlets, as well as paid ads. Most of these were being used or were being developed by conservative think tanks. Powell presents new solutions as well, particularly in regard to changing academia. He recommends businessmen coordinating a staff of scholars and speakers for campus events; an evaluation of textbooks; the "balancing" of faculties; and the enhancement of graduate schools of business. Finally, he urges corporations to stop neglecting the courts and stockholder power as sites of action. In all of these projects, Powell saw the Chamber of Commerce, and not the emergent conservative think tank, as the site through which conservatives could take action. The memo ends by positioning the businessman as under assault if they did not change: "One does not exaggerate to say that, in terms of political influence with respect to the course of legislation and government action, the American business executive is truly the 'forgotten man.' "[33]

Reaction to the publication of the Powell Memo among conservative elites was swift. Discussion of the memo between these elites pervades the archives. However, what was most interesting about the response was the way the memo was repurposed. At AEI, Baroody received a copy soon after Anderson's *Washington Post* columns were published. Upon reading the memo, Baroody knew that it would do him no good in terms of promoting the value of his think tank given that Powell stressed action through the Chamber of Commerce. What Baroody needed to do was reinterpret Powell's message in a way that centralized think tanks like AEI as the key institutional sites for political activity. Luckily, Baroody had just such a place to promote his vision as he was scheduled to speak at a meeting of the Business Council—a loose-knit group of conservatively oriented business owners—in Hot Springs, Virginia, on 20 October 1972. In the first two weeks of October, Baroody wrote a speech that incorporated elements of Powell's analysis but that positioned AEI, not the Chamber of Commerce, as the solution to the problem. Like

Powell, Baroody argues that business had been "persistently losing [the ideological battle] because it had been persistently defaulting." However, unlike Powell, Baroody argues that universities, while certainly a problem for conservatives, were not the main threat. The main threat, instead, "has been a spectacular rise in the number of public policy research centers, both the university-connected and other"—the "other" being the Brookings Institution. Echoing this familiar theme, Baroody argues to the businessmen present that Brookings represented the "citadel of intellectual Democratic liberalism," one that was in a "dominant competitive position, even to the point of providing a virtual monopoly in public policy idea formation" given its vast financial resources. Importantly, however, Baroody contends that he did not fault Brookings for such a bias or such a financial position. Instead, he states that "any fair-minded evaluation would show that Brookings has done a remarkably sophisticated job in mobilizing scholars of stature and competence—of generally the same ideological persuasion." As with Powell, Baroody instead faults the corporate class for not contributing to existing centers, like AEI, which more accurately reflected their own conservative ideological persuasion. He argues that only small changes in "corporate contributions patterns is required" to build an alternative to Brookings. Such a shift would bring "effective competition" to the "intellectual mainstream" in support of a "free society" because the "cornerstone of a free society is rational debate" whereby there must exist a "clash of ideas, effectively presented, to arrive at public policy decisions that will not undermine but rather bolster the foundations of our free society." He closes by arguing that the institutional "monopoly hostile to business" could be broken but not "without reordering priorities in the support patterns of corporations and foundations—at least by those corporations and foundations concerned with preserving the basic values of this free society and its free institutions."[34] This Business Council speech represented the clearest articulation by Baroody—and I would argue by any conservative to that date—of the case for seeing policy not through the lens of the technoscientific ideal but rather as a marketplace. Baroody was effectively, and persuasively, arguing that bias and ideology, whether in Brookings or in AEI, no longer mattered. What mattered was that multiple ideologies were allowed into the marketplace to compete for the minds of policymakers and the public. Whereas earlier rhetoric of AEI appealed directly to "objectivity" and "nonpartisanship" when trying to promote the think tank's activities, Baroody's Business Council speech was more akin to one given at a political rally, urging corporations to stand up for their values in an intellectual and monetary marketplace.

The response to Baroody's speech promoting elite conservative involvement in the marketplace of ideas was positive and he made sure that those elites not present were made aware of his message—particularly those who were interested in the Powell Memo. When John Olin enthusiastically sent Baroody a copy of the Powell Memo for his comments in March 1973, Baroody replied only with a copy of his Business Council speech. Olin replied with great praise.[35] Baroody mailed the speech to the Scaife Family Charitable Trust and received an equally enthusiastic reply in which the representative from the trust asked to share its analysis with his friends. Baroody, of course, enthusiastically agreed.[36] Finally, Baroody was able to publish a version of the speech in the main publication of the National Association of Manufacturers, thus leading to even wider exposure in the business community.[37]

Baroody's new pitch yielded immediate results—especially in regard to specific policy viewpoints that conservatives sought to introduce into the marketplace of ideas. Most interestingly is the way in which AEI was now able to respond to "policy crises" in order to insert their conservative viewpoints into the marketplace. One such crisis was the 1973 oil embargo, which showed the vulnerability of the United States to oil supply disruptions from the Middle East. With the crisis many on the liberal/left, particularly through the Brookings Institution's Energy Policy Project, advocated increasing government intervention and price controls over the energy supply along with a focus on decreased personal consumption and conservation. Such a solution was anathema to conservatives and oil company executives. With this crisis Baroody and others at AEI knew they had an issue at hand through which they could apply their new marketplace rhetoric of policymaking. With former defense secretary Melvin R. Laird at its head, AEI launched its two-year National Energy Project. The planning documents for this new policy research endeavor are revealing for the ways in which Baroody, Laird, and project planner Gordon Hodgson would sell their idea to potential donors. Oil company CEOs and conservative foundation directors were particularly targeted, with Hodgson dismissively referring to them as "the lowest common denominator" for their relative inability to understand how the policy process worked. Because of this inability, Hodgson recommended an education plan of action to convince these groups of people to donate money to the AEI project—as opposed to "trade associations" and "Madison Avenue." Hodgson argued that CEOs were now "ready to listen and to pay more than lip service to the viable option that is contained in [AEI's message] ... to provide a competition of ideas in the intellectual mainstream of policy formation. They will be ready to assist us in getting foundation support."[38]

In the "point paper" that would be sent to these CEOs and foundation directors, AEI employs their policy marketplace rhetoric on the specific issue of energy policy, arguing, "At the present time, in the intellectual mainstream of research and idea formulation on the energy problem, one research center holds a virtual monopoly. This is the Energy Policy Project (EPP) headed by S. David Freeman, a former Research Fellow at Brookings. EPP is sponsored by the Ford Foundation and is currently funded at $3.5 million; some have estimated that this figure may double before the project is completed. With this level of financial backing EPP has a staff of highly competent scholars and the results of their efforts will have a significant and perhaps decisive impact on US national energy policies in the future." AEI argues that the "thrust of many of their studies" would be in the direction of "more government intervention and controls" and that it was "vital in our country's short and long-term interests that all sides of this issue be explored in great depth."[39] AEI's National Energy Project would then provide a "balancing" viewpoint to the Brookings project—one that focused on antistatist solutions to the energy problem. At the press conference announcing the project, Laird drove this point home: "To date a good deal of the published work on problems arising out of this crisis has tended towards simplicity rather than complexity. Their cries of alarm, calls for significant changes in lifestyles, exposés of private corporate abuses, sounds of retreat from international responsibilities, and well-nigh inevitable recommendations for increased government intervention. With the seriousness of the energy crisis in mind, as well as concern over some of the simplistic approaches so far offered for remedying the situation, the American Enterprise Institute is now embarking on a major National Energy Project that will focus deliberately on the highly complicated nature of energy policy and on the diverse options available for solving some of our future energy problems."[40] According to Laird, what was needed was a balancing approach to those out of Brookings that tended to focus on changes in lifestyle, problems with oil companies, and increased government intervention. Left unstated was that the AEI proposals, which were underwritten by oil companies through conservative foundations—or as Laird disguised it, "entirely through private foundation sources"—would be more in line with solutions that tilted in their direction.

However, as Baroody would discuss in a Q-and-A regarding the project, all of these biases were perfectly fine in a new policy world where competition and balance reigned over other values. Discussing the Energy Policy Project at Brookings, Baroody argues that he and AEI "don't believe in criticizing or 'burying' our competitors—the reverse is true—we 'praise' them. That's the core of the AEI philosophy: '*Competition* of ideas is fundamental to a free society. . . .' The energy issue is the best example I know of where there exists a dangerous monopoly and intellectual arena and where research competition is so essential." In essence, Brookings and its project would have their liberal voice funded by liberal foundations, and AEI would have their conservative voice funded by oil companies. Even more interesting, however, than simply promoting a new policy with this new rhetoric, was the way in which Baroody used the new policy, and the discourse that undergirded it, to promote a new *political identity* with AEI as its primary institutional promoter. At this point in time, in 1973, it is probably best to define this identity as "sensible conservatism"—although, as will be seen, it would take on the moniker "neoconservatism" later on in the 1970s. Baroody articulates the identity in this way: "One of the greatest strengths of AEI is that it has no label or ideology. Right-wing conservatives say it is too liberal; left-wing liberals claim it is too conservative. The only label or ideology that is accurate to describe AEI is that it still firmly believes in the basic institutions that made America a great nation and this especially includes the competitive enterprise system."[41] In this way, Baroody's new rhetoric echoed the earlier FSA in its battle against JBS conservatism. Here, Baroody argues that AEI is for a simple defense of capitalism and is happy to have both liberals and right-wing conservatives level critiques against the institution. If you were a "sensible conservative," you turned to AEI for your policy in the marketplace of ideas.

Baroody and AEI's success in implementing the marketplace of ideas, and in using that same framework to create new policies and political identities in the early 1970s, was nothing short of remarkable. In a short period of time, the think tank was able to make itself newly relevant and became flush with new resources and staff. At a 7 February 1974 twentieth-anniversary dinner for Baroody's tenure as chief executive officer at AEI, the think tank celebrated his role in this growth, particularly noting the resident scholars and adjunct scholars now employed by the think tank. And, of course, the growth of the institute's budget from $100,000 a year on his arrival to $3 million a year was stressed as well.[42] President Nixon, despite being in the midst of the Watergate scandal that would end his presidency, took time out to send Baroody a congratulatory message that directly employed the new conservative policy rhetoric Baroody had done so much to promote: "Until your pioneering efforts, the institutions of public opinion molding were largely monopolized by spokesman for centralized big government who felt that every public policy problem could be solved by massive federal spending programs all directed from Washington D.C. This point of view clearly dominated the intellectual debate from the 1930s to the 1960s. Largely thanks to your efforts at AEI, a virtual monopoly in the field of ideas has ended. The competition of ideas so vital to a healthy political order is now being achieved and public policymaking is richer for it."[43] It seemed that AEI was on the cusp of a new era of relevancy in the "marketplace of ideas"— the go-to think tank for conservative policies that would "balance" the "spokesmen for centralized big government" that had so long dominated. What Baroody did not expect, however, was that an open market for ideas meant that new products and services would come to be offered— ones that might be more palatable to conservatives interested in a purer, more activist political identity than AEI was willing or able to offer.

WHERE A MORE ACTIVIST, ideologically pure think tank would come from was open to question—although it was clear many conservatives were thinking about the prospect. The foremost within the Nixon administration was presidential aide Pat Buchanan. Shortly after Nixon's landslide re-election in 1972, Buchanan penned a now-famous memo to Nixon discussing the options for mobilizing elite conservative activism. The memo was in large part celebratory boasting over Nixon's victory, but Buchanan also sought to outline his plan for a more permanent, lasting political majority. The memo and its goal of a lasting majority are ironic given that by the midterm elections in 1974 Nixon had resigned and Republicans were swept from both Houses of Congress in the aftermath. Nevertheless, the memo and its long-term thinking are relevant in that Buchanan had a clear sense of the problem Republicans faced in the marketplace of ideas. Buchanan's language analyzing the problems conservatives faced was strikingly similar to Baroody's. While focused more on building a lasting *Republican* coalition, as opposed to conservatism more generally, the target of Buchanan's ire was the same as Baroody: the Brookings Institute and the Ford Foundation. As was seen in the early part of this chapter, Buchanan and others in the administration had wildly overblown views of Brookings and its power. Buchanan expresses these views but also, like Baroody, has begrudging respect for Brookings: "If we are to build an enduring Republican Majority, then we need to construct institutes that will serve as the repository of its political beliefs. The Left has the Brookings Institution, tax-exempt, well-financed and funded—sort of a permanent political government-in-exile for liberal bureaucrats and Democratic professionals."[44] Contrastingly, and somewhat surprisingly, the Ford Foundation was viewed far more negatively as Buchanan argues that "our political interests dictate public exposure of the ideological bias of the Ford Foundation—and circumscription of its manifold efforts to fund the political activism of the American Left."[45] He goes on, "A public exposure of Ford's record, and repeated political attacks could sensitize the nation to what they are doing, frighten Ford to back away from 'social activism,' and perhaps produce a cornucopia of Ford funds for Republican and Conservative causes—to spare Ford from being taken apart by the Congress at some future tax freeform hearings. Despite the appearance of power and solidity and confidence, the Ford Foundation, like the American left, is a paper tiger."[46] Despite language like this, Buchanan preferred establishing conservative Republican institutions that would counter Ford and Brookings as opposed to scaring or bullying them into changing their behavior. Unlike Baroody, though, Buchanan argues that AEI would not fit the bill. While the memo expresses a clear preference for "the same kind of institution" as Brookings, Buchanan nevertheless argues that "AEI is not the answer." Instead, he states that conservatives needed "something new, initiated in the coming year sometime, and funded both by Government contracts and contributions from American business—and other pro-Republican foundations." Buchanan contends that such a new institution "could serve many purposes," including: "(a) a talent bank for Republicans in office; (b) a tax-exempt refuge for Republicans out of office to stay at work and stay longer; (c) a communications center for Republican thinkers the nation over."[47] Why Buchanan immediately dismisses AEI is left unclear by the memo as AEI is only discussed once—in the brief quote above. One can surmise, however, that Buchanan was only versed in the old AEI model of the 1960s and not the new model Baroody was then working to develop—one that had much in common with Buchanan's own ideas.

Buchanan would have clearly been averse to the older model of AEI, which still sought relevancy within a liberal policy discourse, as opposed to the new AEI, which was studiously working to reframe the policy debate in conservative-friendly terms.

Even if Buchanan and others had a better understanding of the new policy rhetoric and think tank model Baroody and AEI were experimenting with, it is highly likely that he, and other elite conservative activists, would have still been skeptical of the think tank. Buchanan, for his part, was interested primarily in what a think tank could do for the Republican Party. Although Baroody was obviously a Republican who supported Republicans with his think tank, the Republican Party was a secondary concern for him. His first concern was being the premier quasi-academic conservative think tank that was the "go-to" institution for academic, policy, and media elites for the promotion of "sensible conservatism"—both as a policy and as a political identity. By its very nature, such a project involved quite a few elite Republicans. However, it would also—as will be seen later in this chapter—involve former Democrats, so-called neoconservatives, who still in the 1970s did not identify as Republicans. Moreover, whoever was involved at AEI was, by definition, *elite*. These elites existed in a quasi-academic and policy universe that had, at its core, a suspicion of mass movements. As far as Baroody and AEI were concerned, the way to influence idea formation and policy was within elite realms. Baroody was, by the 1970s, soured by his personal experience with mass movements and electoral politics. Buchanan, by contrast, lived his life for this type of politics and would undoubtedly have been suspicious of such the elite institutional mindset that existed at AEI.

As it turns out, other conservatives felt the same way. These activists wanted a think tank that would not only connect with a conservative elite but also one that would connect to the emerging conservative grass roots of the 1970s. Even more accurately, they wanted a think tank *that saw no difference* between the elite and grass roots—one that would just as strenuously advocate for those in corporate boardrooms as they did for conservative activists in the streets protesting *Roe v. Wade* or those organizing against the content of their children's school textbooks in West Virginia. What these new conservative activists desired was a think tank that would speak to the concerns of all movement conservatives and then use its power in Washington to influence, and lobby for, public policy that spoke to these concerns.

Two such conservatives were twenty-eight-year-old Paul M. Weyrich and thirty-year-old Edwin J. Feulner Jr.—both men were conservative activists in every sense of the word.[48] In the early 1970s, Weyrich worked as a press secretary to Republican Senator Gordon Allott, while Feulner was an administrative assistant to Republican Representative Philip Crane. Both were "inspired by Barry Goldwater's principled run for the presidency in 1964 and called themselves movement conservatives."[49] Feulner, in particular, was a true product of the postwar conservative movement. As a freshman in college at Regis College in Colorado, he credits reading Russell Kirk's *The Conservative Mind* and Eric Kuehnelt-Leddihn's *Liberty or Equality* for his conversion to conservatism. He then subscribed to *National Review* and became a member of the conservative student group the Intercollegiate Society of Individualists. He went on to attend the London School of Economics on a Richard Weaver fellowship, an ISI program. Finally, he was a Hoover Institution fellow, where he worked as a policy analyst for Melvin R. Laird, who was head of the House Republican Conference.[50]

The story of how these two young staffers came together to found a new conservative think tank, the Heritage Foundation, has been told again and again by both men and other "movement conservatives"—so much so that it has largely entered into the realm of mythmaking. It is clear, however, that Feulner and Weyrich were envious of liberal think tanks like Brookings as far back as 1969 and that they wanted a similar site for conservative activism. The officially sanctioned Heritage institutional biography describes the outlook at the time: "Envious conservatives watched the powerful liberal coalition of academics, think tank analysts, members of Congress, White House aids, interest group officials, and journalists run much of the business of the nation's capital and wondered: 'Why can't *we* put together an operation like that?'" The same institutional biography caricatures the legislative process of the time in much the same way as Feulner, Weyrich, and Baroody did: "Time and again, a liberal professor would write an article suggesting the creation of a new federal program. The article would be quoted approvingly in the pages of the *New York Times* or the *Washington Post*. Studies of the suggested program would be underwritten by the Ford or Rockefeller Foundation. Scholars at Brookings would meet with members of Congress and their staffs to discuss how the program might be legislatively framed. Special interest groups would endorse the proposed legislation and contact their congressmen and senators. And, finally, a broad-based coalition would emerge—seemingly out of nowhere—backing the bill. The rest would roll smoothly into place: The liberal idea would become law, a new government agency would be created, a new social experiment would begin, and taxes would be raised."[51] Although immensely reductionist, such writing helpfully shows how conservatives like Baroody, Feulner, and Weyrich thought about the policy world in the late 1960s and early 1970s. Brookings and the Ford Foundation were positioned as all-powerful institutions in their implementation of a liberal agenda.

Despite these similarities in analysis, Feulner and Weyrich were frustrated with the ability of AEI to serve as the necessary conservative counter to Brookings. Nearly every article or book ever written that references the story of Heritage's genesis repeats the same story regarding such sentiments. Such mythmaking makes it hard to discern to what extent the story is based in developmental reality or whether it operates in the murkier realm of historical memory. As the story goes, in the spring of 1971, Feulner and Weyrich were working with their respective congressmen regarding a congressional debate over Supersonic Transport (SST) legislation. Both men and the members of congress they represented favored continued federal funding for a supersonic transport plane but lost the final Senate vote by a slim margin. After the vote transpired, the two men received an AEI study on the issue. Weyrich confronted Baroody about the tardiness, to which Baroody supposedly replied, "We didn't want to try to affect the outcome of the vote."[52] Feulner argues in the official Heritage institutional history, "It was at that moment that Paul and I decided that conservatives needed an independent research institute designed to influence the policy debate as it was occurring in Congress—*before* decisions were made."[53]

While there is no doubt that some version of this event occurred, its iconic place in the history of the Heritage Foundation is suspect for two reasons. First, given Baroody's reorientation of AEI by this point, it stretches the imagination a bit to think that he actually spoke the quoted words. Second, as Tom Medvetz has persuasively noted, "there is a seeming discrepancy in Edwards's [the author of the institutional biography] account of the timing of these events" as he cites the SST debate as being seminal but also notes that Feulner and Weyrich were fully engaged in the search for organizational funding in 1969. I agree with Medvetz's interpretation that "it seems to me most likely that the AEI report did not really inspire the idea for the Heritage Foundation, as Feulner reports, but that the incident may nevertheless have focused Feulner's and Weyrich's strategic approach."[54] What Feulner and Weyrich envisioned, as early as 1969, which was crystallized by this incident, was "an activist think tank" that was "designed to influence the policy debate as it was occurring in Congress—*before* decisions were made."[55] As this study argues, this was definitely the direction Baroody was moving in at AEI as all conservative institutions were becoming much more forthright about their politics and the policies they wanted. It is clear, however, that Feulner and Weyrich wanted to enter the marketplace of ideas with something even more aggressive—a think tank that was more activist than academic; nimbler in responding to policy debates; more in tune with the desires of conservative activists in Washington and at the grass roots; and more willing to criticize Republicans for not being forthrightly conservative.

So, like Buchanan (although Weyrich and Feulner never spoke with him about it) the men desired a new think tank with a new focus to be distinct from AEI. The main problem now would be how to fund such an endeavor. Once again, there is a story for how this occurred that is now inscribed as official Heritage lore. As the story goes, Weyrich accidentally received a letter intended for someone else from Jack Wilson, the assistant for political affairs to Joseph Coors. The letter asked how Coors could put his money to use for conservative causes. Coors, who had recently read the Powell Memo, wanted to actualize its recommendations. Weyrich and Feulner arranged a presentation for their new idea with the beer magnate. According to Weyrich, as part of the meeting, they took Coors to the White House, where they met Lyn Nofziger, who "was serving as Ronald Reagan's man in the Nixon administration" and supported their idea. As was seen in this chapter, Coors had already met with Bill Baroody to discuss funding AEI's efforts in the 1970s. According to Weyrich, Coors brought this up at the White House to which Nofziger responded, "'AEI? AEI? I'll tell you about AEI.' He got up from his desk and walked over to his library. He pulled a study off the shelf and literally blew a cloud of dust off of it. 'Their stuff is good for libraries. But it is not timely and nobody around here uses any of it.'" According to Weyrich, Coors told him later "that it was at this moment that he decided to go with us."[56] Once again, this story, along with the SST legislation story, should be seen at least in part as a mythmaking exercise designed to dramatize the founding of Heritage. Nevertheless, it is clear that Feulner and Weyrich, along with Coors, had a think tank model in mind they felt AEI could not fill. AEI, in their minds, was "too academic" and their research was too easily ignored. Coors, Weyrich, and Feulner wanted a nimbler, quick-responsive think tank that was not afraid to get involved in legislative debates. Coors decided on an initial investment of $250,000 in 1971–72 with the promise of more to come.[57] Coors was joined by prominent AEI contributor Richard Scaife, who gave $900,000 in start-up money as well.[58] The men started work under the institutional name the Analysis and Research Association, which was officially founded in late 1971. Unable to get the organization firmly established, they decided to take over an existing foundation, the Schuchman Memorial Foundation, which had become dormant. There were problems with the board of directors at Schuchman, though, as "members of the old board preferred a more traditional approach to public policy, relying on conferences and publication of papers. The new members, led by Weyrich and Feulner, wanted to affect the legislative process promptly and directly."[59] Weyrich and Feulner split off and formed the Heritage Foundation. The think tank was formally incorporated on 16 February 1973.

From the beginning it was clear that Coors, and the two men he funded to start Heritage, did not desire an institution that was overly academic or interested in "sensible conservatism." They wanted an explicitly political think tank that fought intensely tactical fights over legislation, and Coors wanted to see results on his investment immediately. On 29 June 1973, only four months after Heritage's incorporation, Feulner and Weyrich wrote Coors with an update on their efforts in getting the think tank, and other projects, off the ground. It is noteworthy that almost the entire memo is dedicated to legislative battles they were currently engaged in—including killing various wage and price controls; cutting funding for urban mass transit; working to make sure that striking workers did not have access to food stamps; passing legislation to end busing in public schools; and passing a balanced budget amendment, among many, many others. Even so, Weyrich and Feulner urge patience to Coors, reminding him that "Brookings has been working for a decade and a half to gain the prominence it now enjoys in domestic affairs."[60] Throughout much of 1973, the men would have a singular problem with truly getting their new think tank off the ground: lack of tax exemption. Such a status would make it hard to fundraise for their efforts as there were only so many deep pockets like Coors who were willing to donate solely for the conservative cause. The IRS notice of tax exemption came on 27 November 1973, which also served as the formal date on which Heritage was separated from the Schuchman Foundation.[61]

The tax exemption of late 1973 meant that 1974 would serve as the first year in which Heritage's founders would truly work through their institutional model of a rapid-response, unapologetically conservative think tank that spoke for both elite and grassroots conservative activists.[62] The institution's "Prospectus for 1974" is notable for the forthrightness of such a vision. In defining "the problem" Heritage sought to solve, the pamphlet argues the following: "The Problem: One of the most significant trends in recent U.S. history has been the growing influence of foundation 'think-tanks' upon the course of public policy. Institutions such as the Ford Foundation and the Brookings Institute have had a disproportionate influence upon policy decisions at the Federal level in that influence has been consistently liberal-socialist in its viewpoint. Drawing the bulk of the funding from the corporate giants of industry, this has been a case of the viper of socialism in the bosom of the free enterprise system. The result has been increasing economic and social chaos, and the price of that chaos has fallen most heavily upon the middle classes and the non-corporate business community." What is most interesting about this opening is that the writers identify Ford and Brookings in much the same way as those at AEI. However, they were clearly more likely to use incendiary rhetoric like the "the viper of socialism," which was a distinct nod toward conservative populist rhetoric that would soon become commonplace among conservative activists. Positioning the institution as a voice for the middle class and small business also amplified such populist rhetoric. This position of speaking for the "little guys" was heightened further by their stated goal to speak for "traditional American economic and social *values*" and on "behalf of traditional values" that "the vast majority of Americans cherish" because they "know that they have given us the freest and best life in the history of mankind." Such a nod toward "values" was a clear nod to the emerging Christian conservative grassroots movement—which was organizing at a fevered pace in the 1970s, particularly after the *Roe v. Wade* Supreme Court decision. Additionally, the pamphlet argued that the Heritage Foundation would be unafraid to defend such traditional values, unlike "the nation's elected leadership," Democratic and Republican alike. While they argued that "liberal-socialist" think tanks had a head start, they would catch up because they "propose to defend what the people really want." Such a populist institutional positioning, and willingness to take on Republican elites, sought to make Heritage stand out in the "marketplace of ideas" ahead of think tanks like AEI that had been in the game much longer. Finally, in addition to showing the myriad of conservative issues they would be lobbying for, the 1974 Prospectus also outlines a "Student Educational Program" that sought to draw strength from the conservative grass roots in order "to educate young Americans to the kind of government envisioned by the Constitution and to interest them in being active participants in maintaining and strengthening that system instead of 'dropping out' of it or revolutionizing it." Such a program, actively positioning itself as a counter to the New Left, sought to bring young conservative activists to Washington for a semester in order to show them "the practical, inside operation of Congress and to interest them in legislative government as a career."[63] In this way, Heritage continued and amplified the conservative think tank project of creating and maintaining a new generation of conservative activists.

Such direct lobbying on issues and training of new young conservative activists was not all Coors, Feulner, and Weyrich had in mind as Heritage soon took on all the traditional markers of think tanks—policy reports, conferences, media appearances, and so on. Such endeavors were never thought of as merely an intellectual exercise—they were designed to influence legislation in a more conservative direction as rapidly as possible. Given such goals, rigor and academic pretensions such as peer review would be sacrificed to speed of production of reports and gaining influence in public debates. Feulner, in a 1985 speech on how he thought about the role of Heritage from the beginning, was quite clear in this regard. He argued that Heritage specialized "in the area of quick-response public policy research and in marketing academic works for public policy consumption." Such a focus on "marketing" and "consumption" obviously synced well with the emerging consensus of the period around policy being debated in a marketplace of ideas. In the same speech, Feulner further made this link, likening his institution to Procter & Gamble in that the company "does not sell Crest toothpaste by taking out one newspaper ad or running one television commercial. They sell it and resell it every day by keeping the product fresh in the consumer's mind."[64] Incessant and rapid promotion of policies as products, made easier by the hegemony of the marketplace of ideas throughout the 1970s, was integral to Heritage's institutional model from the beginning. And while such a mode of policy debate does not foreclose the idea that liberal and/or conservative policies could be founded on analytical rigor, it does not require it. As has been delineated in this chapter, the only requirement within the marketplace of ideas model, as opposed to the liberal technocratic model, was that there were ideologically different positions being debated—preferably in such a way that could be described as "balanced."

For those like Feulner, Weyrich, and Coors, men who prized speed and relevancy of policy production, such a way of debating policy was a boon. Producing rigorous policies, be they liberal or conservative, takes time. For an institution like Heritage, taking too much time meant losing relevancy. In a policy-debating world where one's institutional identity as conservative was enough to be heard, speed over rigor was rewarded, and Heritage was able to capitalize on this dynamic. Heritage publications from the 1970s reflect these priorities. For instance, a 1974 publication entitled "Federal Child Development: What's Developing?" is notable for its lack of rigor and peer review. The policy primer relies on decades-old "research" to argue against federal aid for child care assistance and against the very ideas of child development, child advocacy, and expertise in early childhood education—all of which are seen as insidious plots hatched by the women's movement in order to free women from their natural roles as caregivers and, ultimately, to undermine "the family, *qua* family, as the basic institution of Western civilization." The document even gives credence to such fantastic claims that "maternal separation and deprivation" can "disrupt the action of the pituitary gland, the 'master gland,' causing abnormal growth and metabolism patterns, even dwarfism."[65] The report was sent to a Heritage trustee for review, but only after it was produced, showing analytical rigor was not a high priority. The trustee argued that the paper's author "let his emotional dislike for working mothers influence his discourse too much" and that he relied on outdated research and "paid no attention to opposing experiences and conclusions."[66] However, such rigor was clearly not the purpose of the study. The author himself, in the paper, argues that he was trying to articulate "what the traditionalist extreme in the preservation of the nuclear family" would look like.[67] He sought to define the new outer right-wing pole on the issue at hand in order to "balance" those who were said to be arguing for a destruction of the traditional family structure.

Issues such as child care assistance, which engaged the emergent Christian religious Right in the 1970s, tended to produce the most over-the-top Heritage research papers and claims—to define the "conservative stance" entering the marketplace of ideas in the most right-wing way possible. Another such example is a 1976 paper on "Secular Humanism in the Schools," which advocates declaring secular humanism a religion and thus making it illegal to teach in public schools on religious freedom grounds. It also notes and supports the growth of Christian schools and homeschooling, arguing that such trends would continue "if the public schools continue to drop the ball and lose the faith of the American people."[68] On issues such as this, Heritage did more than write policy papers. In its early years, Heritage legal counsel James McKenna represented parents in Kanawha County, West Virginia, who went to court over objections to the textbooks being taught in the public schools in their area. McKenna was invited by "one of the ministers who led the parent revolt, the Rev. Ezra H. Grapey." In a 1975 news article, McKenna presents his involvement in the following way: " 'I felt that these parents were getting ground up in an educational system where they had no voice,' McKenna said. 'I committed myself to help them to the extent of my resources. After all, I am Heritage's total legal staff. I represented them in court eight or nine times, and assisted them in making a presentment and help set up a seminar, which was an attempt to balance the inquiry the NEA [National Education Association] had on it.' " This quote is interesting for a variety of reasons. First, Heritage was clearly developing a different project than AEI—one that would be in and of the emergent grass roots of the conservative movement. Second, even this issue is framed by McKenna in terms of "balancing" the public debate—this time against the liberal NEA. In this way, even new issues such as textbook content were framed through the marketplace of ideas. Finally, McKenna's "little guy" framing of the issue is significant as well as he argued that Christian conservative parents were struggling like David against an all-powerful liberal establishment Goliath. Such rhetoric was also infused with victimization as McKenna, in the same article, argues that he "has been stung that some reports which tied his and Heritage's involvement in Kanawha County with the Ku Klux Klan and the John Birch Society. 'It's gotten to be that you can't stand up for a majority without being called John Birch, KKK or Nazi,' he said."[69]

Other research and Heritage activism in the 1970s tended to be less outlandish but entirely predictable as the research merely repeated standard takes on issues of concern to the post–World War II conservatives. Primers on wage controls, natural gas deregulation, national health insurance, Vietnam policy, "Allende and the Failure of Chilean Marxism," SALT treaties, and others merely repeated tried-and-true conservative stances of a hardline defense policy and limited state intervention in the economy domestically. Again, this is not to say that Heritage could not, and would not, in the future produce rigorous "new" policy ideas. The ideas of the 1970s, however, cannot be classified as such. They were old and produced quickly for easy consumption within a policy-debating world where their identity as "conservative policies" was enough to make them heard. Moreover, Heritage's focus on so-called social issues important to the emergent Christian conservative grass roots of the 1970s is particularly noteworthy in that other conservative think tanks like AEI did not focus on such issues at all. AEI instead preferred to articulate policies and political identities that were most important to the business community, anticommunist Cold Warriors, and, eventually, neoconservatives. Heritage, throughout the 1970s and especially into the 1980s catered to all of these AEI positions but also never neglected Christian conservatism. In this way, Heritage and its founders sought to do two things at once. First, they wanted to be the only conservative think tank that spoke to the concerns of the conservative elite and the grass roots. Second, they were trying to be a "fusionist" think tank in the way it sought to speak for all of the impulses of postwar conservatism at once.[70]

Initially, however, there was one way in which Heritage was not a "high" and "low" conservative think tank: in its financing. At first, as previously stated, Heritage received nearly all its funding from conservative elites like Joseph Coors and Richard Mellon Scaife. However, in late 1974, such contributions jeopardized the emergent think tank's tax-exempt status. In that year, Heritage treasurer Lawrence Pratt sent an urgent letter to all Heritage trustees asking for their help in remedying the problem: "In order for the Heritage Foundation to maintain its tax exempt status, it is necessary that one third of the revenues of the Foundation be obtained from what the IRS terms 'qualified sources/monies.' 'Qualified monies' are those contributions in amounts not greater than $6,000, or money received from any federal, state, or local government entity—regardless of amount; or from the sale of publications. It is in this latter regard that I am writing to you. Although our income is adequate to support our present programs for the Heritage Foundation to maintain its present tax exempt status, we must produce several thousand dollars in 'qualified monies,' prior to December 31, 1974. I am sure you can see that this does not leave us much time."[71] The problem was simply that Heritage relied far too heavily on donations of more than

$6,000. To maintain tax-exempt status, that would need to change, and change soon. Pratt suggested as a remedy that all trustees attempt to find companies and institutions that would be interested in buying Heritage publications in bulk—a short-term solution that would do little to address the problem in future fiscal years. Because of this incident, throughout the late 1970s Heritage began to explore small-dollar contributions through direct mail efforts as a way to finance the think tank. Unlike AEI, which had always shunned anything that smacked of a "membership model," Heritage leaders correctly assumed that such a model would work for their think tank since they spoke to issues of concern among grassroots conservatives. The strategy paid dividends as by 1981 Heritage had developed 120,000 small contributors ($2 to $20) annually.[72] Such contributions further solidified Heritage's status as a high/low fusionist model for conservative think tanks.

Such an ability to engage the conservative grass roots financially and on issues of concern became a hallmark of all Joseph Coors's conservative activism. In 1975, the *Washington Post* took notice of Coors's growing political clout in these regards. The paper ran a four-part series where it examined the way in which Coors's activism competed with "old-line conservative organizations" in Washington.[73] The series' final three articles focus on three of Coors's efforts: setting up a conservative television outlet; setting up the "Committee for the Survival of a Free Congress" to oust liberals in Congress within both parties; and, of course, setting up the Heritage Foundation.[74] All three are of interest in terms of understanding the motivations of not only Coors but the men who worked for him. They all clearly saw their projects as being of the conservative movement and attached to the grass roots. In terms of Coors's TV network, he argued that he "got into it because of our strong belief that network news is slanted to the liberal, left side of the spectrum and does not give an objective view to the American public"—clearly echoing the marketplace of ideas rhetoric used against liberal think tanks like Brookings to gain entrance into public policy debates. This rhetoric of "balancing" attracted conservative activists like Roger Ailes, who worked at Coors's network and would go on to help found Fox News in the 1990s using the same rhetorical strategies. The article on the Committee for the Survival of a Free Congress noted how important small-dollar direct mail contributions, headed by "direct mail specialist Richard Viguerie," were for the organization. Viguerie was the same person who began to employ such tactics for Heritage.

Despite all of this notoriety and publicity by the mid-1970s, Heritage was a small think tank by Washington standards. Brookings and AEI still appeared to be the biggest players in town. As to the latter, the mid-1970s saw a monumental surge in AEI's revenue as conservatives put their money where their mouths were in the marketplace of ideas. For the fiscal year ending in 1976, AEI took in $4.725 million from only 194 contributors, nearly 70 percent of which came from just eighteen conservatively oriented private foundations—showing that Baroody's long-term strategy in this regard had paid dividends.[75] Revenues rose even further to just short of $6 million in the next fiscal year, helped along by a new $1 million contribution from the Lilly Foundation.[76] In the mid-1970s, it appeared that Baroody's AEI was on the path to being the dominant conservative voice in the marketplace of ideas. Their position as the "sensibly conservative," Republican-oriented, big-business-oriented, high-dollar donation, elite Washington think tank appeared to be winning the day against upstart Heritage. However, in the midst of this growth for AEI and Heritage in the mid-1970s, outside events intruded as the Watergate scandal shone a spotlight on corporate contributions in politics. These events seemed to threaten both AEI's and Heritage's funding structures in that the scandal might make businessmen and corporations less likely to contribute to anything that seemed too political.

Ironically, when the Watergate-related investigations of the Nixon administration revealed illegal corporate campaign contributions and activities, there was actually little reason for Baroody, Weyrich, Feulner, and their financers to worry. By this point, think tanks were largely shielded from aggressive inquiry given their tax-exempt status as "educational" 501(c)(3) organizations. Such a classification actually made them more valuable institutions in the minds of elite conservative activists because their donations were tax deductible and because the donations were seen as less political than donating to an elected official. For instance, the President of the Libbey-Owens-Ford Company wrote a fundraising appeal on behalf of AEI less than four months before Nixon's resignation, which states the following: "Disclosure of illegal political contributions by a few business organizations to achieve questionable objectives has caused all business relations with Government to be regarded with mistrust, not only by the press but by our citizenry. As a result, even permissible personal contributions by businessmen to political candidates, or business contributions for the purpose of influencing specific legislation, seems certain to be diminished. . . . Points of view traditionally identified as those of business seem likely to get short shrift on Capitol Hill. In such a climate, the analysis of national issues and pending legislation by a credible source such as AEI, fairly presenting pros and cons, seems almost the only way that the business philosophy may receive any serious political attention."[77] Given appeals like this, the increased donations to AEI discussed above should be seen in some ways as a response to the Watergate scandal. This new monetary fuel would launch AEI's profile, and the profile of other conservative think tanks, from the mid-1970s until the end of the decade.

AEI WAS NOT THE ONLY THINK TANK seeing a monetary surge in this period. The Hoover Institution was raising its profile in the marketplace of ideas and in the fiscal year of 1974 took in almost $2.2 million, including $275,000 from the Scaife Family Charitable Trust and $200,000 from the Lilly Foundation—showing a clear ability of Glenn Campbell, like Baroody, to capitalize on the conservative foundation base of support.[78] Both men used their newfound wealth to jointly expand Hoover's domestic policy research and position it as something other than merely an anticommunist think tank. By 1974, the "joint publication venture" for domestic studies was publishing studies at a fast rate.[79] Such activities and fundraising brought new publicity for Baroody and AEI in particular—publicity Baroody used to sell the think tank and the marketplace of ideas rhetorical frame. In a March 1975 *New York Times* article on AEI, Baroody was largely left to expound on the greatness of AEI and its contribution to the "competition of ideas" in the United States, which Baroody asserts was the institute's "only mission." He brags that while still "not in Brookings's ballpark" in terms of funding, AEI was well situated financially because of "foundation support" that "now comprises 80 percent of AEI's income," including the 1972 grant of $300,000 from the Ford Foundation. Such facts would become tried-and-true staples in Baroody's narration of the think tank's position and financial health for mainstream publications. Collected together, they were meant to convey, as the *Times* article helpfully puts it, "that AEI had been accepted as belonging in the policy mainstream."[80] Baroody himself could not have put it better. The article was useful instruction regarding institutional liberalism's embrace of the marketplace of ideas at the expense of more technocratic understanding of policymaking. The *Times* reporter made Baroody's argument for him that AEI was now the institutional representative of "respectable conservatism," a position also signed off on by that paragon of institutional liberalism, the Ford Foundation. In the marketplace of ideas, AEI was now the respectable right voice.

Other mainstream publications would soon follow the *Times*'s lead in the way they positioned AEI as the voice of reasonable, open-minded conservatism in the marketplace of ideas. *Finance Magazine*, in December 1975, quoted Baroody as saying, "It is hard to pin labels" on the think tank, and even though they were "in a competition of ideas" with Brookings, that the institute's relationship "with Brookings is friendly." The article then went on to note that "today AEI receives 75–80 percent of its funds from foundations," which was "pleasing to the staff."[81] Likewise, a May 1976 *Newsweek* article argues that AEI was promoting an increasingly "fashionable premise" that "government was much too big" and on the strength of that premise was approaching Brookings's levels of funding—a $5.3 million annual budget to Brookings's $7 million. The article then helpfully employs marketplace rhetoric when it argues that there would "almost surely be a growing market for those ideas" considering "the current leanings of the [Ford] administration."[82] AEI in particular would benefit from Ford being in office since Ford was one of the longest-running supporters of the institute, starting with his early days as a representative in the U.S. House. After Ford assumed the presidency, he held numerous meetings with Baroody and AEI staffers, including the two separate meetings in April and May 1975.[83] He was also a special guest at a May 1976 AEI dinner, where he gave a speech that helpfully advanced the marketplace of ideas by noting AEI's vital role in ensuring "that there [was] a vital competition in the realm of ideas. Competition of ideas is absolutely essential to the continuation of a free society, for it is diversity which is the strength of our democracy."[84]

This new widespread notoriety, financial strength, and political clout in the White House and Congress increased the "products" AEI was able to sell in the marketplace of ideas. The foremost among these was the political identity "neoconservative." Up to this point in time, the implicit identity AEI had been selling was that of the mainstream/respectable conservative. However, such an identity was lacking coherency and acceptable "selling potential." In this light, it was around 1975–76 that AEI became a key marketer of the identity "neoconservative." Although such a political identity carries immense baggage now, given its nearly forty-year history, at the time it represented something new. From 1973 to 1975, "neoconservative" was created in order to describe liberal intellectuals and policymakers who had become disaffected with the political-cultural ideals of the Democratic Party during that period. Domestically, neoconservatives became immensely skeptical, if not outright hostile, to the welfare state initiatives of the Great Society and to the New Left generally. The leading cheerleader for such a position was Irving Kristol, a New York public intellectual who edited and founded the influential journal *The Public Interest*. Kristol came to AEI as one of its first fellows in 1972 and would write his many public writings under such a title until 1999. Kristol wrote prolifically, including a monthly column for the *Wall Street Journal* from 1972 to 1997. Almost single-handedly he came to popularize this new political identity and to situate AEI as its institutional base. He gave the think tank a clear new product to promote in the marketplace of ideas—one that, while thoroughly conservative in its orientations, had the aura of moderation in that its key promoters were former Democrats. Such a position was the perfect fit for AEI as it sought wide influence. The 1976 *Newsweek* article on AEI already describes it as being the central institution representing "the swing towards neoconservatism."[85]

Kristol was integral at AEI not only for his promotion of this new identity but also for his ability to connect AEI with funding from nonconservative sources of funding with which he had strong ties. One such funding base was the Alfred P. Sloan Foundation—which was part of the constellation of New York–based liberally oriented foundations. The Sloan Foundation tended to fund scientific research but in the 1970s also took interest in economic research. Kristol understood this and encouraged Baroody to apply for funding from the Sloan Foundation for AEI's new 1975 project—its Center for the Study of Government Regulation.[86] Around this period of the mid to late 1970s, as the heavily regulated mid-century economy was faltering, conservative economists began forcefully making an argument rapid deregulation was needed. AEI wanted to develop its Center for the Study of Government Regulation as a place to promote such an idea. In the mid-1970s "deregulation" was seen as one of the key "new ideas" emerging from AEI and conservative economists more broadly. More recent research has shown that the idea of deregulation had been around for quite some time, both within and without the think tank structure.[87] Despite this "oldness" of the idea, deregulation obtained the aura of "the new" as policymakers began grasping for solutions to the economic woes of the United States in the 1970s. Baroody had grand ambitions to situate AEI's Center for the Study of Government Regulation as the central promoter of the idea. With this goal in mind, in 1975 Baroody wrote a letter to the Sloan Foundation requesting the foundation allocate a "three-year grant to AEI in the amount of $500,000" as part of an overall five-year budget of $10 million for the center.[88] In a follow-up letter for the request, Baroody notes, "Irving Kristol has agreed to chair the Advisory Council for the proposed Center and, as you probably know, there's a strong likelihood that he will be at AEI as a Resident Scholar during the forthcoming academic year." Baroody also adds that other foundations had already contributed funding, including, "the Lilly Endowment which has committed $2.5 million over a three-year period; the Richardson Foundation with an initial commitment for one year of $500,000 with an indication that the Trustees will sympathetically consider requests for each of the next two years in like amounts; and the Glenmede Trust with an initial one-year grant of $250,000."[89] Kristol's influence, combined with the financial support of other foundations, secured the money from the Sloan Foundation, with the first of five $100,000 payments allocated in fiscal year 1976.[90]

It is hard to overstate the impact of AEI's Center for the Study of Government Regulation in the marketplace of ideas. If anything, AEI's internal institutional history understates its impact, and the impact of the center's main publication *Regulation*, in the mid- to late 1970s. The authors of the internal institutional history argue that it was *Regulation*'s "jargon-free, scrupulously nonpartisan articles" that "had stimulated debate on regulation, antitrust, and trade and contributed to progress in those areas."[91] Recent research into the history of the "deregulation movement" backs up this assertion.[92] The center and the publication *Regulation* were immensely influential in a variety of ways. First, they gave platforms to key influential architects of deregulation, including Murray Weidenbaum, Marvin H. Kosters, and James C. Miller. Through that exposure, these men became key witnesses at congressional hearings where deregulating various American industries, such as the airline and trucking sectors, became a reality. Second, the style and tone of *Regulation* made it immensely readable for not only academics but members of the general interested public. As such, the idea of "deregulation" took on new life beyond the narrow idea of deregulating certain industries. As Baroody puts it in a letter to *Regulation* subscribers, "In the past federal regulation was directed primarily at business. But today, it touches nearly every aspect of your life. You're being told what is safe to eat, wear, breed, ride in . . . what you can watch on TV . . . what products you can buy and sell . . . what you're working conditions must be . . . even how you can spend your leisure time. On the one hand, you cry out for protection as a consumer, but on the other, your outrage at the growing interference of government in your community, your school, your business."[93] In this way, the center and *Regulation* had much broader aims than simply deregulating various sectors of the American economy. They also targeted the 1970s "consumer movement" led by Ralph Nader for allowing encroachment of the state into the private lives of all Americans. Finally, AEI's promotion of deregulation had an even more profound effect as Gerald Ford lost to Jimmy Carter in the 1976 election. Essentially, the election of Carter, and his support of many of the ideas and policies of the deregulation movement, further entrenched AEI as the most influential conservative think tank. When combined with the support of deregulation policies by Democrats in Congress, including such luminaries as Senator Ted Kennedy, AEI saw its influence rise even further. Now the institute could further position itself, through deregulation and its neoconservative identity, as a conservative think tank within the mainstream of American political thought and practice.

Ironically, Ford's loss of the presidency, and the attending support of key Democrats for much of what AEI was promoting, actually enhanced AEI's position in the marketplace of ideas. Ford's exit from the White House helped in other ways as well. First, Baroody's son, William Baroody Jr., was on Ford's White House staff and immediately after Ford's loss began talks for a position for Ford at AEI as a "distinguished fellow." He assumed such a position in 1977. Such a move raised AEI's profile even further with mainstream publications arguing that the move "highlighted the emerging importance of the Institute as a conservative center for research in economics, political science, and foreign affairs."[94] Additionally, these same mainstream organs immediately began to argue that AEI would now house the next Republican "government-in-waiting." AEI was now considered to have the same relationship to the Republican Party as Brookings had to the Democratic Party—the institution where policymakers would find employment until a member of their party was in the White House. The *New York Times* set the tone in this regard when they published a November 1976 article entitled "Casting Begins for the Next 'Shadow Cabinet.'" In it, AEI is identified as the primary place where Republican policymakers would wait out the next Republican administration. The *Times* helpfully argues that this was the case because while AEI used to have "the reputation of being so conservative it was positively far-out," this was now "no longer the case" and the institute would surely "become an important source of valuable conservative criticism of the Carter Administration policies" in the same way Brookings staff criticized Republican presidents while in office.[95]

Ironically, at this same time Brookings itself was undergoing changes in the opposite direction as the institution was taking great pains in order to be viewed as *less* partisan. There were many reasons for such a change. The first involved the new financial realities of the United States in the 1970s. James Allen Smith, in his official biography of Brookings, notes that for all Bill Baroody sought to raise money from elite conservatives using Brookings's massive endowment as a counterpoint, the stock market decline of the mid-1970s had significantly eroded that endowment "from a peak in 1972 of about $49 million to less than $33 million in 1976."[96] After this setback, Smith argues that the board of trustees at Brookings desired a new president who could "seek out new sources of financial support to supplement the foundation resources that had been hard hit by declining financial markets and the inflationary surge of the early 1970s."[97] The board wanted such "new sources" to include corporate support. However, by this point, Baroody and others at conservative think tanks had done much to tar Brookings as fundamentally biased against corporate interests within the marketplace of ideas. Given this fact, Brookings wanted a new president in 1977 who would signal that such a perceived bias was not true. The man they hired for the job was Bruce K. MacLaury, an economist who "was chosen because he was viewed as 'professionally nonpartisan'" despite serving two years in Nixon's Treasury Department.[98] The hope was that MacLaury's reputation would attract more ideologically diverse funding streams.

The choice of MacLaury also shows the effectiveness of conservatives' marketplace rhetoric in that liberal institutions began to ideologically discipline themselves to appear more "balanced" at the very same time conservative think tanks were becoming more forthrightly conservative. The effect of this was profound in that it shifted the entire political spectrum to the right in that all think tanks, *including Brookings*, were moving rightward throughout the 1970s. Financial concerns at Brookings undoubtedly contributed to this dynamic. But it was also clear that those at Brookings simply did not want to be viewed as a liberal Democratic institution and were particularly concerned with conservative critiques that said they were. And although efforts to internally address this critique began most forcefully under MacLaury, there is evidence that Brookings trustees were already wounded by such accusations as early as 1973. In that year, a friend of Baroody's who was on the Brookings board of trustees sent him a letter indicating that "Brookings is getting a better balance of personnel than it had a year ago" and that he "was personally impressed by the understanding and concern that the Board of Trustees expressed relative to the liberal reputation which Brookings has received in the past few years."[99] MacLaury's arrival simply signaled that the board was now willing to address such concerns with a new president who would appoint more ideologically diverse people to the staff of the institute. Mainstream media outlets covered, and in many cases lampooned, the Brookings shift. The *Los Angeles Times* ran a fake "help wanted" ad that read: "Republican. Deep thinkers with high level experience in government, economics, foreign affairs. White House background helpful. Apply Brookings Institution, Washington, D.C." The *Times* writer then noted, "Dignified Brookings isn't about to do anything as crude as place a want ad. But the fact is that the renowned think tank, which many regard as a citadel of liberal Democratic ideas, has a new president, Bruce K. MacLaury, who wants to recruit some prominent Republican scholars. MacLaury hopes to obtain for Brookings a more balanced ideological image and, in the process, to obtain more financial contributions from the corporate world."[100] Joking aside, it is hard to understate the significance of this move and the success it represented for conservatives in implementing their new policy rhetoric. In the beginning of implementation, conservatives like Baroody had simply hoped the "marketplace of ideas" rhetoric would situate AEI as the conservative voice in the debate that balanced Brookings. Now the rhetoric was having a different effect as Brookings was *balancing its own institution* ideologically—what MacLaury described to one publication as the need to have "a diversity of views to keep the place credible."[101] Such a move weakened any liberalism actually contained in Brookings while conservative think tanks became more forthrightly conservative. As historian Donald Critchlow suggests, such a move by Brookings "signaled the abandonment, or at least the fundamental transformation, of the nonpartisan ideal, with its perhaps naïve assumption that social scientists could stand above the political fray and act in the public interest, which had motivated Robert Brookings and other progressive era architects of independent research institutes. Their zeal for objectivity and efficiency in the distrust of politics, embodied in nonpartisanship, gave way to the very different conception that political knowledge was somehow inseparable from fundamental values, and thus—in the Brookings case—to a quest for ideological balance." Such a shift, argues Critchlow, is encapsulated in a quote from one MacLaury era Brookings official, who argues, "There is no such thing as 'nonpartisan' research. At best research can only be bipartisan."[102] Such a quote, particularly in the overall context of this study, is revealing in the way it highlights the differences between liberal and conservative think tanks by the late 1970s. While conservatives were striving for more ideologically oriented think tanks, liberal think tanks were disciplined by the marketplace of ideas to strive for the opposite—a think tank that was more "bipartisan."

This is not to say that conservative think tanks were in agreement on what conservative identities and policies should be promoted. By 1976–77, in fact, there was intense disagreement on both matters of ideology and tactics among leading conservative think tanks. By this period, Heritage has grown to a point where Baroody at AEI and Glenn Campbell at Hoover were pressed by donors to help them make sense of the upstart think tank—and to possibly ally with it. For instance, in 1976 a donor wrote Campbell, arguing that "if I'm correct in my understanding of the goals and purposes of Heritage, it appears that the Heritage Foundation, Hoover Institution and American Enterprise Association [*sic*] should have much in common." He went on, "It seems to me, if we could forward some kind of effective working alliance between Heritage, Hoover, and American Enterprise [*sic*], we might ultimately prevail against Brookings and their liberal establishment allies."[103] Although there is no record of Campbell responding to the letter, Bill Baroody undoubtedly conveyed Campbell's feelings when Baroody responded to a similar inquiry in 1977 from a donor who asked, "How long has [Heritage] been in existence and what's it been doing that is not already receiving the attention of AEI?"[104] Baroody dismissively replied, "As you know, many of our friends are very busily engaged in 'reinventing the wheel.' To answer your question directly, I know of nothing that some of these outfits are doing which is not already receiving the attention of AEI."[105] Although undoubtedly self-interested, it is actually quite possible that Baroody believed what he was saying about Heritage.

From inside Heritage, things looked very different. The mid-1970s marked a period of extensive growth and change at Heritage, and if Baroody had known about these changes, he would have had reason to worry about AEI's relative strength in the marketplace of ideas. The biggest reason for such changes was a change in leadership. In 1975, Paul Weyrich left the presidency of Heritage to become more directly involved in electoral politics and to more directly organize the Christian Right. For a brief period, the think tank was then managed by California businessman Frank Walton. Walton's biggest contribution to the organization during his brief tenure was in fundraising as he was largely responsible for Heritage's direct mail small-dollar donation efforts referenced earlier in this chapter. From late 1975 until his term ended in April 1977, Walton had boosted the Heritage budget from $743,000 annually to more than $1 million annually. In April 1977, Walton was replaced by Ed Feulner, who would remain as Heritage's president until 2013. Under Feulner, fundraising increased at a rapid pace—both at the large- and small-donor level. The 1977 budget was $2 million, by 1979 it was $4.1 million, by 1980 it was $5 million, and by 1981 it was $5.3 million—with 24 percent of the 1981 budget coming from small donors.[106]

Heritage's success under the tenure of Feulner in the late 1970s was not simply due to his ability to raise money. Feulner in this period worked to refine and hone the "Heritage model" for the conservative think tank—which in the 1980s would pay dividends over the AEI model. Most important in this regard, Feulner worked to hone Heritage's role as a quick-response think tank. In a 1981 interview, he argued that this meant Heritage "was a second-hand dealer in ideas," whereby "we take the ideas from the seminal thinkers, translate them into policy concepts, refine them, publicize them and make them usable within the policymaking process" so "pressure groups can advocate them, build coalitions around them and ultimately trigger some action."[107] Such timeliness could only be accomplished if policies were marketed in the briefest way possible. Feulner argues that when he came to Heritage, he instituted the "briefcase test," which meant that a "study should be as brief as possible. Arguments should be concise and clearly presented. Because of the vast number of issues addressed in Congress, there is a desperate need for concise studies which cut through the rhetoric and lay out the arguments to help members of Congress make informed choices on issues before them." What this meant was first developing a new type of Heritage publication, the *Backgrounder*. Feulner argues that Heritage tries "to limit our *Backgrounders* to ten pages—a document which stands much greater chance of being put into a briefcase and read before the debate than a book which generally ends up on a bookshelf."[108] Even shorter formats were developed. First came *Heritage Issue Bulletins* in the 1970s, which were quickly produced studies of specific pending legislation.[109] Later, once Reagan was in office, came the *Executive Memorandum*, a series that outlined "an argument in its briefest form—one sheet front and back—and it's written, printed and hand-delivered to the concerned Washington offices in twenty-four hours, often all the time available before a crucial decision is made."[110] During the late 1970s, Feulner made sure that Heritage began amassing a databank of contacts so all of these quick-response publications could be quickly written and then get to the right people in government on time. Finally, in the late 1970s Feulner also developed a twice-monthly newspaper column, the *Heritage Foundation Forum*, which by 1981 was used in more than 450 newspapers around the country—ensuring that the think tank's conservative message was heard outside Washington.[111]

Besides developing Heritage's quick-response capabilities through new publications, these new forums also furthered Heritage's goal of becoming a fusionist think tank that represented all strands of conservatism as well as both the concerns of conservative elites and the conservative grass roots. The earlier publications of Heritage cited in this chapter made many think that the organization was solely dedicated to the concerns of the Christian New Right. In some sense, this reflected the concerns of Weyrich who was definitely of this movement. When Feulner came in as president, he reduced the overall research of Heritage in this area from 25 percent to only 10 percent by 1981.[112] The think tank still spoke to such concerns, but just as one part of the overall conservative coalition they sought to unite. Feulner created several new publications to speak to all parts of the conservative coalition: "For the traditionalists and the neoconservatives, there is the *Policy Review*, a scholarly quarterly [created in 1977] with articles by such intellectual lights as Senator [Daniel Patrick] Moynihan, Milton Friedman and economist George Gilder. For the foreign policy and defense community, there is the 'National Security Record,' a monthly newsletter that alerts readers to upcoming Congressional issues and carries well-researched articles arguing for such conservative causes as the unmanned bomber. And for the New Right, there is 'Educational Update,' a newsletter that attacks sex education, advocates school prayer and otherwise supports the social views of the Moral Majority."[113] By the late 1970s, Feulner was truly creating a new conservative think tank form—fast-acting and able to represent all voices in the conservative movement.

By the late 1970s Heritage was not the only new upstart in the marketplace of ideas. By this point, libertarian conservatives began to feel unrepresented by conservative think tanks. Although places like AEI and Heritage undoubtedly spoke a libertarian language when it came to free-market capitalism, their commitment to such a perspective often was unevenly applied. Into this void stepped the Cato Institute—which was truly organized and incorporated as a think tank in 1976–77. Cato was largely the brainchild of libertarian Edward H. Crane III, who was also president of Cato from its inception until 2012. A financial analyst by training, Crane felt that libertarian ideas were largely absent from American political debates and that existing conservative think tanks were not interested in remedying this problem. So, like Feulner at Heritage, Crane found a key financial backer of his idea: Charles Koch, who, along with his brother, headed up Koch Industries. Although Koch Industries began as an oil-refining and chemical production business under their father, the brothers would expand it into a multibillion-dollar company with projects as diverse as commodity trading and the production of various consumer products. Libertarian writer Brian Doherty, who is clearly a fan of both Koch and Cato, argues that Koch contributed monetary funds to the Cato Institute as a way to "increase the amount of libertarian capital goods" in the marketplace of ideas. Koch, in an interview with Doherty, says that Cato was part of an "integrated strategy . . . to bring about social change, from idea creation to policy development to education to grassroots organizations to lobbying to litigation to political action." Such a strategy saw "academia and think tanks" as key "scriptwriters" for politicians who were ultimately "just actors playing out a script." Up until this point, Doherty argues, there was no think tank serving as such a scriptwriter for the libertarian position. There was the Foundation for Economic Education, which sought to influence the public through numerous publications from the end of World War II onward, but not a think tank that tried to do this and also be an "in-the-debate public policy house" was well.[114]

Such a dual role, so integral to the modern conservative think tank, was hard to achieve because Cato established its offices in San Francisco—as opposed to Washington, D.C. The choice of San Francisco was nevertheless an interesting reflection of what Cato was trying to do as an institution and with its first publication, *Inquiry*. *Inquiry* editor Ralph Raico, in a letter to heavyweight libertarian economist F. A. Hayek, notes that the magazine's "main purpose will be to establish a dialogue between libertarians and those who in the United States are called 'liberals.'"[115] Given this, the choice of San Francisco seems apt. In announcing the magazine to the public, Crane argues that such an alliance would be formed through *Inquiry*'s commitment to the "humanist values of peace" and "toleration in individual rights." The magazine would do this through an emphasis on "investigative reporting and analysis on such topics as enforcement of victimless crime laws, civil liberties and threats to the Bill of Rights, government underwriting and subsidizing of corporations, the abuses by the U.S. domestic and foreign intelligence agencies, and U.S. government interference in the affairs of other countries."[116] With such an agenda, it is clear that many liberals would find much to like about Cato's libertarian philosophy and that such an institutional philosophy would be markedly different from the positions emanating from Heritage and AEI. In addition to publications like *Inquiry*, Cato copied much from other conservative think tanks. A letter from Crane to Cato supporters notes the development of a "Cato Sponsors Program" to develop a small donor base in addition to their big-money corporate supporters like Koch. The same letter notes that such funding would go to Cato's Academic Affairs program, which sought to develop policy frameworks for lawmakers. Finally, much like Heritage, Cato developed a program that sought to recruit and educate young Americans to the conservative cause.[117] Titled "Summer Seminars in Political Economy," Cato promotes them as "intensive eight-day programs . . . integrating history, philosophy, public policy, and economics into the kind of worldview that gives an individual confidence to think for himself."[118] Cato would continue such activities until 1981, when it moved its headquarters to Washington, D.C., in order to have a more direct impact on the policymaking process.

In the late 1970s, despite the differences between Cato and places like AEI and Heritage, the institutions had much in common—particularly in the way all of them sought to bury the last vestiges of the liberal technocratic edifice of policymaking and replace it with the marketplace of ideas. A powerful new paradigm for advancing this goal was provided by AEI's Irving Kristol in a highly influential 1977 *Wall Street Journal* op-ed entitled "On Corporate Philanthropy." While in many respects the op-ed echoes now familiar conservative messages on the importance of corporations giving to institutions that support their values, Kristol also introduces a term to the general public to define the enemy of corporate values: "the New Class." This framework, to Kristol and his neoconservative allies, was not new. They had been developing it in publications like *Commentary* and *Public Interest* for almost a decade by this point. To the general public, however, it was new and very power-ful. Kristol and his allies used it to characterize those who displayed "a habitual animus to the business community" and who sincerely believed "that the larger portion of human virtue is to be found in the public sec-tor, and the larger portion of human vice in the private sector." Accord-ing to Kristol, the New Class primarily resided "in our universities, in our foundations, and in our media too," and the members were biased toward the position that "'constructive social change' is always something that government does for and to people, never something that people do for and to themselves—and most definitely nothing that American busi-ness does for or to anyone." Kristol's rhetoric here is particularly notable for the way he includes the media along with foundations and academia as the primary components of the New Class who were biased in favor of welfare state liberalism and against "American business." Such a for-mulation would become reliable conservative rhetoric heading forward and situated conservative think tanks and conservative media outlets as necessary balancing agents to such a bias.

Kristol, of course, goes on to argue that it was the duty of business-men and corporations to fund such conservative institutions, who were ultimately "'dissident' members . . . of the New Class." In tandem with this funding, businessmen had to also "decide *not* to give money to sup-port those activities of the New Class which are inimical to corporate survival." In making such an argument, Kristol clearly argues that there should not be a "naked contest with the New Class" but rather that "you can only beat an idea with another idea, and the war of ideas and ide-ologies will be won or lost *within* the New Class, not against it."[119] Kris-tol's formulation here performs a powerful rhetorical trick that was always implicit in the new conservative rhetoric of policymaking—that corporations, businessmen, conservative intellectuals, and, quite simply, anyone who advocates for the virtues of capitalism are persecuted for such beliefs by an all-powerful New Class. This is particularly striking in the case of Kristol, who by this point was earning a living as an intel-lectual that well exceeded the wildest dreams of any liberal intellectual. Nevertheless, by situating himself as a "dissident" within the New Class and in situating corporations and businessmen as the "little guys" in a "war of ideas and ideologies," Kristol engaged these groups in an ex-tremely powerful way by situating those who benefited the most from American capitalism as its populist underdogs.

Other conservative think tanks followed suit and employed Kristol's rhetoric for their own ends. For instance, in an early Cato Institute publication, Edward Crane argues that there is "a danger of public policy institutions becoming part of the New Class of bureaucrats, technocrats, academics, and politicians who more and more are presuming to have the ability to make decisions for the rest of society." According to Crane, "In recent years Americans have started to react much more skeptically to the pronouncements of the New Class. But skepticism is not enough. In order to establish a renaissance of the spirit of self-reliance and individualism that marked the founding of our nation, it will be necessary to create a broad constituency of intelligent, informed Americans." Such an informed citizenry "can't be intimidated into believing the 'experts' know better; this will be required to restore our natural rights as free human beings."[120] In this way, Crane goes beyond Kristol in speaking a populist conservative discourse on behalf of all the American people and not simply the corporate class. In this formulation, Americans had "wised up" and would continue to with the help of Cato. Heritage also made use of the same rhetoric in their publications. An article in *Policy Review* entitled "The Dilemma of Conservatives in a Populist Society" argues that conservatives need to get in tune with populist American culture to "confront and perhaps vanquish welfare liberalism." In particular, "the heads of the great corporations must themselves accept more widely than they now do the values of conservatism," namely, through sponsoring "important work in education, research, the arts and other areas of American culture once left strictly alone by American business enterprise."[121] Furthering Kristol's addition of the media to his New Class paradigm, another *Policy Review* article argues that among the press there are "troublesome signs of a homogeneity of political, social and economic attitudes" as journalists were largely "drawn from a social and educational elite" that was influenced by an "adversary culture." Such a culture, which Kristol also mentions when discussing the New Class, made "journalists see it as their function to place before the public the needs of society as they see them" as opposed to leaving political agendas to the politicians. Americans would need to be educated about such a "media bias" so as to increase their skepticism of this part of the New Class.[122]

As the decade of the 1970s closed out then, conservative think tanks were making immense headway in changing the way Americans thought about and debated public policy. The liberal technocratic edifice was crumbling and new conservative voices, in think tanks and elsewhere, were entering the new marketplace of ideas. The only remaining question is how many institutional representatives would gain entrance to the debate. With four main conservative think tanks now in place—AEI, Hoover, Heritage, and Cato—would all their "voices" be equal, or would there need to be a battle for supremacy for one "top spot"? If the latter were the case, as the 1970s closed, all bets would have likely been on AEI or Hoover to take top billing. They had been around the longest, had the highest budgets, and were most clearly associated with the Republican Party. Elite media organs were placing their bets on AEI as the late 1970s saw a spate of articles in high-profile news outlets trumpeting the institute as the premier conservative think tank, with Hoover as a possible second place.[123] Heritage and Cato received nary a mention. With the benefit of hindsight, however, AEI's position showed vulnerabilities. First, in March 1978, William Baroody Jr. took over for his father as head of AEI.[124] The younger Baroody had worked in the Ford administration but had never led an organization before, thus the appointment subtly smacked of nepotism. Second, AEI's cultivation of the "neoconservative" identity led many conservatives to the suspicion that AEI cared little about the grassroots conservative movement—especially since so many neoconservatives identified as Democrats at one time or another. Ed Feulner at Heritage would seek to inflame such concerns in interviews, saying things like, "Unlike AEI . . . we have not moved to the mushy middle of the political spectrum. We are unabashedly and unashamedly conservative."[125] Feulner's position was more likely to gain favor from the beginning upon Ronald Reagan's election in 1980. Finally, there was a big unknown in the late 1970s—Heritage's immense preparation for the possibility of a Reagan election. When compared with AEI, Heritage's institutional model of a fast-acting policy shop aligned with both the conservative elite and the grass roots would pay dividends with a new conservative president in the White House. In contrast, AEI was woefully underprepared. However, although Heritage would ultimately win out in terms of overall influence by the end of the 1980s, it was still AEI that had the most marked impact on the first key policy decision of Reagan's first term—the enactment of "supply-side economic" policies. It is to this story we now turn.

3
Think Tanks in the Age of Reagan

When examining "supply-side economics," and the role of think tanks in implementing such an idea, it is not enough to look solely at the Reagan presidency. AEI, Heritage, and other conservative think tanks recognized that the very idea of "supply-side economics" was a new one that needed to be "sold" to the public and policymakers well before a conservative was in the White House. Given this fact, it is necessary to return once again to the important period of the 1970s, for it was then when the intellectual groundwork was laid for the eventual implementation of "supply-side" economic policies. Conservative think tanks were integral in selling this new product in the marketplace of ideas. As the name suggests, "supply-side economics" as an idea was meant as a contrast to Keynesian "demand-side" solutions to economic problems. With the rising economic problems of the 1970s—including inflation, slow economic growth, and rising unemployment—conservatives in think tanks and elsewhere correctly recognized that this was the time to sell more conservatively oriented economic policies. The seeming inability of Keynesian economic prescriptions to deal with the problems of the 1970s made even more fertile ground for conservative economic policies. Additionally, because the marketplace of ideas paradigm of policy debate was becoming dominant at this same time, new conservative ideas would be easier to introduce. Under such a framework, all that was needed was the policy's identity as "conservative." The very name "supply-side economics" accomplished this goal as it "balanced" the liberal, Keynesian side of the economic policy debate. Taken together, all of these factors meant that the entry barriers for "supply-side economics" into the economic policy debate were very low.

In the mid-1970s, the Heritage Foundation was still growing as a think tank, and only AEI had the resources to introduce supply-side economics into the marketplace of ideas. What this meant was that such an idea came to be associated with AEI's neoconservative identity. Given these factors, it is unsurprising in hindsight that the key nexus for the germination of the idea occurred between AEI, Irving Kristol, and the *Wall Street Journal* editorial page. As senior fellow at AEI and as a member of the *Journal*'s Board of Editorial Contributors, Kristol had the time, resources, and centrality within the marketplace of ideas to put forth supply-side theories. As editor of the *Public Interest* and as professor of social thought at New York University's Graduate School of Business, Kristol was uniquely situated to promote and support supply-side economics and its centrality to the neoconservative political identity. Shortly after being named to his post at the *Journal* in 1972, Kristol met Jude Wanniski, a writer for the *Journal*'s editorial page.[1] In this capacity, Wanniski began telling Kristol about the theories of two relatively unknown economists: Arthur Laffer of the University of Chicago and Robert Mundell, a Canadian economist at Columbia University. Wanniski told Kristol that he wanted to start writing about their ideas but worried that people would not publish his papers because the ideas were "considered heretical"; he worried that he would get a lot of "flak from the economists."[2] Kristol immediately agreed to run a column in the *Journal* on the subject as well as two articles in the *Public Interest*.

Here we see the key importance of the marketplace of ideas for introducing policies that lacked significant rigor: the barrier for entry of those ideas into the policy debate was now extremely low. In some sense, the more provocative and "heretical" the idea, the *easier* chance it had of entering the marketplace given the overriding need to "balance" the debate. Kristol, since he had done so much to make this way of debating policy dominant in the 1970s, understood this fact better than most. He knew he could introduce such controversial ideas with ease and without the rigors required by academic research—namely, peer review by other economists. Kristol knew that the *Wall Street Journal* and the *Public Interest* were not bound by such constraints and that the barriers for entry in the marketplace of ideas did not require such expertise or rigor. In 1974, Wanniski published his first popularization of Laffer's and Mundell's views in the *Journal*. His column provides the first introduction to the very idea of "supply-side economics." Wanniski, who had no professional training in economics, immediately posits his economic policies as the solution to the economic crises of the 1970s. He argues that the United States cannot "climb out of the deepening recession by harking to either the classical economic advice of tight money and balanced budgets or to the neo-Keynesian nostrum of easier money, public-service employment and wage-and-price controls." According to Wanniski, the correct prescription is "a $30 billion tax cut and the temporary halting of open-market operations by the Federal Reserve to assure monetary restraint." The tax cut would include an across-the-board cut on "both personal and corporate incomes." Most provocatively, Wanniski asserts that there would be a "balance-of-payments equilibrium"—that is, the cuts would not produce an overall drop in federal revenues and would have the added effect of pulling "the whole industrial world out of its slump."[3] As Wanniski correctly notes in this op-ed, both liberal and traditional conservative economists at the time and in the future would disagree with such a view. The idea that tax cuts would produce a "balance-of-payments equilibrium" when not paired with spending cuts was rejected by all mainstream economists. However, this idea of "revenue neutrality" in the face of massive tax cuts became *the central tenet* of supply-side economics as proposed by its neoconservative promoters in the 1970s. In the marketplace of ideas, it was merely another position in the debate to balance, in this case, both the ideas of liberals and traditional "balanced budget" conservatives.

With his articles in the *Public Interest* in 1975 and 1978, Kristol gave Wanniski an additional platform to sell his idea within the marketplace. By this point, *Public Interest* was read by policymakers at both the local and national levels. It was in many ways the perfect venue to showcase supply-side theorizing while still imparting an academic aura. The journal itself had the aesthetic makeup of an academic peer-reviewed journal without actually being peer reviewed. Most articles in *Public Interest* were simply run with nothing but Kristol's approval. For instance, Wanniski's 1975 piece, "The Mundell-Laffer Hypothesis—A New View of the World Economy" was written after Kristol simply told Wanniski, "Write it, and I'll run it." Wanniski then "wrote the article . . . in four weekends."[4] What stands out most in the piece is its almost complete lack of rigor through source citation, footnoting, and any sort of modeling. The research of Mundell and Laffer is discussed in generalities given that Wanniski only expressed their views from conversations he had with the two men. Buried in one of the few footnotes is the pertinent fact that there was "no Mundell-Laffer paper" to explain their ideas.[5] The entire article seeks to convey to a popular audience academic research that did not actually exist. Wanniski boldly asserts that research was not needed because the Mundell-Laffer Hypothesis "easily explains phenomena that other theories can explain only with immense difficulty and complication."[6] Wanniski argues that Mundell-Laffer's simple, easy-to-understand theories are the answer for the "economic nightmare" through which the world has been passing because their solutions "would not involve a period of suffering by the world's population in order to achieve improvement."[7] Unlike the "neo-Keynesians" and traditional conservative economists who insisted on pain, Wanniski presented Mundell and Laffer's theories as both utopian in their simplicity and politically attractive because their simple solutions would cure all. These solutions consisted of *"tight money and fiscal ease"*—the former as a return to the gold standard and the latter preferably taking "the form of tax reductions" aimed at "augmenting supply."[8]

Wanniski buried an even more controversial claim in another of the article's few footnotes. This is where he expounds on what would become the key supply-side myth introduced in the earlier *Journal* op-ed: that you could cut taxes, keep "government spending maintained," *and at the same time* "raise output and the tax base" in enough quantities to offset any adverse effects on the deficit. Wanniski is very clear on this point, arguing that "the tax cut numbers are only 'implied' in the sense that Mundell and Laffer believe deficits would not materialize in those amounts since the tax base would rise" to make up for any possible deficit. Once again paraphrasing Mundell and Laffer from conversation, Wanniski argues that all of this was possible because the United States was in a unique historical moment where "special conditions exist." These "special conditions" exist when a nation was being "choked, asphyxiated by taxes" to such a point that a massive cut would not yield lost revenue because of the productive energies the cut would unleash. Additionally, the longer the United States waited to institute cuts, the *larger the tax cut would need to be* in order to make up for the continued "asphyxiation" produced by the dawdling of policymakers. This led to the constantly increasing nature of the cuts advocated by supply-siders over time. In May 1974, they advocated an immediate tax cut of $10 billion; in October 1974, $30 billion; and in February 1975, $60 billion."[9] When describing all of these tax cuts, Wanniski, Mundell, and Laffer always employed the word "implied" given that revenues would supposedly not be lost if the cuts were implemented. In this context, it is easy to see why the idea of "supply-side economics" began to gain traction. In a moment of absolute world economic crisis and dislocation, this group of men offered the easiest solutions imaginable for policymakers: tax cuts, no lost revenue, and a return to the gold standard to cure all ills. The lack of rigor in formulating this view was striking, but it is undeniable that such an understanding of supply-side economics was extremely appealing to lawmakers and the public at large.

Academic economists responded in force to Wanniski's ideas with rampant skepticism forcing Wanniski "to learn more . . . just defending the piece."[10] His second *Public Interest* article in 1978 is best seen as an attempted response to the critics. In this piece, Wanniski first presents the now-famous "Laffer Curve"—an idea once again related to Wanniski in conversation with Laffer. The curve purports to show that "there are always two tax rates that yield the same revenues"—one high and one low. If you reduce taxes from the high rate (which the United States was supposedly at in the late 1970s) to the low rate, there would be no change in revenues because of the productive energies unleashed by the cuts. The "simple curve" was not from an article by Laffer, but rather what Laffer drew freehand when asked to explain his ideas to an aide to President Gerald Ford.[11] After presenting the curve, Wanniski narrates its "simple points" historically since "the idea behind the 'Laffer curve' is no doubt as old as civilization, but unfortunately politicians have always had trouble grasping it."[12] This section of the article was most likely designed to rebut critics who questioned Wanniski's research methods. The critics no doubt assumed that there must have been some sort of modeling behind the theory. However, rather than such modeling (beyond the simplistic Laffer Curve), Wanniski proceeded to quote long sections from classical political economy, including David Hume and Adam Smith. These sections do not reference anything resembling "supply-side economics," and given that Wanniski rarely chose to interpret the passages in the context of an argument, it is hard to read them as anything but performative. Playing on nationalist and anticommunist sentiment, Wanniski assures his readers that "the Politburo of the Soviet Union has the same problem as the Finance Office of New York City: It also rejects the idea behind the 'Laffer Curve.'" Additionally, "The Founding Fathers of the United States" were supply-siders one and all.[13] Finally, in a twist undoubtedly designed to turn more liberals into neoconservatives, Wanniski insists that "a welfare state is perfectly consistent with the 'Laffer curve'" because the government will have no lost revenues. Wanniski insists that supply-side tax cutting had been done before by liberal John Kennedy in 1962–64. Wanniski argues that although the cuts were sold "in Keynesian terms," the "reductions successfully moved the United States economy down the 'Laffer curve,' expanding the economy and revenues."[14] Again, what is striking about this article is its intense lack of rigor despite being on the same public policy debating field as academically trained economists in the marketplace of ideas. The barrier for entry in the marketplace was now so low that drawings on napkins and large block quotes from David Hume were taken seriously by many, including the president of the United States.

Wanniski's new *Public Interest* article brought a rash of new criticism, which prompted him to write a book on the subject—a book that was put into the marketplace of ideas directly by AEI itself. The ability of people like William Baroody and Irving Kristol to leverage the developing foundation/think tank nexus enabled neoconservatives like Wanniski to produce his book with ease, rapidity, and low barriers to entry. Wanniski wanted to write his book, but his editors at the *Wall Street Journal* would not allow him to take leave of his role as columnist unless he found a paying academic fellowship. Kristol connected him with Baroody and Leslie Lenkowsky of the Smith Richardson Foundation to make this happen. Wanniski had a conversation with Baroody about the book, but submitted no formal proposal—only a nine-month budget of $39,550.[15] In fact, from the archival record, it appears that Baroody was the only person who put something in writing regarding the project's actual content. In a letter dated November 1976, Baroody reminded Wanniski that during his nine-month fellowship in 1977 he would "pursue research to explore the interaction of progressive personal income tax systems and currency inflations and the effects of this interaction on output and employment in various countries throughout the world."[16] Baroody also tried to raise the stipend Wanniski would receive from the Smith Richardson Foundation given that Baroody was interested in making a splash with his first "Journalist Fellowship." Lenkowsky pushed back, and eventually Wanniski was welcomed on as "Journalist in Residence at the American Enterprise Institute" with a stipend of $22,000 plus $8,000 for expenses for the first nine months of 1977.[17] At AEI he would write his book, eventually titled *The Way the World Works*.[18] As this process shows, the conservative think tank and foundation nexus had by this point in time greatly decreased the entry barriers into the marketplace of ideas while at the same time providing enormous monetary compensation to such efforts. Both of these were in direct contrast to the rigors of academic publishing and even publishing at a think tank like Brookings. Wanniski was able to secure a book contract and funding for his book with remarkable ease—seemingly without having to propose the contents of the book to anyone. He was selling a hot commodity in the marketplace of ideas, and Baroody, Kristol, and AEI wanted to strike while they were still able to sell it to policymakers and public at large.

Before getting to the book, its reception, and its role in selling supply-side economics, it is first important to note how Wanniski's residency at AEI was important in other ways. In short, his time there provides a perfect example of the way in which think tanks, internally, can be an institution where conservatives were able to work through the seeming contradictions of their own conservatisms. As has already been shown, think tanks like Heritage wanted to become "fusionist" institutions for all the various strands of conservative thought—a place where libertarians, traditionalists, anticommunists, neoconservatives, and the religious Right all felt represented and where the contradictions between these impulses were worked through. AEI, by contrast, largely felt comfortable only representing neoconservatives and anticommunists during this same point in time. However, Wanniski's time at AEI showed how this was beginning to change. A 1986 *Washington Post* article provides a unique lens into this change. The article profiles Antonin Scalia upon his nomination to the Supreme Court under Ronald Reagan. In particular, the article profiles Scalia's time as an AEI scholar in 1977—the same year Wanniski was writing his book at AEI. As the *Washington Post* put it, 1977 was something of a banner year at AEI for conservatives who would go onto prominence in the 1980s. By happenstance, many of these key conservatives were employed by the institute during that year and participated in an informal discussion group within the think tank. As the *Post* put it, "Among the other members of the AEI discussion group [besides Wanniski, Scalia, and Kristol] were Robert H. Bork and Laurence Silberman, both now on the U.S. Court of Appeals; Jeane J. Kirkpatrick, a former UN ambassador; and Rudolph G. Penner, director of the Congressional Budget Office." Silberman, in the article, describes the "synergistic impact" of being at AEI together: "We were all friends, and it sparkled. A cross-pollination took place." Wanniski describes one such "synergistic impact" that took place in his conversations with Scalia and Bork: "We would talk about prostitution and the tax codes, which have both been with us since the beginning of time. The higher the taxes the more prostitutes you have. It's logical according to the law of supply and demand. I felt that Bork and Scalia were especially positive toward the things we talked about. They were intrigued by the impact that economic growth would have on social mores." Wanniski notes that Bork in particular loved "a theory that explains everything."[19] Here Wanniski worked to convert Bork and Scalia to his supply-side economic doctrine through an appeal to their traditionalism, their concern for religiously grounded "social mores." Wanniski fused the seemingly disparate strands of conservatism—a tactic he and other supply-siders would take in the future.

Wanniski avoids this type explanation for supply-side economics in *How the World Works*. However, the book betrays the same simplicity and lack of rigor found in the earlier *Public Interest* articles. For these reasons, academics largely ignored the book. For those who did pay attention, the reviews were scathing. For instance, Benjamin Cohen declares, "Wanniski has rushed in where even college sophomores fear to tread. Should it be any wonder that his reach exceeds his grasp?" Cohen argues that Wanniski's " 'theory' itself (which is really no theory at all—in the sense of a rigorously specified set of relationships among a key number of variables—but rather merely a hodgepodge of unsubstantiated economic and political propositions) boils down to the idea that 'civilizations rise and fall with their tax rates. The success of economies is assured when taxes are cut.' " Honing in on the op-ed nature of the book, Cohen writes, "If all of this sounds remarkably like an editorial from the *Wall Street Journal*, that should not be surprising. Wanniski makes his living writing editorials for the *Journal*. What *is* surprising is that we are expected to take it all seriously. The book would be much less distressing if we were permitted to read it as satire rather than as scholarship." Cohen also strikes at the heart of the problem of much of conservative think tank writing at the time: "For all of his erudition, he does not appear to appreciate the dangers of the colorful historical generalization, the univariate theory of history. For all of his sophistication, he still insists on trying to reduce complex reality to trite oversimplification." Cohen ends his review, "Serious scholars can expect to learn little from this type of approach to historical problems."[20] While certainly correct, Cohen misses that these problems are precisely why the theories can gain traction in a new marketplace of ideas. In such a world, totalizing, breezily written studies, as opposed to rigorous academic research, ruled the day.

And in a strange way this type of academic reception undoubtedly gave force to the argument Wanniski makes in his book and articles. Given that conservative think tanks and their inhabitants were explicitly counterpositioning themselves to academia, negative reviews like this were used to declare such "liberal institutions" as still being "out of touch"—in need of balancing in the marketplace of ideas. Such a stance was reinforced by the book's immense popularity as it went through five printings. The book also opened new doors for Wanniski to policymakers. After the book's publication, Kristol "urged Wanniski to go by Congressman Jack Kemp's office in Washington to introduce himself." From these meetings "came Kemp-Roth, the bill to reduce taxes by some 33 percent" with "the Laffer curve analysis [as] the linchpin of the bill."[21] Journalists also treated the theories of Wanniski/Laffer as merely "one side of a debate" that needed to be taken seriously. For instance, Geoffrey Norman, writing a 1979 article for *Esquire* about the rise of neoconservatism, wrote that Wanniski's theories "sound almost too good to be true—free beer *and* wide roads—but there is historical evidence to support the argument," including "the tax cut that was passed during John Kennedy's presidency." The same article also asserted that "Laffer's analysis became the theoretical basis for the current tax-cutting movement—including Proposition 13" in California, without noting that the huge cut in property taxes brought about by Proposition 13 did not produce the increased (or even sustained) governmental revenues predicted by supply-siders.[22]

The lack of additional revenues from supply-side tax cutting under Proposition 13 did not concern Irving Kristol. It was clear even at this early point in 1978 that Kristol was unconcerned with the veracity of the empirical claim. For Kristol, the main concern was electoral victory through the populist potential represented by supply-side tax cutting. After Proposition 13 passed, and echoing his earlier critiques of the "New Class," Kristol declared in the *Wall Street Journal* that Prop 13 was a victory in "a new kind of class war—the people as citizens versus the politicians and their clients in the public sector. And the people won."[23] Traditional conservative economists like Milton Friedman agreed with neoconservatives like Kristol that Prop 13 was indeed a victory for conservative populism against the New Class. Writing for the Heritage Foundation in 1978, Friedman declared it a victory for "the grassroots movement that Governor Ronald Reagan began in that state."[24] Unlike Kristol, Friedman allied himself with traditional fiscal conservatives who argued that tax cutting would need to be accompanied by spending cuts. Traditional conservatives like Friedman rejected the central claim of neoconservative supply-siders at AEI that tax cutting would unleash new energies to sustain or increase government revenue. Writing in the same article about the Kemp-Roth federal supply-side bill, Friedman argued, "We should be clear, however, that it is in reality not a tax reduction bill; it is a proposal to change the form of taxes. As long as high government spending remains, we shall have the hidden tax of inflation. The only true tax cutting proposal would be a proposal to cut government spending." Such reservations did not stop these conservatives from supporting the cuts. In the same article, Friedman declared, "I support this bill since I believe that any form of tax reduction under any circumstances must eventually bring pressure to bear to cut spending."[25] As many at Heritage would do, Friedman articulated the newly emerging conservative "starve-the-beast" mentality—one that believed that any tax cuts would force spending cuts.

As for the supply-siders associated with think tanks like AEI, even they began to have reservations about some of their claims. However, like Kristol, they chose instead to focus on the electoral benefits of the policies. Forgotten for now was the link between the supply-side tax cuts and reinstituting the gold standard. When confronted with the assertion that their cuts might not yield additional tax revenues, supply-siders simply dismissed these concerns. Laffer himself told *Newsweek*, "There's more than a reasonable probability that I'm wrong. But . . . why not try something new?"[26] Kristol took a slightly different route when arguing for the full supply-side agenda of tax cuts that "must be very large indeed" combined with increased military spending and no cuts in social services. He argued that both liberal and traditional fiscal conservative economists were being too "gloomy—and rather boring." His agenda was much more fun and had "considerable political appeal."[27] Given the proclivities of Kristol, Laffer, and Wanniski to rely on concepts such as fun and newness to sell their policies, it was left up to Paul Craig Roberts, a senior research fellow at the Hoover Institution, to make a more academically minded case. Roberts's background included graduate training in economics, which provided an additional aura of expertise for those looking to make the supply-side case for the Kemp-Roth bill. Once again in the *Wall Street Journal*, Roberts wrote an op-ed citing a "Chase Econometrics" study to assert, "The federal government would recover in revenue reflows 41% of the $25 billion tax cut in the first year. This rises to 72% in the seventh year. The remaining deficit is more than covered by the increase in personal savings, retained earnings, and state and local government surplus." According to Roberts, the Kemp-Roth cuts "would get us out of the high deficit, high inflation, low productivity, low growth doldrums, and save transfer programs like Social Security."[28] Writings like this allowed Roberts to eventually procure employment, first as an economist for Kemp himself and later in Reagan's Treasury Department.

As the 1980 presidential campaign heated up and supply-siders like Roberts, Kristol, and Wanniski saw Reagan as a possible vehicle for their policies, these individuals moved to even more simplistic frameworks for explaining their policies in the marketplace of ideas. Given the popularity of his book, Wanniski moved from the *Wall Street Journal* and AEI to op-ed holy ground of the "liberal media" at the *New York Times* as the *Times* sought to add neoconservative voices to balance the liberal ones on their op-ed page. It was at the *Times* that Wanniski made his case for supply-side cuts and, ultimately, ending progressive taxation. As to the latter, he asserts that "tax progressivity" was the "central problem" supply-siders sought to remedy with a reduction in "the progressivity of the tax system" or a total elimination of "it with a proportional rate that does not punish extra effort." Additionally, Wanniski once again turns to the gold standard along with tax cuts as an economic cure-all: "The central problems will go away, and with it the malaise. Will there be a deficit? Maybe not. But if so, so what? Restoring the links between an individual's effort and reward, and enabling individuals to save in dollar assets that hold their value, will encourage millions of Americans to increase their efforts and increase their savings, which will open opportunities for millions more. Deficits would soon go away, and so would the worst of our social problems. Instead of a society smothered, crushed by disincentives, with all its tensions, there would be air, light and hope." The promotion of an economic policy that would bring "air, light, and hope" moved Wanniski's utopian framework a great deal further. Such utopianism was also likely an appeal to religious conservatives who may not have had supply-side tax cuts as their top priority. In this vein, Wanniski finishes his op-ed with the following benefits of the supply-side tax cutting: "For the individual American, who now spends all of his or her time in this sea of social tension, consumed in survival tactics, the very first dividend for solving this central problem will be a moment of 'spare time,' a concept that has become almost obsolete. With moments of spare time multiplied, moments free of tension or anxiety over what The System will do to you next, the drugs and alcoholism and divorce and personal abuses may begin to recede. We will once again feel confident about ourselves as a nation, and the Russians would view us in a different light."[29] Here again we see the ability of conservatives coming out of think tanks to posit their policies in ways that broke down divides between conservative camps. Here, tax cutting, supposedly only important to "business conservatives," is articulated within a Cold War framework ("the Russians would view us in a different light") for anti-communist conservatives as well as being articulated in a way that is palatable to religious conservatives (ending divorce, alcoholism, allowing more free time to families).

With Reagan's campaign heating up, Kristol was also making the holistic case for supply-side tax cutting. In May 1980, Kristol wrote the *Journal* op-ed that was easily the clearest statement of why he was advocating the supply-side doctrine. For Kristol, the cuts were about a "battle for Reagan's soul" and for "the self-definition of the Republican Party, and the vision of the Republican future." In such a battle, compromise between neoconservative supply-siders and traditional conservative academic economists (who wanted spending cuts with the tax cuts) "may not be possible" or "even desirable." In other words, conservative Republicans like George H. W. Bush, who famously called supply-side tax cuts "voodoo economics" before agreeing to be Reagan's vice president, should not be compromised with. Instead, what was needed was a bold neoconservative ideological agenda for the Republican Party that included supply-side tax cutting as a main pillar. Instead of merely existing to "clean up the mess" of big-spending liberals, Republicans needed to become big spenders too. They needed to "appeal to nationalist sentiments by advocating a larger and more formidable defense establishment, with the budget a distinctly secondary consideration," and they needed to "vigorously advocate tax cuts, also with the budget remaining a secondary consideration." Kristol continues: "For what if a massive increase in the military budget, not matched by (and it will not be matched by) corresponding cuts in social programs, does create a fiscal problem? And what if the traditional-conservatives are right and a Kemp-Roth tax cut, without corresponding cuts in expenditures, also leaves us with a fiscal problem? The neoconservative is willing to leave those problems to be coped with by liberal interregnums. He wants to shape the future, and will leave it to his opponents to tidy up afterwards." In the end, "The important thing, in the politics of the 1980s, is to have a vision of the kind of society you wish your country to become, to align your strategy along the sights of this vision, and then plow ahead." With supply-side economics and increased military spending at its core, Kristol argues that the Republican Party would be able to "plow ahead" and win elections. The rigor, truthfulness, or problems created by the policies would take a distant second to creating a neoconservative vision for the nation.[30]

Kristol was continuing the long-term conservative think tank project of creating a holistic ideological conservatism that sought to fuse different strands of conservatives and build a larger movement. Only now, rather than screaming into the ideological wilderness as think tanks had done from the 1950s through the early 1970s, this project was becoming thoroughly mainstreamed. Kristol was now directly lobbying a man who would become president to accept his position. And, lest there be any doubt that this is what Kristol was advocating, he clarifies his position in a July 1980 *Journal* op-ed entitled "The New Republican Party," where he fully acknowledges that his conservatism was in many ways a break from tradition. He argues that Republicans need a "sharp ideological identity." He acknowledges that this would not be easy for conservatives to accept "since modern conservatism was born out of a rejection of, and contempt for, the ideological politics of the French Revolution." Kristol states that such an ideological sharpness is nevertheless needed to rally "supporters around a vision of the future." Up until 1980, he argues, conservatives had permitted "the Left to shape the society" with conservatives only left as "efficient managers" once in office. He claims this was no way to create a movement as "for better or worse, ideology is now the vital element of organized political action." According to Kristol, only neoconservatives could provide such ideological ammunition.[31] Kristol would soon find out if a President Reagan and his policymakers agreed with this sentiment.

ON 5 NOVEMBER 1980, the day after Ronald Reagan's presidential election victory, it was unclear to which conservative think tank his administration would turn for staff appointments and policy ideas. Reagan had deep, long-standing ties to Hoover as a result of its base at Stanford University, and AEI was still viewed as the premier Republican Party think tank. These facts seemed to leave Heritage largely on the outs. Undoubtedly aware of this, Ed Feulner and Heritage prepared to make sure Heritage was not left in the dark. Throughout 1980 the think tank had been preparing a major policy book in the event that Reagan won the election. By 1980, Heritage had honed their new, rapid-response, short policy primers as the new model for the less rigorous marketplace of ideas. Feulner recognized that something else would be needed for an incoming conservative president: a massive book that would shine the spotlight on Heritage as the premier up-and-coming conservative think tank. In addition to garnering publicity for the think tank, Feulner and others at

Heritage were also keenly aware of what happened the last time a Republican president won a presidential election—he was not armed with conservative policy proposals. As Herb Berkowitz, Heritage's public relations director in 1980, put it, "We knew that when the Nixon administration took over, so much time was spent learning who was who and what was going on that it was months before anyone could look at policy matters . . . so the trustees decided, why don't we come up with policy initiatives on our own?"[32] Heritage threw $100,000 into the project in the nine months before Reagan's election, engaging some 250 conservative policy activists in the process.[33]

The result was a 3,000-page document entitled *Mandate for Leadership* that sought to cover every policy area imaginable for the incoming administration. As Feulner tells it, "Seven days after the election . . . we met with Martin Anderson, Dick Allen, Ed Meese [key members of the Reagan transition team] and others in the basement of the Hay-Adams and we delivered them the first draft copies of *Mandate for Leadership*."[34] The administration was greatly appreciative. Edwin Meese said, "The study was very impressive. The Reagan administration will rely heavily on the Heritage Foundation." David Stockman, who would go on to become the office of management and budget director, was even more effusive: "The scope and depth of the work is unprecedented. It stands as a blueprint for the policy options available if we are to meet the challenges of the 1980s. Leaders in both the new administration and the Congress will find in this work all they need to hit the ground running."[35] *Mandate* led to the appointment of fourteen Heritage staff members to Reagan transition teams. Feulner was appointed to the transition executive committee.[36] Just as important, the press took notice—focusing nearly all the publicity garnered by conservative think tanks squarely on Heritage. By early December, the *New York Times* was confidently asserting that *Mandate* was "being used as a guideline by the Reagan team."[37] Liberal publications were even taking envious notice. *New Republic* published a lengthy article that argued that liberals needed to copy the Heritage model. The article contends, "Heritage is astoundingly good at packaging and promoting conservative proposals in the media. Hardly a week goes by without some major newspaper or magazine publishing a story or an op-ed piece based on a Heritage report. One of the great publicity master strokes of the year was Heritage's *Mandate for Leadership* project, the 3,000-page report to the new administration on what needed to be done to impose conservative government on the country."[38] The final part of this "publicity master stroke" was the repackaging of *Mandate* into a 1,000-page book for wide public consumption. The book made the *Washington Post* bestseller list, establishing it in the media as "the bible of the Reagan transition."[39]

Such acceptance by the incoming administration, and such publicity in the press, caught conservative think tanks like AEI and Hoover off guard. Both think tanks had key people on the transition team and on the White House staff.[40] However, AEI, under the new leadership of William Baroody Jr., was trying to cultivate a more moderate image for the think tank. Such an image was not received well in the Reagan administration. A dual *Washington Post* profile of AEI and Brookings argues that "despite their traditional liberal versus conservative labels, Brookings and AEI are also edging closer together in their focus: away from the moderately far left-and right-of-center, toward the more pragmatic—and less blatantly ideological—midpoint of the political spectrum."[41] For AEI, this was ultimately a misreading of the current political moment and one that would have long-term consequences for the think tank in the marketplace of ideas. For a think tank that had always been identified as firmly conservative, the election of a conservative president hardly seemed the time to argue for moderation in the institute's institutional mission. Ed Feulner certainly realized this at the time when he told a reporter, "Unlike AEI . . . we have not moved to the mushy middle of the political spectrum. We are unabashedly and unashamedly conservative."[42] In the marketplace of ideas, Heritage was selling the stronger product—a forthright conservatism with a new president ready to implement it.

However, it remained to be seen how such a conservatism, exemplified by *Mandate*, would be translated into real-world public policy. Part of this was due to the fact that *Mandate* contained little that was new in terms of conservative policy. In fact, news reports at the time often struggled to identify anything in the book that had not been central to conservative thought and policy for years, if not decades. The *New York Times* reported that "the foundation's extraordinarily detailed twenty volume report, which is being used as a guideline by the Reagan team, includes proposals that range from abolishing the department of energy by 1982, to returning most functions of the Environmental Protection Agency to the states or other government offices, to increasing the 1981 military budget by $20 billion."[43] None of this was new in that it synced with long-standing conservative ideological and policy goals. The *New Republic* report was even more direct: "All Heritage's intellectuals really have not produced an abundance of original ideas. The one cited most often as a Heritage product is that of low-tax enterprise zones to encourage investment in high-unemployment areas. Even that idea, as it happens, originated in England—and with a Socialist, at that—and was imported here by Heritage staff members."[44] Strikingly, Feulner agreed with such an assertion and argued that such a focus on promoting "new conservative ideas" misunderstood the institutional role of Heritage. He argued instead that Heritage was a "second-hand dealer in ideas" that took "the ideas from the seminal thinkers, translated them into policy concepts, refined them, publicized them and made them usable within the policy-making process. Then the pressure groups can advocate them, build coalitions around them and ultimately trigger some action."[45] In a 1985 talk on Heritage's mission, Feulner was even more forthright when he argued that Heritage seeks to "market an idea" and to "help popularize and propagandize" existing ideas. In the same talk, Feulner went even further and explicitly likened what Heritage did to a company or advertising agency: "Proctor and Gamble does not sell Crest toothpaste by taking out one newspaper ad or running one television commercial. They sell it and resell it every day by keeping the product fresh in the consumer's mind."[46] Here we see just how comfortable conservatives had become with marketplace metaphors of policymaking. Feulner saw Heritage's policies in the same light as a consumer product like Crest toothpaste. The metaphor can be taken even further in the debate over old versus new conservative policies given that Crest itself is one of the oldest brands of toothpaste on the market. What Feulner was implicitly saying was that it did not matter how old a policy product was—all that mattered was its incessant marketing in the marketplace of ideas.

Such marketing was what *Mandate* was about—making a "splash" in the marketplace of ideas by promoting and marketing old conservative ideas and centering Heritage as the main policy ad agency for the conservative movement and the Reagan administration. However, it remained to be seen how exactly such marketing would translate into the implementation of actual policy ideas, especially supply-side economics and its central old conservative idea of cutting taxes. Given that Heritage, through Milton Friedman, had mildly questioned supply-side claims in the past, it was slightly unclear how they would advocate for the claims during Reagan's first years. *Mandate*, however, left no question that Heritage was on board with the supply-side agenda embodied in the Kemp-Roth bill. In the section of the book on the Treasury Department, Norman B. Ture declares that the "top priority in refocused tax policy should be given to substantial across-the-board marginal rate reductions. The rate cuts provided in the Kemp-Roth bills afford an excellent model for this basic tax revision."[47]

Reagan undoubtedly agreed with such a recommendation. Before he took office, however, another influential supply-side tract was published with think tank support—one that would go further than Wanniski's *The Way the World Works* in garnering support for supply-side tax cutting. The book was George Gilder's *Wealth and Poverty*, which was published in late 1980 to much fanfare. The book would go on to sell a half million copies. President Reagan read the book and, because of it, Gilder asserts that "according to a study of presidential speeches" he "was President Reagan's most frequently quoted living author."[48] Sections of the book had appeared previously in Heritage's *Policy Review*, but the main support Gilder received in writing it was from an upstart conservative think tank in New York, the Manhattan Institute for Policy Research. The Manhattan Institute was founded in 1978 in part by Antony Fisher—a British libertarian who had worked his whole life to establish libertarian-oriented think tanks in Britain and elsewhere around the world. By the last decade of his life, Fisher had begun setting up new think tanks in the United States like the Manhattan Institute.[49] In its first two decades of existence, the think tank was mostly dedicated to influencing New York City and state governments in a rightward direction. With work like Gilder's *Wealth and Poverty* and, later, Charles Murray's *Losing Ground*, the think tank has also sought to involve itself in national politics.

In many respects, *Wealth and Poverty* reads much like Wanniski's *The Way the World Works*. In short, it is hard to even read the book as concerned with policy per se. Rather, much of the book is a freewheeling, free-form meditation on cultural conceptions of wealth and poverty. In the brief sections of the book where Gilder actually does discuss the substance of policy, he does so fleetingly and in a way that disregards any and all analytical rigor. The book openly mocks the very idea of analytical rigor in policymaking, especially in the discipline of economics. In the book's preface, Gilder writes, "Wealth and poverty are the prime concerns of economics, but they are subjects too vast and vital to be left to economists alone. Although economists have provided me with some of my most valued counsel—and I will be acknowledging them in numbers—this book is in part an essay on the limitations of contemporary economics in analyzing the sources of creativity and progress in all economies." Gilder largely took his ideas from "unpopular figures among the professional economists" like "Arthur Laffer, Irving Kristol, and Jude Wanniski." Gilder liked the latter more because of their ability to "capture the high adventure and redemptive morality of capitalism" as opposed to the "'good' or 'sound' economists who contribute most to the development of the science" but who exaggerate the discipline's "scientific rigor." Such a view of economics and policy-analysis, led Gilder to declare *The Way the World Works* "one of the great inspirational works of economic literature." *Wealth and Poverty* would follow "the supply-side trail that Wanniski so boldly blazed."[50]

Given this view, it should come as no surprise that Gilder, in the fleeting moments where he does discuss the actual policy details of supply-side economics, fully accepts the boldest claims of its adherents while dismissing all criticism emanating from liberal and traditional conservative economists. Gilder argues that Laffer and Wanniski had definitively shown "that lower tax rates can so stimulate business and so shift income from shelters to taxable activity that lower rates bring in higher tax revenues. The private sector can be relieved of its onerous tax rates without requiring cuts in public sector services. The idea was simple and demonstrably true." Considering the case now closed, Gilder then returns to dismissing the "liberal economists who derided" this conclusion and the conservative ones who "were coolly skeptical." His dismissal is worth quoting at length in order to fully illuminate his ideals of policymaking:

> The critics used an idiom of rejection that is becoming familiar in all the social sciences, as they eschew original reasoning and adopt the role of programming and interpreting their computers.... In all cases novelty, creativity, imagination, and surprise—the elusive variables of all our lives—are left out. Nonetheless, the computers provide an all-purpose mode of refutation for any theory the experts dislike or did not think of first. The technique is to run regression equations with ever larger numbers of variables and ever more refined and therefore dubious statistics until all meaning

washes out. Then they announce that "more recent analysis and breakdown of the data indicates there is no evidence . . . absolutely no evidence . . . not a shred of evidence . . ." or especially "only anecdotal evidence . . . not a bit of data"—in this case—no persuasive testimony to indicate that the United States has reached the upper portions of the Laffer curve [and] that American tax rates are at a point where tax reductions can enlarge revenues.[51]

A clearer sense of a shift from a technocratic view of policy to a *felt* sense of policy could not be written. Here Gilder dismisses *the very idea* of claims to conclusions or truths grounded in evidence—especially evidence gained from "the computers" as such conclusions "eschew original reasoning," and "novelty, creativity, imagination, and surprise."

At this point, Gilder then makes the next logical leap, and indeed one openly allowed in the marketplace of ideas—the exaltation of the "common man," or the "nonexpert" in policymaking. He argues that America's "most sophisticated and interesting economists were incapable of comprehending an economic reality—the greatly excessive marginal tax burden on American income and investment—that was manifest to a former football player trained in physical education, Congressman Jack Kemp; a *Wall Street Journal* editorial writer with little economic training, Jude Wanniski; and an economist, Arthur Laffer, who was widely seen as most 'unsound' by all his more prestigious colleagues."[52] In a twist, lack of expertise in a subject of study is now deemed more worth than expertise—indeed, such "common sense" in seeing "economic reality" is the sole purview of the non-expert. In this passage, Gilder largely criticizes conservative economists like Milton Friedman for not accepting the "economic reality" that cutting taxes will increase federal revenue. Later in *Wealth and Poverty*, he also criticizes liberal economists for ignoring this "reality" since such a "truth" would be fantastic for their professed politics: "For liberals concerned with the distribution of income . . . the Laffer curve offers a promise as seductive as any of the Keynesian strictures against austerity and thrift. Regressive taxes help the poor! It has become increasingly obvious that a less progressive tax structure is necessary to reduce the tax burden on the lower and middle classes. When rates are lowered in the top brackets, the rich consume less and invest more. Their earnings rise and they pay more taxes in absolute amounts. Thus the lower and middle classes need pay less to sustain a given level of government services."[53] Gilder seems unable or unwilling to realize that liberal economists simply do not accept his "economic reality" that regressive taxes ultimately help the poor.

However, such an assertion by Gilder—that more regressive taxes will help the poor—is one of the more unique developments of supply-side theorizing found in the book. Gilder devotes so much time to it that it needs to be examined separately from the claim that tax cuts would produce more federal revenue. By adding such a controversial view to the marketplace of ideas, Gilder undoubtedly furthers another common think tank goal—seeking to reconcile and "fuse" the various impulses of modern conservatism in the 1970s and 1980s. At the time Gilder wrote, the emergent Christian Right, which did so much to elect Ronald Reagan, had other concerns at the top of their agenda besides tax cuts. For instance, most were primarily concerned with a constitutional amendment to ban abortion and with allowing prayer in public schools. Religious conservatives needed to be convinced that a more regressive tax system synced with their self-described "pro-family" politics. Much of *Wealth and Poverty* thus becomes an intellectual exercise in fusing neoconservative supply-side economics with the emerging "pro-family" politics of the religious Right.

In performing such a fusion, Gilder was intellectually fashioning what is best described as a "family values economy"—one that sought to articulate supply-side economics through a discourse of morality, faith, "values," a sense of right and wrong, and concern for the poor.[54] Early on in *Wealth and Poverty* Gilder forwards this line of thought when he argues that the current tax system of the United States forced Americans to act in a fundamentally immoral way by concealing income to evade high taxes. He argues that such unlawfulness, while relieving "financial pressures on some families" leads to "severe tensions and anxieties ... whether from paying imposts that they feel are unfair or avoided by others, or from violating their own sense of what is right. Either way, the results are rage into demoralization. Such experiences, happening to the fast-growing group of American families, explain much of the pain in protest of the ostensibly affluent middle classes. These problems also demonstrated why large tax cuts are needed both to reduce illegal and concealed activity and to help strengthen families."[55] In addition to ending such immorality and strengthening the family, large tax cuts would once again restore "faith in man, faith in nature, faith in the rising returns of giving, faith in the mutual benefits of trade, faith in the providence of God," which are "all essential to successful capitalism." The tax cuts "are necessary to sustain the spirit of work and enterprise against the setbacks and frustrations it inevitably meets in a fallen world; to inspire trust and cooperation in an economy where they will often be betrayed; to encourage the foregoing of present pleasures in the name of a future that may well go up in smoke; to promote risk and initiative in a world where the rewards all vanish unless others join the game."[56] Such rhetoric firmly situated regressive supply-side tax cutting as *inherently moral* and even Christian in its implications. It also shows how conservatives were not separating so-called values issues from economic issues. In works like *Wealth and Poverty*, they sought to explain them as one and the same. Anyone who disagreed with policies such as supply-side tax cutting was eroding "upward mobility" among the poor, which, according to Gilder, "depends on all three principles—work, family, and faith—interdependently reaching toward children and future. These are the pillars of a free economy and a prosperous society."[57] This is why, in the preface to *Wealth and Poverty*, Gilder comfortably asserts that the "central theme of *Wealth and Poverty*" is "the need to extend to the poor the freedoms and opportunities, the values of family and faith, that are indispensable to all wealth and progress." He then asserts that this used to be a "central theme of American liberalism. Yet today, and in a great historic irony, Phyllis Schlafly, Connie Marshner, Edwin Feulner, Jack Kemp, and others on the 'New Right' have become the best friends of the poor in America, while Liberalism administers new forms of bondage in new fashions of moral corruption to poor families."[58]

Gilder sought to garner the support of religious conservatives, and forward the trope of the family values economy in other ways as well—namely, a heavy reliance on normative gender roles. He argues that supply-side economics would "strengthen the male role in poor families," which should be "the first priority of any serious program against poverty." Here, implicitly, Gilder argues that all men, but especially poor men, would see higher wages, more money, and better work opportunities though his "antipoverty" politics of supply-side economics. Such a result would prod male household heads to channel their "otherwise disruptive male aggressions into his performance as a provider for a wife and children."[59] According to Gilder, such a change would clear up the "natural" differences between men and women in the household: "Money is far more immediately decisive in the lives of men than of women, and women often fail to understand what is at stake among men at work. The man's earnings, unlike the woman's, will determine not only his standard of living but also his possibilities for marriage and children—whether he can be a sexual man. Man's work best finds its deepest sources in love."[60] Gilder posits his sexism as necessary truth-telling that seeks to end taboos that had developed in the United States around the topics of sex and money. As to the former, supply-side tax cutting would restore men to their "natural" places at the head of households, even restoring their lost libidos. As to the latter, he argues supply-side tax cuts would hopefully diminish the "hostility to [America's] great benefactors, the producers of wealth" who "on every continent and in every epoch . . . have been the victims of some of society's greatest brutalities."[61] He argues that such "hatred of producers of wealth," especially among the "intelligentsia," was now equivalent in its virulence to racism.[62] Such ideas were clearly the product of the same sort of thinking that animated Irving Kristol's writings about the "New Class" in the 1970s. Supply-side economics, in such formulations, thus served an array of goals: ending the hatred of the wealthy; saving poor families from the policies of liberalism; restoring the male to the head of all households, and, in turn, restoring his flagging sex drive; restoring morality and values to the American family; restoring faith in capitalism and God; and, of course, sharply cutting taxes regressively without seeing any drop in federal revenues.

Supported by conservative think tanks, and buttressed by the new marketplace of ideas discourse of policy debate, writings like Gilder's, Kristol's, and Wanniski's went mainstream as simply "another side of the economic debate." Despite the fact that their claims were increasingly taking to the realm of the fantastical, they were widely read, widely disseminated, and widely debated. Most important, Ronald Reagan agreed with these sentiments, and, immediately upon entering office, he began pushing for the passage of the Kemp-Roth bill. Additionally, key appointments were staffed with supply-side adherents. For example, Paul Craig Roberts—who was last seen writing in favor of supply-side cutting for the Hoover Institution—assumed the position of assistant secretary of the treasury for economic policy. As 1981 progressed, it appeared more and more likely that Reagan and those who supported the Kemp-Roth Bill were going to get their way. It was at this point that traditional conservative economists began to express their concerns. Along the same lines as Milton Friedman had in 1978, these traditionalists, like neoconservatives, absolutely favored the tax cuts, just not without spending cuts as well. Once again, the Heritage Foundation served as an outlet for such a position. Writing for the Heritage publication *Policy Review* in the spring of 1981, Carl Christ (a professor of economics at Johns Hopkins) and Alan Walters (chief economic adviser to Margaret Thatcher) took to questioning key supply-side assertions as passage of Kemp-Roth seemed imminent. Directly challenging Wanniski, Gilder, and the "Laffer Curve," the authors asked whether it was true, as the men had said, that outputs will "rise so much that tax *revenue* will rise, thus cutting the federal deficit? Even if government expenditures are not cut?"[63] Plainly, the authors concluded that "tax cuts in the U.S. will reduce tax revenue, not increase it, even though output may rise," and that supply-side adherents who argued otherwise were relying on Wanniski's "serious error" in his "interpretation of the Laffer curve."[64] They concluded that the "moral of the story" is that the United States must adopt their traditional conservatism. Specifically, "When we advocate tax cuts, we must be prepared to advocate cuts in government spending at the same time, or else advocate bigger deficits." Asserting otherwise, they claimed, was tantamount to "offering pie in the sky, without adequate evidence that we will ever taste it."[65]

Showing the credibility and authority think tank publications were bringing, Paul Craig Roberts himself responded directly to Christ and Walters in *Policy Review*, arguing that "all of [their] points have been carefully considered by Administration economists and found to be deficient," including their central assertion that "a tax cut will reduce government tax revenues."[66] However, Roberts then went on to declare: "The success of the Administration's economic policy does not depend on the tax reductions fully paying for themselves with revenue feedbacks. The policy is not based on the 'Laffer curve.' However, it would be incorrect to say there would be zero revenue feedback. What the Administration does argue is that the combination of increased savings, revenue 'reflows' and budget cuts more than pay for the tax cut."[67] On one hand, Roberts declares their points regarding the supply-side cuts to be deficient, but then tells them not to worry because administration policy was not based on the "Laffer curve." This assertion was hard to reconcile with the fact that the bill being discussed was Kemp-Roth, which Wanniski, Laffer, and others had helped plan. The bill eventually signed into law on 13 August 1981 was known as the Economic Recovery Tax Act of 1981 or the Kemp-Roth Tax Cut. While the bill itself was not exactly the form advocated by most supply-siders (they wanted even bigger tax cuts than the final bill gave), it nevertheless contained the key element of an across-the-board cut but one tilted heavily toward upper-income earners. The bottom marginal income tax rate dropped from only 14 percent to 11 percent, while the top marginal rate was reduced from 70 percent to 50 percent.

Almost immediately after the bill's passage, worry set in among conservatives that their claims regarding the tax cuts would not come to fruition. These worries were exacerbated by continuing inflation in late 1981. Despite such worries, all the various promoters of supply-side policy had intellectual "outs," so to speak. In the *New York Times* Wanniski declared that supply-siders "had predicted this situation," and that the problem was that "the die was cast when it was arranged that the supply-siders would dominate the fiscal side of Treasury and monetarists would get the monetary side." This disabled the implementation of his full vision—namely, the return to the gold standard given that "gold [was] the only answer" to the current problems of high inflation and deficits. In other words, the tax cuts that they had advocated for were not the problem. Rather, the fact that they were not coupled with a return to the gold standard was the true problem. According to Wanniski, if their full conservatism could be implemented, everything would be fine: "Nothing bad will happen. Interest rates will plummet, and the $106 billion cost of financing the national debt will plummet too, balancing the budget. Auto workers and carpenters will exchange with each other again, and the savings and loan institutions will be saved. The third world will be able to refinance its stupefying debt at low rates as interest rates tumble worldwide, keying on the dollar. The financial crisis we are now going through will be ended. The dollar will be as good as gold."[68] In many ways it was easiest for neoconservatives like Wanniski to explain away bad consequences because their thinking had always been the least tethered to realism or small claims. This op-ed was but another example of this phenomenon. Wanniski could simply continue to make even more outlandish claims for additional policies that he knew would never be implemented.

Irving Kristol, still at his *Wall Street Journal* post in late 1981, and still writing as an AEI distinguished fellow, took a slightly different route—while still using rhetoric that asserted that the current situation was not the fault of the policies he had advocated. While declaring Wanniski's gold standard critique "extremely cogent," he nevertheless declared himself "agnostic on the issue."[69] However, like Wanniski, when answering the question, "Why did the economy collapse?" Kristol also sought to assign blame elsewhere. In this way, he too was allowed to continually reassert his policies without taking on blame for problems they may have produced. Declaring that the economy's collapse "obviously" had "no connection with 'Reaganomics,'" Kristol instead laid the blame on "the swollen Carter budget for fiscal 1981" and, like Wanniski, on the "tight money policy of the Fed." If supply-siders had been listened to "earlier and to a more substantial degree" (that is, larger tax cuts), "it would at least have made the economy's fall less precipitous and even (as 'supply-siders' hoped) might have prevented it altogether." According to Kristol, the problem was simply that neoconservative supply-siders had not been listened to enough. Even with the Kemp-Roth bill, the problem was that supply-siders had not totally gotten their way with a "populist" bill that "called simply for a 30% tax cut on all income tax rates for all taxpayers" as had originally been proposed in the 1970s. In this formulation "the Democratic leadership in the House" was really to blame for lowering the individual tax cut a bit and phasing it in more gradually than the supply-siders had hoped. In the end, according to Kristol, "the only ones who were unhappy were the 'supply-siders'!"[70] Consequently, Kristol disavowed his group of conservatives of blame, while actively blaming others who did not fully listen to and accept his agenda.

Traditional conservative economists at the Heritage Foundation noticed these explanations and began to form a response of their own that insisted that their own agenda should have been followed. Along these lines, Tim Congdon, economic correspondent for the *Times* of London, wrote a scathing critique of neoconservative supply-side views for Heritage's *Policy Review* in the summer of 1982. By this point, it was becoming abundantly clear that the predictions supply-siders made for their policies were not coming true. Congdon wrote that President Reagan "embraced their nostrums" with "vigor, enthusiasm, and naiveté" because of their promised tax cut cure-all.[71] But now that their policies were followed by a year of "major contraction in business activity and a fall in tax revenues" that added $100 billion to the federal deficit, it might be too late to reverse "the damage [that] has already been done."[72] Congdon even correctly describes the neoconservative "gold standard evasion" of responsibility—which he argues made their position "empirically impregnable at the level of debate (editorial columns and political dinners) where the supply-siders specialize and excel. No one can prove what might or might not have happened if a particular hypothetical state of affairs had or had not existed."[73] However, in correctly identifying the problem with supply-side conservatism, Congdon asserts that what was needed was a return to his traditional fiscal conservatism; in particular "lower public expenditures and less government regulation [to] enable the private sector to operate more efficiently."[74] As for increased taxes to counter the huge new deficits, Congdon does not go there, declaring that the "damage has already been done." In essence, then, Congdon gets to have it both ways as well by keeping the cuts and arguing for more austerity. Reagan and Congress did not agree as they jointly passed the Tax Equity and Fiscal Responsibility Act of 1982, which rolled back one-third of the previous year's reduction (although not on the highest income earners) in an attempt to reduce the deficit caused by the supply-side cuts. The 1981 act would go down as the biggest tax cut of the 1968–2006 period, while the 1982 act would go down as the biggest tax increase of the same period. Even so, the 1981 act, contrary to long-standing neoconservative supply-side claims, caused federal revenues to drop by an average of $111.4 billion per year in the four years after its enactment. Revenue as a percentage of GDP dropped –2.89 percent per year in the same four years.[75]

The essential fact of this revenue drop, in tandem with the massive 1982 tax increase, were two facts supply-side theorists in think tanks would have to grapple with and explain. The former directly contradicted the central claim of their most vocal adherents, while the latter called into question the commitment of Ronald Reagan to their tax-cutting strategy. As would be the case with so much in the rest of the 1980s, the Heritage Foundation took the lead in developing responses. Ed Feulner, in a 1985 speech on the question of "what Heritage does," shows that part of Heritage's central intellectual project surrounding supply-side economics in the early to mid 1980s was rewriting the history of the idea in a way that removed some of the most outlandish ideas that emanated from neoconservatives like Kristol, Wanniski, and Gilder. In the speech, Feulner downplayed all AEI-affiliated writers and their role in promoting "supply-side economics." Instead, he argues that Heritage was "active in bringing ideas concerning Supply Side Economics to the attention of opinion leaders in Washington. Together with the Institute for Research on the Economics of Taxation (the only Supply Side economic 'think-tank' in Washington) we produced a book titled *Essays in Supply Side Economics* which laid out the theoretical case for Supply Side Economics.

We co-hosted a conference to introduce the publication and discuss the ideas that were put forth in the book. The conference was attended by 400 congressional aides, members of Congress, administration officials, professors and representatives from the media." Feulner argued that it was this book, and Heritage's promotion of it, that "made significant inroads in the myth that Supply Side theory was dreamed up while economist Arthur Laffer was doodling on a cocktail napkin."[76] What Feulner elides here is that the book was published and released *after* the passing of the 1981 tax cuts most associated with supply-side economics. So Feulner's speech and the book itself instead need to be read as historical reinterpretations designed to centralize Heritage in promoting supply-side tax cuts while downplaying the most outlandish claims of the neoconservatives who *did* drive the debate. In some ways, historical reinterpretation made quite a bit of sense because Heritage, while always explicitly advocating the tax cuts, never went as far as AEI-affiliated neoconservatives in saying such cuts would increase government revenues or would require a return to the gold standard. Instead, and surprising given Heritage's inclination to publish at the absolute fringes of the debate in the 1970s, Heritage had always positioned their support of supply-side tax cuts along with spending cuts and a rejection of monetary policy associated with returning to the gold standard.

Essays in Supply Side Economics participates in this same historical rewriting. In the foreword, written by Feulner, he argues that the essays in the book are designed to put "to rest many of the popular misconceptions that have been expressed by the press, policy-makers, and the public concerning the legitimacy of supply-side economics and implications of the Reagan administration's economic policies." Feulner argues that there was a lack of legitimacy because of the "political success of the Tax Act of 1981," which encouraged the notion that "supply-side economics is a political movement with little or no economic theory behind it." Strangely, then, Feulner closes the foreword by admitting that such a notion was indeed true: "Heretofore there existed no comprehensive explanation of supply-side economic theory or of the evidence that policies based on supply-side economics will work; this volume supplies that explanation."[77] In the foreword Feulner is at his most honest in what the book seeks to accomplish—providing an economic veneer for a policy that had already been passed and had never been subjected to any sort of analytical rigor. In doing so, the more outlandish claims of the neoconservative writers who had truly helped sell the policy to policymakers and the public alike would be elided in favor of a much more reasonable-sounding definition of supply-side economics—one that focused on the more uncontroversial assertion that government could affect conditions of supply and not just demand. David Raboy, in his essay in the book entitled "The Theoretical Heritage of Supply Side Economics," makes such a shift away from the neoconservative definition when he asks, "Do supply-side policies flow from logical, consistent, empirically verifiable economic theories or are they merely the whims of fanciful, fast talking political operatives?" Of course, he argues that he former was the case as there were really two camps of supply-side thought with "the popular press [having] seized on the fringe ideas that stem from different sources to produce one giant, seemingly bizarre set of theories. If one derived all of one's information about supply-side economics from the popular press and made a kind of composite supply-sider, one would have to conclude that a supply-sider categorically rejects monetarism and considers Milton Friedman to be the most dangerous heretic since Keynes; believes not only that tax cuts are self-financing, but that all cutting of taxes can cure any economic ill; and, most astonishing of all, that taxes can explain any event from the Great Depression to Third World Revolution."[78] Here the theories of Wanniski, Kristol, and others, which did drive the debate in advance of the 1981 cut, are positioned as being a media conspiracy of sorts, designed to "freeze out" more reasonable conservative positions like those held by Milton Friedman and, of course, the Heritage Foundation.

Think tanks like Heritage were also central in the debate surrounding what would become the conservative response to the 1982 tax increases. In many ways, this hike was the first Reagan policy that enabled think tank conservatives to sell their various identities in the marketplace of ideas by *disagreeing* with Reagan—as now they could simply argue that Reagan was not a true conservative, libertarian, and so on, because he chose the tax hikes. This allowed think tanks to reassert their identities in the marketplace while not appearing beholden to Reagan and/or the Republican Party. It established a tried-and-true policy employed by conservative think tanks of critiquing elected Republicans from the most right-wing position in order to pull Republican elected officials in that direction. Feulner, in a 1983 *New York Times* article, discusses how Heritage used "report cards" to further such aims: "On the anniversary of Mr. Reagan's first twelve months in office, Heritage gave Mr. Reagan a 62 percent 'compliance rating' on major conservative issues. 'Our job is to run the flag all the way up the flagpole and hope people salute,' said Mr. Feulner. 'The fact that Ronald Reagan saluted 62% of the time wasn't bad at all as Jimmy Carter would have saluted 20% of the time.'"[79] In regard to the tax hike, Heritage and other think tanks like the Cato Institute leveled a critique from the right. For instance, in late 1983, Cato president Edward Crane wrote a brutal op-ed against Reagan in the *Wall Street Journal* that at the same time sought to sell Cato's libertarian outlook. Crane wrote that, if Reagan was a conservative, "there is little in conservatism today to distinguish it in any meaningful sense from liberalism." Reagan, unlike libertarians, had no "internally consistent set of principles" and he was ultimately a spendthrift executive who "directed all of his manifest lobbying talents toward pushing a $100 billion tax increase through Congress" in 1982. In conclusion, according to Crane, Reagan's conservatism, and those who supported it, was "devoid of anything approaching a commitment to individual liberty" and "cannot help but lead us to a bigger, stronger central government."[80] Only Cato's libertarianism was the true pathway to these goals.

Heritage had similar retrospectives regarding Reagan's first-term performance that they published in late 1984 as part of a symposium entitled "What Conservatives Think of Reagan." Adam Meyerson, who introduced the forum, notes that among the forum's participants there was "universal approval for Mr. Reagan's tax cuts, tied with a universal concern over his failure to cut spending, particularly entitlements programs. Virtually all of those featured here blame deficits on spending, not on tax cuts; on the contrary, they tend to oppose the tax increases of 1982."[81] Paul Weyrich, writing in the forum, concurs with this assessment, "The radical surgery that was required in Washington was not performed. Ronald Reagan made a pledge not to touch entitlements programs, and that's one of the few pledges he has kept absolutely. But until we come to grips with entitlements, no amount of tinkering with tax increases is going to get the budget in order." Continuing with his metaphors of the body and surgery to it, Weyrich argues, "The correct strategy for Reagan would have been to take the 'Economic Dunkirk' approach outlined by Kemp and Stockman. He had an unprecedented opportunity to say you don't understand what a mess Jimmy Carter left us in, to say radical surgery was required and I'm ordering something that will hurt but will save the patient's life. He could have cut much more if the program was fair to everybody, in the sense that everyone's benefits were cut. Instead he was seen as cutting out benefits for poor people, while still subsidizing the International Monetary Fund, the Ex-Im Bank, and businesses like Chrysler."[82]

As these critiques show, think tanks like Heritage were, by Reagan's second term, integral outposts in the project of critiquing conservatives from the right. Such a project had many effects. First and foremost, it kept Republican legislators constantly worried about their right flank and more likely to hew to the positions put out by places like Heritage. Second, it allowed conservative think tanks to often deny the results of their policies as there could always be a retreat to their pure position which allowed them to assert that "real conservatism had never been tried." Finally, continually asserting new right flanks, on a myriad of issues, expanded the entire "acceptable" mainstream political debate as the right wing in the marketplace of ideas continued to move rightward. The entire spectrum of political opinion shifted right as these positions entered the realm of debate, requiring others to respond to them. These "right moves" of the entire political spectrum were facilitated by not only Heritage's advancement as an institution in furthering such a project but also, as we will see, the willingness of other think tanks to acquiesce to this shift.

BY THE MID-1980S, Heritage was enormously successful in ways beyond merely "setting the right flank" in the marketplace of ideas. In short, their institutional model was running circles around old-timers like AEI and Brookings. The press coverage of Heritage's tenth anniversary in the fall of 1983 reflected its newfound place of importance in Washington as both the *New York Times* and the *Washington Post* ran glowing profiles of the think tank and its president. The *Times* story writes glowingly of Heritage's new headquarters and its tenth-anniversary celebration keynoted by none other than President Reagan.[83] The *Post* story goes into much greater detail regarding Heritage's enormous success in such a short period of time. What the report shows was that Heritage was truly in the process of perfecting the new model conservative think tank that it began developing in the 1970s. Once again, such a model had key components which were designed to make Heritage the top conservative think tank in the marketplace of ideas. First and foremost, it prioritized the speed, production, and influence of policy over rigor. Interestingly, this goal was in some ways perfected by the think tank in 1981 when Feulner hired a former reporter and editor from *Time* magazine as the think tank's research director. By 1983, Burton Pines had streamlined the research and influence peddling in a profoundly effective way. According to Pines, the first shift he made was when he "ordered the Heritage research staff to get out and pound the quarters of government the way reporters do. As a result, there is a fresh, newsy quality to the scholarly research in the 8-to 14-page ('about the length of a *Time* cover story') 'Backgrounder' reports that Heritage turns out at the rate of two or three a week." Such "newsy" research was then focused in a way whereby it would be most effective. Once such research was produced, "Feulner and his lieutenants [routed] them to every key congressman and senator" and made phone calls to get them to the right aides. As Feulner puts it, "Our concept is to make the marketing of the product an integral part of it ... our role is trying to influence the Washington public policymaking community ... most specifically the Hill, secondly the executive branch, thirdly the national news media.'" As for the news media, always now willing to print conservative voices so as to balance the marketplace of ideas, "An aggressive public relations staff distributes the foundation's outpouring to the media, where it is often fuel for editorials and the subject of news reports."[84]

In addition to perfecting the speed, production, and influence of its policy production, the article shows that Heritage was also perfecting their model in other important ways. They were becoming more effective in "channeling a lot of conservative thinkers and policy specialists into the White House and agencies," especially "the Republican Study Committee, a congressional staff of fourteen serving 145 mostly conservative members of the House." They also moved people into influential areas by maintaining "a computerized file of 1,000 conservative academics on call for speeches (countless), seminars (many) and expert testimony before Congress (about 50 times a year)." Heritage was perfecting the model of developing and supporting conservative policy people and then moving these people into places where they would have the most influence. Heritage could do all of this because of their perfection of a fundraising strategy that targeted both the elite and the grass roots of the conservative movement. Where places like AEI were still getting all of their funding from a small number of individuals, corporations, and conservative foundations, Heritage was tapping these sources plus broadening its base "with an aggressive [direct] mail campaign" that "had brought in 138,000 individual contributions in the past eighteen months." Finally, the article shows how Feulner was increasingly selling Heritage as the "fusionist" think tank in the marketplace of ideas where the foundation would be seen "as an 'honest broker' within the conservative movement, bringing together libertarians, neoconservatives, and traditional conservatives in the new right under one roof."[85]

While Heritage was perfecting its model in the marketplace of ideas by the end of Reagan's first term in office, its competitors were struggling to keep up. Although Brookings was still seen as the most prestigious of all think tanks, and still had the largest budget and endowment, there was enormous concern that that it was losing relevance, especially to the new Heritage model. A December 1983 *New York Times* report reflects such concerns and the changes this brought about at Brookings—changes that further entrenched the marketplace of ideas and pulled Brookings to the right in its institutional identity. According to the report, in order to keep up with places like Heritage, there was a "very overt fashion change" in the "character of [Brookings's] product." What this meant is that there was "less a disposition to produce complete analyses in book form, and a more pronounced disposition to comment in either testimony, short form or very brief monographic form." Such short-form work even had names that aped Heritage publications: "'Brookings Review,' Brookings 'Discussion Papers,' and handsomely published 'Brookings Dialogues on Public Policy.'"[86] Additionally, Brookings hired a full-time public relations director and invited journalists to regular briefings to make sure Brookings was receiving the kind of publicity that Heritage was. Such changes were unsurprising given that they came about under the head of a Republican, Bruce MacLaury, who would have had less problems with conforming to the models of conservative think tanks and publishing papers that were more likely to be accepted in the marketplace of ideas. MacLaury, in 1984, continued to make other controversial changes as well. Donald Critchlow, a historian of Brookings, notes that in 1984 there "were charges of trustee interference, of the devaluation of genuine scholarship in favor of short-term policy research, of staff appointments going to Republicans to achieve political balance, and of a forced consensus in the formation of an institutional perspective when it came to writing such studies as *Economic Choices 1984*." I concur with Critchlow, who argues that such changes in part came as a result of the criticisms of Brookings. The institution moved right in a number of ways, and helped reinforce the marketplace of ideas way of debating policy, in order to maintain relevance and to prove it was not "liberally biased." As Critchlow correctly notes the changes were most important for the rightward drift of policy debates in that they "signaled the abandonment, or at least the fundamental transformation, of the nonpartisan ideal" that had motivated Brookings even during the postwar period where it was associated with New Deal and Great Society liberalism. As Critchlow notes in an analysis that obviously syncs with my own, "Their zeal for objectivity and efficiency in the distrust of politics, embodied in nonpartisanship, gave way to the very different conception that political knowledge was somehow inseparable from fundamental values, and thus—in the Brookings case—to a quest for ideological balance." Critchlow even quotes a Brookings official at the time, "There is no such thing as 'nonpartisan' research. At best research can only be bipartisan."[87] Such a wholesale abandonment of the technocratic ideal and embrace of the marketplace of ideas model by Brookings arguably did more to shift policy debates rightward that any development by Heritage. Now all think tanks were working within this new conservative-friendly way of debate. In such a world, conservative think tanks like Heritage and AEI could be openly conservative as they were still "balancing" Brookings, the mainstream media, and academia. At the same time, Brookings and the media were becoming more amenable to conservative changes in policy debate and achieving "balance" internally within their own spaces. Taken together, such shifts meant a rightward shift of the *entire* marketplace of ideas.

Reagan's second term saw an exacerbation of such a trend as all the key think tanks took Reagan's victory as a sign of the rightward movement of the American electorate and responded to move their institutions accordingly. As the think tank now most closely associated with Ronald Reagan, Heritage reaped the rewards in Reagan's second term. The financial records of the think tank show a steady upward trend for the rest of the 1980s, and by 1985 it was taking in more revenue than any other think tank in Washington. In 1985, total revenue for Heritage was $11.4 million, and by 1989 it was $16.3 million. Most impressively, a full 43 percent of the 1989 revenue came from individuals as opposed to 38 percent from foundations and corporations—showing the success of Heritage's direct mail fundraising efforts.[88] This is not to say that such individual contributions came from "little-guy" small donors—far from it. Such widespread notoriety for Heritage as "Reagan's Think Tank" meant that big-money conservatives were seeking them out—more and more at the expense of AEI. For instance, in a letter from Ed Feulner to Heritage Trustee Clare Boothe Luce, Feulner brags that from the period from 1975 to 1985, Richard Mellon Scaife, individually and through his trusts and foundations, had provided the think tank more than $10 million. In the same letter he tells Luce that at the recent "April meeting of the Heritage Foundation Board of Trustees in Dallas, Texas, Joseph Coors announced that he and his wife, Ali, were making a $2 million gift above and beyond their annual support."[89] Feulner was, of course, using all of these facts to prod Luce, a longtime conservative donor and wife of *Time* publisher Henry Luce, to make similar donations. She responded with a donation of $250,000 to Heritage.[90]

Heritage then used this new windfall to even further expand the reach and influence of their institutional model. In particular, by late 1985, it was becoming the go-to institution for young conservatives who wanted entry into Washington power circles. A November 1985 *New York Times* article notes, "Many analysts are bright graduate students recommended to Heritage by conservative professors on selected campuses; others walk in off the street, attracted by Heritage's reputation for hiring and promoting the careers of young conservatives. Heritage says it has placed a few dozen of its own employees in government jobs in recent years, has helped to place more than 250 other conservatives in policymaking jobs over the past fourteen months and still has 3,000 resumes on file."[91] Such an influx of young conservative activists allowed Heritage to situate itself as the key institution devoted to the identity formation and employment of young conservative activists. By the end of Reagan's second term, Heritage had set up regular meetings for these young activists and called them "Third Generation" meetings. An article in Heritage's *Policy Review* asserts that "Heritage Foundation senior vice president Burton Yale Pines coined the term in reference to three generations of conservative opposition to liberal policies beginning with the New Deal. (The First Generation refers to the intellectual groundbreakers who coalesced around William F. Buckley Jr. in 1955 to publish *National Review* and who later launched the Draft Goldwater movement; the Second Generation refers to the political activists and organizers who helped elect Reagan in 1980.) The Third Generation was swept into politics on the heels of a Reagan victory. Unlike the previous generations, it entered politics not when conservatives were in opposition but when they held power."[92] Such a moniker was used to give meaning, history, and importance to young conservative activists. By centralizing Heritage as the key storyteller, the think tank gained even more importance within all levels of the conservative movement during Reagan's second term.

Not so coincidentally, Heritage's surge in Reagan's second term coincided with AEI's decline and near shuttering. Heritage's new institutional model left AEI without a clear identity as Heritage increasingly came to be seen as the intellectual opposite of Brookings—a placement previously occupied by AEI in the 1970s. It seems that William Baroody Jr.'s plan from early in Reagan's first term to "moderate" or "balance" the perspectives at AEI was the wrong institutional goal at the wrong time. In an era of ascendant conservatism, Heritage's model was immensely more lucrative in the marketplace of ideas. Moreover, AEI's funding base was much more insecure in such an environment. Given that both Baroodys had always resisted a small-donor model like the one Heritage had cultivated, AEI was at the funding whims of a very small number of high-dollar conservative donors. According to a December 1985 article on the situation at the think tank, many of these donors were now moving to funding Heritage, putting AEI in a rough position financially. Moreover, William Baroody Senior's plan to set up a permanent AEI endowment for just such a situation was never followed through with by his son. Such a situation forced Baroody Jr. to announce in 1985 that "staff would be cut immediately by 15 to 20%, publications scaled back, and a planned move to a newer, posher quarters abandoned because of financial troubles."[93] Unfortunately for the younger Baroody, AEI was finally getting the "competition of ideas" his father had been demanding throughout the 1970s, and it was undeniable that Heritage was winning with its nimbler, more forthrightly conservative product.

By June 1986 the situation at AEI was dire with many speculating that the once prominent think tank would shutter itself. In that month, long-term funder the Olin Foundation cut its financial support, saying to the *Washington Post* that the think tank had "gone very far downhill, on a managerial and philosophical basis." According to the article, many "within the conservative philanthropic community" like Olin were worried about the "creeping centrism" at the think tank. The *Post* piece describes the problem as such: "With so many policy institutes seeking money, AEI's drift away from a sharply defined right-wing position became a vulnerability. 'There is no serious supply-side economist there,' [conservative donor] Lenkowsky points out. 'The foreign-policy program, with the exception of Jeane Kirkpatrick, has long been an object of criticism of people outside AEI. . . . The general attitude of the conservative donor community is watchful waiting. There are fears for AEI's overall institutional viability. It's a role-definition problem.'"

In addition to this lack of identity in the marketplace of ideas, particularly when looked at alongside Heritage, the *Post* article also highlights near-universal condemnation of the managerial practices of Baroody Jr.[94] Although he fought it, the younger Baroody was eventually forced to resign in the summer of 1986, leaving many speculating what was next for AEI. In the fall of 1986, longtime AEI hand Paul McCracken took over the institute on an interim basis. Showing the depth of the think tank's funding problems, McCracken sent supporters letters that they could no longer send out complementary publications to AEI supporters.[95] In December of 1986, Christopher DeMuth was named AEI's president—a position he occupied until 2008. DeMuth is accurately credited with returning the institute to prominence, particularly in the George W. Bush years. Given that AEI was on the verge of bankruptcy when DeMuth took over in late 1986, it was striking that by September 1987, he was already sending out appeals for new projects at AEI, a testament to how fast he was able to turn the think tank around and get it on a stronger financial footing.[96]

In 1987, the Cato Institute, celebrating its tenth anniversary, was also enjoying limited success as the libertarian product in the marketplace of ideas. Such a product is accurately described in a *New York Times* profile of their birthday as a "dedication to the freest conceivable free market economy, the least possible government, lower military spending, smaller American military commitment abroad and full civil liberties for all." Ironically, Cato found that they were particularly successful in selling such an identity to "younger people of the post–World War II 'baby boom' generation." The vice president of Cato, David Boaz, argued that this was due "to their disaffection with the Vietnam War, suspicion of government and major political parties, personal economic conservatism and dedication to civil liberties." However, Cato's budget of about $2 million per year showed that such an identity was not going to be the priority of big-money conservative donors. Given this fact, Cato saw their purpose as a think tank in much more limited ways. William A. Niskanen, the chairman of Cato in 1987, forthrightly claims that "our audience is not the voting public." Rather, he said, "We hope to shape the perspective of the policymaking community so that its members are conscious of alternative solutions when the demand for change arises. Our audience is the Washington community."[97]

As Reagan's time in office came to a close, there can be no doubt that the Heritage Foundation was dominant in the marketplace of ideas. Cato was limited in reach, AEI was working on keeping its doors open, and Brookings was trying to maintain relevancy by moving rightward and abandoning their once proud technocratic ideal. This left Heritage with the only clear funding base and institutional identity of all major Washington think tanks. Their model was best tailored to being successful in the marketplace of ideas; hence, Heritage was well positioned to be dominant for some time to come. However, as Reagan neared the end of his second term in office, many at the think tank openly wondered what would come next and whether Reagan had truly accomplished enough while in office. On this issue, Heritage continued its role as the right pole of the political spectrum toward which all Republicans should move. And according to Paul Weyrich in an end-of-term retrospective in *Policy Review*, Republicans would need to do better in the future as they had just witnessed "The Reagan Revolution That Wasn't." According to Weyrich, this was the case because future Democratic presidents "understand that, with the exception of his judicial appointments, almost everything that President Reagan has accomplished can be swiftly undone by a single session of a heavily Democratic Congress, or by the stroke of a pen from a new Democratic president himself. In short, while some significant changes have been made, there has been no Reagan Revolution." Moreover, Weyrich contends, Reagan did nothing to create "new conservative constituencies" while "the same old liberal establishment is in place." He argues that this had much to do with the fact that "conservatives are monarchists at heart. They *love* the Presidency. They think that if you own the presidency, that is all that really counts. Richard Nixon should have proven the case against that theory once and for all, but the idea" persisted under Reagan leading to much conservative disappointment.[98] Instead of such a focus, Weyrich recommends a renewed conservative focus on state, local, and congressional politics as opposed to putting so much faith and energy in the presidency, only to be inevitably disappointed.

Weyrich's end-of-term Reagan retrospective was illuminating in many ways regarding where conservative organizing, particularly within think tanks, would go in the 1990s. Conservatives would, more and more, try to influence state and local politics through a network of state-based conservative think tanks. Much less faith was placed in the presidency as George H. W. Bush disappointed conservative elites in think tanks and elsewhere for his more moderate domestic and foreign policy. By the time Bill Clinton took office in 1992, conservative think tanks had already invested new energies in Congress. But, in other key ways, Weyrich was off in his assessment—particularly when it came to liberal and/or Democratic politics. As will be seen in chapter 4, Democrats had been chastened by the advance of conservatism in the Reagan years and with the success of conservative institutions like Heritage. The ability and willingness of the "same old liberal establishment" to roll back the gains of the Reagan years, or to advance new liberal projects, were severely diminished. Rather, what we will see in the late 1980s and 1990s was an entirely new phenomenon whereby a new conservative think tank that catered directly to the Democratic Party would actually help in the overall advancement of conservatism in American political culture. This think tank, Progressive Policy Institute, and its political umbrella, the Democratic Leadership Council, helped shift the parameters of the debate even more to the right in the 1990s. We now turn to this story.

4

Think Tanks, New Democrats, and Committed Conservatives

This chapter seemingly makes an abrupt shift. Whereas previous chapters have been largely concerned with those think tanks that defined themselves as conservative, this chapter moves in a somewhat new direction. The success of conservative think tanks should largely be credited for this shift. By the late 1980s and early 1990s, Heritage, AEI, Cato, Hoover, and others had thoroughly altered the political, media, and intellectual landscape. The marketplace of ideas paradigm of policy debate was thoroughly entrenched. No matter the issue, and no matter the topic, conservatives in think tanks and elsewhere could reliably depend on the marketplace of ideas to get their voices heard. Heritage was the voice that set the right flank of American conservatism; AEI continued, as it recovered from its financial troubles, to represent neoconservatism; and Cato was the voice for libertarianism. As we will see in this chapter, this influence would remain largely unchanged and unchallenged in the late 1980s and 1990s. All of these conservative institutional voices continued to make their voices heard in the marketplace of ideas. They continued to influence legislators in a rightward direction, and they continued to reliably insert their voices into mass media in the name of "balancing" policy debates.

Given such influence, and given the hegemony of the marketplace of ideas model by the 1990s, this chapter does not focus undo attention on explicitly conservative think tanks except in those moments when their influence and hegemony were threatened. This is not to say that institutional historical change did not occur during this period, only that the primary site of such change was not in think tanks traditionally identified as conservative. Rather, what is most important to examine in the late 1980s and 1990s was the change underwent by those institutions that were historically thought of as liberal. As was seen in the previous chapters, many of these institutions, which conservative think tanks rose to power "balancing," were becoming less and less dedicated to the project of technocratic liberalism. Brookings was now being run by a Republican dedicated to "bipartisan" policy debates. The mass media had so thoroughly internalized the marketplace of ideas model that any liberalism that existed there was tamed by an obsessive need for balance. Academia, particularly the social sciences and humanities, was the only holdout in this trend. But as they maintained a liberal cast, the academic social sciences and humanities were outflanked by conservative think tanks when it came to policy influence. In the late 1980s and 1990s conservative think tanks solidified their marginalization of liberal/left academic voices and those same academic voices largely marginalized themselves.[1] Thus, at the same time that conservative think tanks were introducing more and more conservative voices into the marketplace of ideas, liberal voices were becoming less and less influential or more and more conservative. The entire political spectrum was moving rightward.

The Democratic Party of the 1980s and 1990s was caught up in this dynamic as well. As the final pillar of the liberal technocratic edifice, the Democratic Party had to decide how it would react to ascendant conservatism and to the hegemony of the marketplace of ideas model of policy debate. Ultimately, this chapter argues that the Democratic Party chose the path of the other main liberal institutions in the United States—that of accommodation to rising ascendant conservatism and the marketplace of ideas. Pushed by a new think tank, the Progressive Policy Institute (PPI), and its political arm the Democratic Leadership Council (DLC) the Democratic Party moved rightward in a whole host of ways and, with such movement, moved the entire American political spectrum to the right. This think-tank-inspired historical dynamic was arguably the most important conservative political transformation of the 1990s and, as such, is the primary focus of this chapter. Without the PPI/DLC working to move the party of American liberalism rightward, the hegemony of conservatism and the marketplace of ideas would not have been nearly as strong by the end of the twentieth century. When combined with the acquiescence and/or support of other liberal institutions to the same trends, the rightward movement of American political culture in the 1990s was immense.

THE LANDSLIDE REELECTION OF RONALD REAGAN to the presidency in 1984 led to significant psychological trauma for national Democrats and to a debate regarding how best to counter the growing tide of conservatism in the 1980s. Throughout the decade two schools of thought developed as to how the party should deal with this political tide: the politics represented by Jesse Jackson and his followers and the politics represented by a new Democratically aligned political group, DLC and its head Alvin (Al) From. Jackson's view emerged from his civil rights background and stressed coalition politics whereby traditional Democratic constituencies—labor, women, African Americans, and so on—would unite under a clearly defined progressive agenda and grassroots organizing efforts. This project was crystallized in Jackson's run for the presidency in 1984 and 1988 under the mantra of the "Rainbow Coalition." Al From saw his project at the DLC (founded in 1985) as not only the opposite of Jackson's vision, but also (in the beginning) fundamentally defined by the fact that *it was not* Jesse Jackson's politics. In other words, the DLC, although not technically a think tank itself, used the structure and position of the think tank to counterpose their project to that of Jackson's.[2] This became even more the case once PPI was created in 1989. The think tank, in this formation as the DLC/PPI, did not derive its support from social movements. Rather, From saw his institutions as sites that could marshal elites, in this case elected Democratic leaders and policymakers, to wield power in a top-down way against the energies of a social movement like Jackson's Rainbow Coalition. Especially in the early years, the DLC's members were primarily Southern white men—thus embodying the group's differences from Jackson's social movement even further.

The particular choice of the think tank and think-tank-related political group as organizational structures for elite political movements should not come as a surprise given Al From's background. From had been active in the national Democratic Party since the early 1970s when he directed the U.S. Senate Subcommittee on Intergovernmental Relations under Senator Edmund Muskie. He was then a deputy advisor on inflation to President Jimmy Carter, and then the executive director of the House Democratic Caucus in the early 1980s.[3] This experience gave From the necessary connection with national Democratic politicians to get the DLC off the ground in 1985. Also, it led to what would be the primary organizational purpose of the DLC in its early years—that is, having a "moment of party." In the DLC's early years, its primary focus was getting national Democrats to accept the more conservative political identities that the DLC sold in the marketplace of ideas. These identities, the "Mainstream Democrat" and the "New Democrat," were positioned as counters to the social movement politics of Jesse Jackson.

It was not until four years later that the PPI was established in order to give these new positions policy underpinnings.

However, even before the official establishment of PPI, From borrowed various elements from conservative think tanks for the DLC itself. Like conservative think tanks such as Heritage, Cato, and AEI, he recognized his group as a unique space from which to sell new political identities and policies within the marketplace of ideas. The Mainstream Democrat and the New Democrat could be sold to the media and to Democratic Party elites through the DLC and then later through PPI. Such identities and policies would have a decidedly conservative cast to them as the DLC/PPI sought to position itself and its supporters as a moderating influence over the Democratic Party. Such a project was similar to the move Brookings made during the 1980s as it sought to counter the impression that it was reliably liberal. Pushing back on this perception, Brookings hired conservatives and sought bipartisanship in the name of balancing their institution's voice in the marketplace of ideas. The DLC and PPI sought the same influence over the Democratic Party in order to counter the impression of the party as monolithically liberal. To do so, the organization took on a decidedly elite cast and funding much like AEI. The top-down/bottom-up model Heritage cultivated was of little use to From. In fact, it would have made little sense given that the groups sought to counter the grassroots liberalism of Jesse Jackson and his allies among traditional Democratic constituencies.

From the announcement of the DLC's formation in March 1985, many elected Democrats were already open to the identities the think tank was selling in the marketplace of ideas. At the announcement, From and those present reported that their membership already included ten governors, fourteen senators, and eighteen representatives.[4] At this point in time, the DLC was selling the identity of the "Mainstream Democrat." In nearly every early news report on the group, the adjective "mainstream" was used by supporters to identify who they were and who they were not. This position was not only counterposed to the social movement politics of Jesse Jackson, but it was also situated inside a certain historical narrative that saw "the mainstream" as being a reaction against the overall heated political climate of the 1960s and 1970s—and thus conservative in its orientation. Senator Sam Nunn of Georgia, a founding member of the group, articulated this view in the group's first press conference when he argued, "There is a perception our party has moved away from mainstream America in the 1970s."[5] Likewise, Representative Steve Neal of North Carolina, another founding member, argued that the group "represents the mainstream of American thinking—sensible, pragmatic and moderate."[6] But perhaps the best expression of this position and its relation to a particular historical narrative came from Al From himself in a 1988 interview with conservative Paul Gigot in which he argued the following: "When the great Roosevelt coalition shattered in the 1960s . . . the party consensus shattered as well. The post-Vietnam generation turned isolationist. Organized labor, which had been a force for internationalism, was buffeted in the 1970s by economic change and turned protectionist. A 'cultural radicalism' also infected the party . . . producing other special interests. The traditional Democratic message of 'economic growth with equity' and national strength got lost amid the kaleidoscope of demands."[7] These appeals toward a "traditional" or "mainstream" voter, posited within a particular historical narrative of conservative backlash, show how From and the DLC were not simply responding to the Reagan victory in 1984. Instead, they were selling an identity that had antiradicalism and antiliberalism at its core.

However, beyond this anti-social-movements sensibility, the DLC lacked the ideological and policy content its more conservative counterparts were selling in the marketplace of ideas. Whereas Republican-centric conservative think tanks had a clear ideological and policy agenda, the political category of "Mainstream Democrat" did not have a clear policy agenda attached to it. Quite simply, in its early years, the organization was devoid of any actual fully formed policy content. As the policy debating world of the marketplace of ideas allowed for, the group did not have to have fully formed policy ideas. Rather, simply selling the sensibility of the "Mainstream Democrat" was enough to enter into the debate. Members admitted as much. Chuck Robb, a DLC founder who was governor of Virginia from 1982 to 1986, and a senator from the same state from 1989 to 2001, argued in 1985 that the DLC was "trying to be careful not to identify with a specific ideology."[8] As the 1980s progressed, vague policy outlines began to form. The 1988 quote in the preceding paragraph from Al From presents hazy policy positions such as "economic growth" and "national strength." Likewise, Robb acknowledged "that several of the group's leaders had been described as 'neoliberals' who generally favor many of the historical goals of liberals on social issues but want a more conservative approach to economic and military issues."[9] Several news reports noted that policymakers who aligned themselves with the think tank "generally look favorably on deregulation, and support the easing of antitrust laws, especially in those industries facing stiff foreign competition." However, even though some members paid lip service to such a policy agenda, another news report is undoubtedly more on the mark when it asks the question, "So where do the DLC Democrats stand on trade? All over the lot—approximately where they are on tax reform, deficit reductions and the defense department budget."[10]

This lack of a coherent policy program is why it is hard to overstate the extent to which the early years of the DLC focused on defining the politics of the "Mainstream Democrat" largely by what it was not: left-liberal and grassroots. In the DLC's rendering, catering to these types of politics meant catering to "interest groups" or "special interests." These two terms were variously employed by DLC Democrats to define what they argued should be the periphery of the Democratic Party—positioned in opposition to a "center" or "mainstream" that was defined by their organization. The racial and gender connotations of such a paradigm are hard to ignore. Moreover, given the DLC's initial makeup of "nearly all white men" from the South and West (two black men and no women founded the group), the group often, although never explicitly, equated the "center" or "mainstream" of American politics with white, middle-class, male voters.[11] Two months after its founding, the group added four women, one African American, and two Latinos, but this was now out of a total of seventy-seven members—hardly representative of the party's base.[12] In this vein, and with apparently no pun intended, an aide to the newly elected Democratic National Committee chairman, Ron Kirk, argued that the DLC "wants to take the cream of the party's leadership and leave Kirk with Jesse Jackson and the single-issue interest groups."[13]

Jesse Jackson's coalition was not the only thing the DLC sought to define its new political identity against. Their "Mainstream Democrat" was also defined more generally as an opposition to both "old" and "new" left social movements. Once again, Al From put the point most succinctly in 1986 when he argued, "Labor's views are important, but we're not going to labor and adopt their ideas, and go to gay, lesbian, black, Hispanic, Jewish caucuses."[14] This sort of dismissive attitude to the various elements of the Democratic base was part and parcel of defining the Mainstream Democrat and it was an attitude readily embraced by those Democrats who defined themselves as such. Labor, along with African

Americans, took the brunt of the criticism from Mainstream Democrats as these Democrats moved not only to jettison Democrats' association with "new" social movements, but also with "old" labor-based social movements they saw as being too hostile to big business. As with Republican-centric conservative think tanks in the 1970s and 1980s, such an identity allowed the DLC, and later the PPI, to finance its existence with large corporate donations—giving those same corporations a much larger voice in the marketplace of ideas given that they now had institutional reach in both parties. The DLC was not shy about promoting this fact as a way to articulate that Mainstream Democrats were friendly to corporate interests who were willing to give them a "balancing voice" within the Democratic Party. A March 1989 *Washington Post* article is instructive in this regard. It discusses the DLC's annual conference and how it was funded. The article notes that although "the DLC doesn't have to report its donors and can take contributions larger than those allowed for political candidates and committees," Al From nevertheless "provided a list of the sponsors for this conference." The list "showed three corporate 'hosts' who paid $25,000—the food and tobacco conglomerates RJR Nabisco and Philip Morris, and SmithKline Beckman, a pharmaceutical firm. Another 25 businesses, trade associations and individuals signed up to be $10,000 'sponsors,' and 27 are listed as $5,000 'patrons.' In addition, more than 40 'friends of the DLC' are paying $25,000 each." This type of financial support allowed the companies to not only underwrite the event but also to gain access to the DLC legislators who would be at the conference. The contributors were even allowed access to the "thirteen Democratic senators and 38 of their House colleagues" on a private train taking the attendees to the conference. From told reporters that "he didn't know why the corporations and lobbyists paid to go on the trip" but that he had no problem with gaining support from these "special interests." As From puts it, "Let's face it: Everybody is in some special interest group.... There's no question you can define 'special interest' as our sponsors." Clearly, such a quote and such a story served a dual purpose. First, the story and the way it was reported demonstrated that Mainstream Democrats were not hostile to corporate interests and would "balance" the Democratic Party's liberal wing. Second, it showed that "special interests" were really not a problem for the DLC as long as those interests were not associated with left/liberal social movements.[15]

Because of such an increased corporate funding base, by the end of the 1980s the think tank saw its influence growing within the Democratic

Party. At their 1989 meeting, for instance, the DLC was now "influential enough that the Speaker of the House, the majority leader of the Senate and the chairman of the Democratic National Committee felt compelled to take part in the meeting, as did [Jesse] Jackson."[16] This was not the first time Jackson felt compelled to confront the DLC directly. At their 1987 meeting he spoke to the group for the first time and made the case for détente: "The party has a progressive wing. It has a conservative wing. But it takes two wings to fly." He suggested that the DLC recognize this and support as "members of our family . . . environmentalists, women, American Indians, peace advocates, farmers and many others."[17] However, by the 1989 meeting—with another Democratic presidential loss in 1988 behind them—the tone was not as friendly and the lines hardened in the debate with each side determined to win out with their respective visions. This debate would be carried into the 1990s and, most immediately, to the next presidential election.

FOR THE DLC TO FULLY CREATE their new political identity, the think tank needed to articulate a more coherent ideological and policy platform. Not unlike AEI two decades earlier, the "Mainstream Democrat" needed to be given meaning in the same way "neoconservative" was given meaning in the 1970s. At the end of the 1980s, such a project of identity articulation was harder for the DLC than it had been for AEI. This was largely due to the fact that even though the DLC wanted to be viewed as a "think tank," and sometimes was within the media, it was at risk of being seen merely as a lobbying group. It needed a coherent policy agenda behind its new identity to change this perception. Adding to this urgency was the fact that, by the late 1980s, the lack of a coherent policy program was being noticed by mainstream publications. For instance, in 1990, pundit Thomas Oliphant observed in the *Boston Globe* that the DLC had spent much of its first five years "bashing away at 'liberal fundamentalists' for capturing the party apparatus." Now, finally, the group was "moving onto Chapter Two—the promulgation of 'new ideas' to help the party and its next presidential nominee."[18] This move to articulate the ideological and policy positions of the DLC came in two forms. First, the DLC decided to set up a more formal policy-oriented think tank apparatus through the creation of PPI. The PPI would be the DLC's formal policy arm with researchers churning out fast ideas for policymakers, while the DLC would focus more on the media/public relations role of the think tank. In this way, the DLC was copying and even advancing Heritage's model of a rapid-response think tank targeting policymakers and the media. Secondly, the DLC and PPI created their own publication, the *Mainstream Democrat*, in order to promote their ideology and policy to the party and the public. With the establishment of the PPI in mid-1989, and with the first issue of the *Mainstream Democrat* published soon after, the group's policy and ideology became much clearer—giving their political identity a new coherency.

This did not mean that the DLC abandoned the anti-social-movements core of their new identity, only that they coupled it with a policy agenda as was traditionally done by conservative think tanks. Early PPI documents continued to rail against so-called liberal fundamentalism— defined as the doctrinarian set of Democratic policies produced by "minority groups and white elites" within the party. Such an agenda included "tax and spending policies that contradict the interests of average families; with welfare policies that foster dependence rather than self-reliance; with softness toward the perpetrators of crime and indifference toward its victims; with ambivalence toward the assertion of American values and interests abroad; and with an adversarial stance toward mainstream moral and cultural values." Jesse Jackson, of course, represented the "purest version of liberal fundamentalism" that must be rejected.[19] Such a document, while railing against Jackson and the social movement politics he represented, now did set forth policies the think tank was against. Most significantly, in their acceptance of conservative framings of liberalism, the authors also accept much of the way conservatives discussed liberal policy on a whole host of issues including welfare, crime, foreign policy, and "cultural values."

However, at this point, the DLC/PPI still parted ways from conservative Republican framing on some economic matters. In the first issue of the *Mainstream Democrat*, members repeatedly point to the widening of the income gap that had taken place during the Reagan years and that was "eroding the middle class"—a message Republicans and think tanks like Heritage would never promote. Although he uses much of an early *Mainstream Democrat* article to rail against "the Left," Senator Charles Robb nevertheless seeks to articulate an agenda interested in poverty and "the middle class." Robb writes that "unlike many Republicans, mainstream Democrats believe that society has both a moral obligation and a practical interest in intervening on behalf of the poor and the powerless." Robb goes on to argue that "the growing gap between rich and poor not only offends basic Democratic values, but also depletes our national stock of intellectual capital."[20] Senator Daniel Patrick Moynihan then puts a policy proposal behind the problem of growing inequality in the next issue of the publication. He argues for repeal of a recent payroll tax increase and a further cut in the rate to benefit 132 million lower income workers who were disproportionately affected by these increases. Moynihan calls payroll taxes the "most regressive taxes on Earth." His article was the beginning of the PPI taking on the payroll tax cut as a central issue over the next three years.[21] Such a policy not only allowed the think tank to target a huge segment of voters who crossed racial lines but also would not offend their business constituencies since payroll tax cuts would reduce their overall tax burden.

The irony of this early policy articulation was that it could be construed as economically progressive. While the rhetoric, emphasis, and tone in promoting such economic policies may have been different from the way Jesse Jackson chose to promote similar policies, Jackson took it as an opportunity to support and co-opt the think tank's messaging. Jackson made this crystal clear at the DLC's annual meeting in 1990 when he delivered an address entitled, "Delighted to be United." In the speech, "Jackson welcomed the DLC to what he called the 'new mainstream' and congratulated it for embracing his views on progressive taxation, military budget cuts and investments in education and economic development."[22] The speech, while aimed toward unity, was also a dig at the DLC, which, despite having long criticized Jackson, nevertheless ended up articulating some policy he agreed with. Moreover, by hijacking the DLC's "mainstream" identity in his speech, Jackson showed that he was more than willing to fight the DLC on its own rhetorical ground. The speech rankled many at the DLC who were still concerned with defining their think tank's identity in contrast to Jackson's. Al From called the speech "bizarre, absolutely bizarre" and argued that it was "foolish for anyone to think that the party has moved in Jesse Jackson's direction."[23] Likewise, Governor Bill Clinton of Arkansas, who was now the chair of the DLC, argued that "the DLC's endorsement of tax progressivity differed from Jackson's rhetoric of 'class warfare,' and he said its support for 'measured' reductions in defense spending differed from Jackson's advocacy of deep cuts."[24]

Clinton's and From's reactions to Jackson's speech showed that they needed to do more work articulating the uniqueness of their political position in the marketplace of ideas. Out of this dilemma, the now-familiar political identity the "New Democrat" was born and the "Mainstream

Democrat" cast aside. This switch in positioning should not be seen as merely rhetorical. Coming so soon after Jackson's speech, it was a clear attempt by the DLC/PPI to truly counterposition their politics and policies to Jackson's. The "New Democrat" identity, like the Mainstream Democrat, was still defined as being against the grassroots politics and "liberal fundamentalism" of Jesse Jackson's Rainbow Coalition. Likewise, the new identity would still claim for its acceptors a unique ability to speak for middle-class economic interests and "values." The "new" element of the New Democrat largely centered on the role that the state would place in advancing these interests and values. A New Democrat, according to the DLC/PPI, recognized that government needed to be more effective by doing less, "streamlining," and leaving as much activity as possible to market mechanisms that would work better to alleviate social and economic problems. Fealty to "the market" would now be given priority in policymaking by not only Republican-aligned think tanks but also think tanks like the DLC/PPI.

Just as important as this newly defined position, and role for the state it entailed, was the overall "feel" the New Democrat was supposed to impart its adherents and give to its detractors. First and foremost, the position was clearly intended to advance a feeling of modernity—of being ahead of one's time in understanding the world as is. In this vein, the new role of state action (or in this case inaction) was always positioned within a wider, pop-futuristic narrative. Such a narrative focused on "new developments" that, New Democrats argued, fundamentally altered the role of the state in economic affairs. Most important among these developments were new technologies and the end of the Cold War. New Democrats argued that these had already created fundamental changes in business and society while government was left behind to operate in an "old" paradigm. New Democrats argued that only they recognized this new world-historical epoch and the altered state role it entailed. Second, the identity of the New Democrat imparted a feeling onto its opposite as well. Whereas "Mainstream" never really had an effective opposite to impart onto its other, "New" immediately brings to mind "Old." If a New Democrat recognized and understood the break with the past taking place in the early 1990s, "Old Democrats," or "liberal fundamentalists" like Jesse Jackson, did not. Because of this ability to both define the positive and the negative, New Democrat became a much more powerful political identity in the marketplace of ideas than Mainstream Democrat.

The unveiling of the New Democrat shortly after Jackson's speech had the intentional feel of a marketing campaign "rollout." The contours of the position, but not the position itself, were introduced by Al From in the March 1991 issue of the *Mainstream Democrat*, in an article entitled "The New Politics." In rhetoric that would become commonplace soon after, From declared the emergence of a new historical period where "the industrial order has yielded to a new information age, and the politics that once united Roosevelt's coalition no longer command its loyalty." According to From, the federal government was not innovating for this new period like "governors, legislators and local officials" who were actively "inventing new institutions and new approaches to governing that serve the needs of ordinary men and women in today's fast changing, information-intensive world." In this vein, the "New Politics" would still be for the middle class (that is, "ordinary men and women") but would also recognize that in the new "fast changing, information-intensive world" government would play a different role: "Above all, the new choice means a new way of doing business. It means a radical change in the way government works [and] reinventing government. The new choice is an approach to governing that is as different from the old bureaucratic system as the computer is from the manual typewriter." According to From, "Just as the New Deal shaped the political order for the industrial age, the new politics can define a political order in the information age."[25]

Shortly thereafter, at their annual meeting in 1991, the DLC chose to use the emerging position as a bludgeon against Jesse Jackson and his politics. For the first time, the group simply chose to not let Jackson speak at their annual meeting and used their new political identity as the silencing mechanism. Before the meeting, From said that neither Jackson nor George McGovern would be asked to speak given that they represented "old-style politics." Catherine Moore, spokeswoman for the group, took the critique one step further, arguing emphatically that "we have a specific goal at this convention. That is to unveil what we consider to be the new politics that will move this party forward." According to Moore, Jackson was "representative of an old style of politics that has not done much to help our party win the White House." In terms of defining what the "new politics" was, Moore told reporters that it "involves expanding opportunity, not government; spending money more wisely, but not raising taxes; responding to the needs of the majority of Americans, not specific groups."[26] This quote effectively demonstrated the increased usefulness of the New Democrat over the Mainstream. The

"New" position was much more pernicious in the way it situated its own subjects on a higher plane of understanding while simultaneously denigrating its opponents as out of touch.

Jackson's reaction to the annual meeting slight was probably exactly what From desired: "At one time you had the Dixiecrats ... Now they are organized up north in the same spirit—the Mason-Dixoncrats."[27] The reaction was the exact opposite of the tactic Jackson exercised a year previous. Instead of making himself the high-minded conciliator, he came off as aggressive—magnifying the importance of the DLC and their new identity in the process. From this point on, the DLC had found the most effective way to marginalize Jackson and his grassroots politics—ignore him and situate him within the paradigm of a bygone era. This would be done while positioning their politics and political identity within a narrative of modernity and elite understanding. It was at this point that the position of "New Democrat" was officially unveiled; in May 1991 the title of the DLC/PPI publication was changed from *Mainstream Democrat* to *New Democrat* as the editors argued that they would be for a fundamentally "new way of thinking."[28]

What the DLC/PPI meant by "a new way of thinking" was made clear in the first issues of the publication. For instance, an article entitled "Reinventing Government" argues, "The kinds of governments that developed during the industrial era, with their sluggish centralized bureaucracies, their preoccupation with rules and regulations, and their hierarchical chains of command, no longer work very well" because "hierarchical, centralized bureaucracies designed in the 1930s or 1940s simply do not function well in the rapidly changing, information-rich, knowledge-intensive society and economy of the 1990s." This sort of quasi-populist sensibility (that is, a denigration of "rules," "regulations," and "chains of command") became typical of the New Democrat position and neatly formed a consensus with Republican-centric think tanks throughout the 1970s and 1980s—particularly when advocating policies of deregulation. Likewise, appeals to new technology as defining the new historical epoch (that is, "information-rich, knowledge-intensive society and economy") became ubiquitous. And, as always, the federal government fell behind in recognizing this fact while corporations were out front "making revolutionary changes: decentralizing authority, flattening hierarchies, focusing on quality, getting close to their customers—all in an effort to remain competitive in the new global marketplace." The authors then present "ten principles of entrepreneurial government" that, they argued, would bring the government up to speed in the "information age." Borrowing language from new business management theory, these principles included "Customer-Driven Government: Meeting the needs of the customer, not the bureaucracy" and "Market-Oriented Government: Leveraging change through the market."[29]

In addition to articles like these that focused on defining the new epoch in terms of technological advances, the end of the Cold War was also seen by DLCers as ushering in a new politics—one that New Democrats saw more clearly than others. In an article entitled "Privatization and Its Discontents," author John Donahue takes a trip to a city in Czechoslovakia to find out how the mayor there is dealing with the demise of the Soviet Union. Donahue is surprised to find that the mayor is privatizing the public utilities. The mayor says, "But how can I say it is the wrong thing to do? To choose otherwise, to put the city workers first, is to say that the citizen who needs the services and who pays for them, should not count. . . . It is time to start to catch up to the way you do things in the West." Donahue sees this as an opening to liken liberals in the United States to old-style Soviet communists: "After an inner struggle I decided it would be more charitable not to tell him that a good many American officials in his position would have wilted under the political heat the privatization option promised to generate." Donahue asserts that "Mayor Borbely would have been baffled to learn that many Americans who consider themselves progressives reflexively dismiss contracting out, voucher schemes, and the like as an oversold policy fad—at best irrelevant, at worst a sinister assault on traditions of good government." While admitting that not all privatization is good, Donahue argues that American liberals oppose all privatization because "privatization is often opposed by public workers, and support for public workers is a durable component of the liberal creed." Donahue concludes, "One ironic—no, make that bizarre—consequence is that elected officials in Trnava and scores of other recently-Communist cities are moving to privatize services that are stubbornly stuck in the public realm in most American communities."[30] This short travel narrative of a post–Cold War Eastern Bloc country does an enormous amount of ideological work in such a short space as a former communist official is enlisted to sell the New Democrat identity.

Writers like Donahue, PPI policymakers, and promoters like Al From had now begun to firmly define the New Democrat within the marketplace of ideas. But the question still remained as to which Democratic politician would be the best marketer. Bill Clinton stepped in to fill this void by becoming the group's chairman in early 1990. Many in the group suspected all along that he would use the DLC's power base to launch his 1992 presidential campaign.[31] As early as June 1991, From conceded that there was "a good possibility" that Clinton would be the group's first choice to run.[32] In October 1991, Clinton made the move official by announcing his candidacy. However, unlike in past primaries, Clinton's position as a DLC "New Democrat" occurred in a changed political environment. Most importantly, given that Jesse Jackson ultimately decided not to run again, Clinton had no powerful liberal candidate who was explicitly positioned as the grassroots candidate. In fact, in a testament to the influence of the DLC at this point, Clinton's main opponents were either to Clinton's right (Paul Tsongas) or amorphous reformers like Jerry Brown. In such an environment, the DLC's "new politics," as articulated by Clinton, could take on the appearance of being the most progressive. A reporter notes that after winning several southern primaries in March 1992, Clinton's "recent populist appeals drew strong support among blacks, poor whites and the middle class." Clinton himself argued, "I think what Georgia and South Carolina and hopefully these other votes show today is that the DLC message will sell among traditional Democratic constituencies, and we know from our experience in Arkansas that if they listen it will also sell among independents and Republicans." Some in the media and the DLC, however, began to wonder whether Clinton was going beyond the DLC's "New Democrat" position by sounding more "populist" than the think tank generally advocated. The same news report noted that "while campaigning in the South, Clinton rarely mentioned the [DLC]."[33] PPI policy analyst Bruce Reed, who had now become Clinton's campaign manager for policy, was not worried. Reed argued that this seeming shift leftward was "rooted in the nature of the primary process and the press coverage."[34] Moreover, the DLC/PPI was ecstatic when Clinton picked another one of their own, Al Gore, to run as his vice presidential nominee.

Likewise, Clinton's July 1992 Democratic National Convention speech largely promoted the think tank's "New Democrat" identity. In particular, Clinton was eager to promote the New Democrat's vision for the state: "A government that is leaner, not meaner; a government that expands opportunity, not bureaucracy; a government that understands that jobs must come from growth in a vibrant and vital system of free enterprise." Clinton argued that "the choice we offer is not conservative or liberal. In many ways, it is not even Republican or Democratic. It is different. It is new. And it will work." Clinton also gave three lines of the speech to an emerging PPI issue of importance when he delivered the soon-to-be-familiar edict that his administration would "end welfare as we know it." At the same time, Clinton claimed to speak for a broad middle class when he argued that George Bush had "raised taxes on the people driving pickup trucks and lowered taxes on the people riding in limousines." Finally, Clinton sought to co-opt conservative "family values" rhetoric when he intoned that he was "fed up with politicians in Washington lecturing the rest of us about family values. Our families have values. But our government doesn't. I want an America where family values live in our actions, not just in our speeches. An America that includes every family. Every traditional family and every extended family. Every two parent family. Every single-parent family. And every foster family. Every family." While strident, such rhetoric reflected emergent rhetoric where the family would now be central to organizing economic life given the state's retrenchment. The end of Clinton's speech, with its rousing defense of the Democratic grass roots, was probably the only element of the speech that gave New Democrats pause: "And so we must say to every American: Look beyond the stereotypes that blind us. We need each other—all of us—we need each other. We don't have a person to waste, and yet for too long politicians have told the most of us that are doing all right that what's really wrong with America is the rest of us—them. Them, the *minorities*. Them, the liberals. Them, the poor. Them, the homeless. Them, the people with disabilities. Them, the gays. We've gotten to where we've nearly them'ed ourselves to death. Them, and them, and them. But this is America. There is no them. There is only us."[35]

Judging by a lengthy profile of Al From published in the *Washington Post* shortly after the convention, he clearly did not feel that Clinton deviated from the New Democrat identity. From was positively giddy with delight that Clinton had won, arguing, "I think we will be for the Clinton administration what the Heritage Foundation was for the Reagan administration . . . An idea factory to help Bill come up with new approaches." Such a direct parallel to Heritage was striking, especially given that the Republican-aligned think tank was loathed by many in the Democratic Party by this point. However, From clearly felt that his think tank's "moment of party" had achieved such an advanced state that such a similarity between the DLC/PPI and Heritage was not going to be problematic. Not only did two of their members make up the presidential ticket but they also had a 3,000-person membership that included "750 elected officials nationwide, with 32 U.S. senators and 142 current and former House members, and chapters in 28 states in every region of the country." In addition, their budget was now $2.5 million a year. Strikingly, none of this really seemed to bother Jesse Jackson, who was interviewed for the same article and who saw much more ambivalence toward the "New Democrat" position and politics in Clinton's speech. Moreover, Jackson argued that the actual party platform was a liberal document through and through.[36] Only Clinton's first term would determine if the New Democrat position would win the day.

DURING PRESIDENT-ELECT CLINTON'S TRANSITION to the presidency in late 1992, it seemed that the New Democrat identity was winning out as the DLC/PPI sought to solidify its role in the administration. As with Ronald Reagan's incoming administration and the Heritage Foundation, key members of the groups were working on the transition team by early December 1992. Most significantly, Al From was selected by Clinton to prepare the domestic agenda, and Bruce Reed was moved from campaign manager for policy to a post working on policy for the transition team.[37] Like Heritage before them, PPI produced a policy manifesto for Clinton modeled after Heritage's *Mandate for Leadership*. The PPI's *Mandate for Change* created enormous buzz in December 1992, which suggested it would play a similar role for the Clinton administration as Heritage's *Mandate* had for Reagan. With chapters on the economy, health care, education, the family, crime, the environment, welfare, foreign policy, and "reinventing government," PPI hoped Clinton would use the outline in the same way Reagan used *Mandate for Leadership*. Those in the think tank were not shy about such a parallel. As PPI president Will Marshall argued, "Heritage played a key role in defining a new direction in national politics which became Reagan conservatism. We are trying to play an analogous role in reinvigorating progressive politics."[38] The choice of "progressive" here was an interesting one given that the agenda defined by *Mandate for Change* was largely conservative by Democratic standards. Very often in the think tank's early years, this adjective was used to describe the New Democrat agenda.

Despite this seemingly influential start in the coming administration, many observers began to notice that *Mandate for Change* often went well beyond what Clinton himself advocated. For instance, while the book argues that Clinton "should spend his political capital on a substantial effort to reduce the federal budget deficit next year, including new restraints on entitlement programs and the elimination of subsidies for many industries," this message goes "well beyond what Clinton was willing to embrace during his presidential campaign and would cut more from the federal budget than Clinton so far has said he is prepared to do."[39] More liberal think tanks such as the Economic Policy Institute (EPI) were taking credit for "framing the government spending debate in terms of 'investment,' and Robert Reich, an EPI founder, [was] the top transition adviser on the economy."[40] Despite these mixed signals, the DLC/PPI was guardedly optimistic heading into 1993. They opened their January 1993 issue of the *New Democrat* with the article "Mandate for Change," declaring that the "election signals a shift in American politics" and a victory for their agenda. However, it still remained to be seen whether they would get the chance to implement that agenda.[41]

Disappointment almost immediately set in among "New Democrats" at the beginning of Clinton's first term as he appeared to be abandoning their political project. Despite championing many DLC causes in his first State of the Union (welfare reform, national service, a new crime bill), Clinton led his first term with the issue of allowing gays and lesbians to openly serve in the military, which New Democrats saw as embracing liberal "special interests" they sought to reject. Just four short months into Clinton's first term, DLC members were making public their frustration with his presidency. In an article in the *New York Times*, they question whether "the President, who won office as one of their breed, has come to look very much like the same old—liberal—thing." Joe Lieberman, a Democratic senator from Connecticut, and vice chairman of the DLC, argues that there "has been some disappointment both on a policy ground and personnel ground." DLCers report a long list of grievances: "A budget that favors raising taxes over cutting spending; a Cabinet dominated by liberal Washington insiders; a fondness for ambitious and expensive programs like the proposal to overhaul health care; a solidly liberal stance on issues like homosexual rights and abortion, and the nomination of controversial interest group advocates to highly visible positions." In essence, the group worries that Clinton is wholly abandoning their New Democrat brand in the marketplace of ideas while wholly embracing "liberal fundamentalists" whom the DLC thought it had effectively marginalized. Instead, Clinton is, as the author of the same article writes, "torn between the New Democratic promises of the campaign and the political realities of dealing with the national Democratic Party, controlled by Old Democrats, elected officials and interest groups of a determinedly liberal ideology." The author of this story helps advance the DLC's concerns as he harkens back to a moment from the 1992 campaign: "In 1992, Mr. Clinton publicly criticized the Rev. Jesse Jackson's Rainbow Coalition for inviting Sister Souljah, a black rap artist who has been accused of making anti-white statements, to a coalition meeting." The author then quotes a DLC foreign policy adviser who argued, "But since he's been elected, he's done everything Jesse Jackson could have asked for." This quote and this article are significant for multiple reasons. First and foremost, they show that DLCers were still overwhelmingly concerned with rebuking the social-movement politics personified by Jesse Jackson. They clearly wanted their agenda enacted, but they were just as concerned with dealing a deathblow to "liberal fundamentalism" and grassroots Democratic constituencies. Second, and more positively for the group, it is important to note the way in which this supposedly disinterested news report is unproblematically framed within the terms of the debate that the DLC/PPI has chosen. The author employs both "Old Democrats" and "New Democrats" in precisely the way the same way as "New Democrats" would do. The reporter himself clearly accepts the New Democrat identity as his own, a dynamic that would help the think tank advance its position through supposedly neutral arbiters like elite political reporters for the *New York Times*. These patterns would continue as the 1990s progressed—evidencing the fact that the DLC advanced their New Democrat identity even as they appeared to be on the defensive.[42]

Even more explicitly good news for the DLC/PPI came as the first year of Clinton's presidency progressed and he seemed to be moving toward the New Democrat position. By June, Al From wrote from the pages of the *Washington Post* that "President Clinton has returned to the Democratic Leadership Council agenda—the New Democrat ideas that formed the basis of his campaign."[43] In particular, From cited Clinton's recent return to the issues of "welfare reform," budget austerity, and "reinventing government"—issues that were the core of the New Democratic brand in the marketplace of ideas.[44] From also cited changes in White House management as a sign of progress for the New Democrat agenda. In particular, Clinton's appointment of Republican David Gergen as a senior adviser was cited by From as being important. Gergen told the *Washington Post* that he only took the job after Clinton assured him that he "really saw himself as a DLC New Democrat." From argued that Clinton should build on these accomplishments and "push hard for approval of the North American Free Trade Agreement" as NAFTA had long been central to the New Democrat position.[45]

Clinton did just that in the second half of his first year in office—effectively pushing through a long-term project that, until the 1990s, primarily had support among conservative Republicans and their think tanks. Importantly, the debate over NAFTA fundamentally engaged the question of what the post–Cold War political-economic environment would look like and was thus a perfect fit for the New Democrat brand in the marketplace of ideas. Additionally, NAFTA was one of the first policies that signaled a key area of agreement between Republican- and Democratic-aligned think tanks in the post–Cold War world. Staunchly supported by nearly all Republicans, the DLC/PPI had been pushing for the idea since the late 1980s. The issue had long been blocked by most national Democrats and their labor allies because of the damaging effects it would have on high-paying industrial jobs in the United States—among other factors. Clinton's embrace of the pro-NAFTA position opened an intense internal debate within the party. As with the coming debates over health care and welfare, the New Democrat position on the issue created a powerful consensus with Republicans and their think tanks. This consensus helped dictate how the issue was covered in the elite media—and thus how the issue was perceived by the public at large. The elite narrative on NAFTA went as follows: if some Democrats who were defined as "New" largely agreed with Republicans on the issue, then that position must, by default, have more merit. Conversely, if the position taken by those Democrats who were (now objectively) defined as "Old," then that position must have less merit and be associated with a bygone era. Al From put it best when he argued, "The New Democrats have always been on record in favor of expanding trade, the old Democrats have too often taken the other position. . . . The losers in the battle for the heart of the Democratic Party are joining ranks against NAFTA."[46] It was this powerful dynamic of "New" versus "Old" and winners versus losers that helped propel NAFTA to passage. The DLC/PPI, having worked to use the think tank as a site of expertise to promote the issue, was better positioned in the media to argue that it had the correct view. Finally, given that so many elite political reporters who covered the issue accepted the New Democrat position as their own political identity, the reporting on NAFTA (and other issues) inevitably skewed in the DLC/PPI direction.

The centrality of NAFTA within the New Democrat identity, however, was not easy to explain and seemed to reveal a fundamental contradiction at the heart of the DLC/PPI agenda. While the issue clearly made sense in that it reflected the DLC's emerging political economy and supposed forward-looking approach, it nevertheless was seemingly out of sync with the group's message that Democrats needed to woo a broad middle class. An analyst at EPI put it best when he argued, "For years, the so-called New Democrats have been skewering the left for alienating 'Bubba' by taking up elitist social positions [on affirmative action, abortion and defendants' rights]. Now, when push comes to shove, they are willing to abandon Bubba for elitist economic positions."[47] When the act passed, though, the DLC/PPI argued that NAFTA was firmly in the interest of a broad middle class even if that middle class and their "Old Democrat" allies could not see it for themselves: "Sadly, the opposition of so many Democrats to NAFTA was to be expected. The pact has become a vessel filled with past grievances about jobs lost to foreign competition. Paradoxically, if all politics is local, the politics of foreign trade is the most local of all. The narrow interest is easily defined (protect my job now) while the national interest looms as an intangible promise on the horizon (higher national income tomorrow)."[48] The acceptance by New Democrats of the conservative Republican view of trade and industrial policy here is striking and would not go unnoticed by Republicans and their conservative think tanks as they debated how to respond to a Democrat in the White House.

THE DEBATE AMONG republicans and Republican-aligned conservative think tanks in the aftermath of Clinton's victory was two-sided. On one side of the debate, many Republican moderates contended that their party's stance on social issues alienated voters. A column from the *San Francisco Chronicle* in late 1992 is typical in this regard: "As happened to the Democratic Party B.C. (Before Clinton), the Republican Party of the '90s has been co-opted by extremists. Just as radical leftists imposed their out-of-touch notions on mainstream Democrats, GOPers from the religious Right took over the party platform in 1992—nationally and in California—and poisoned it with stands contrary to the beliefs of most members."[49] This led some of these moderates to form an organization called the Republican Majority Coalition that, mimicking early DLC-speak, argued that Republicans should move the party "'back to its mainstream' and end its focus on such divisive issues as abortion and homosexuality."[50] In this regard, the group was very open about the parallels to the DLC: "The new coalition is modeled on the Democratic Leadership Council, the centrist group that served as a launching pad for President-elect Bill Clinton's successful campaign and provided one of its main themes, that Democrats needed to abandon liberal orthodoxies."[51]

This project, however, did not convince many in the Republican-aligned conservative think tank world. This largely had to do with the fact that, at places like Heritage, many saw the Clinton victory as good for the cause of conservatism. This was largely due to how those at conservative think tanks viewed the legacy of Clinton's opponent, President George H. W. Bush. The view of Bush was not kind and had been so since well before Clinton took office. In the run-up to the 1988 election, Heritage held a forum on the question of who conservatives should support for the Republican nomination, and only one conservative luminary chose Bush to "inherit the Reagan legacy."[52] By 1991, and particularly after Bush broke his "no new taxes" pledge in his first term as president, leaders at think tanks like Heritage were seething at his leadership. In early 1991, Ed Feulner wrote to Heritage supporters, "Only in America as we enter 1991, are advocates of bigger, more-intrusive government on the ascendency again. It's not because conservative ideas have been found wanting. It's because George Bush decided to become a consensus politician in 1990, and the technocrats within his administration and the tax-and-spend crowd on Capitol Hill wasted no time taking advantage of it."[53] In such a framing, Heritage continued its standard project of critiquing Republican politicians from the Right for not being conservative enough—or in the case of Bush for being a liberal technocrat in practice. Feulner took such a critique even further in early 1992 when he gave a speech that issued "a vote of no-confidence in the president" and argued that "conservatives supported George Bush and they got Michael Dukakis."[54] By the time Bush lost in late 1992, Feulner was taking to the pages of the *Wall Street Journal*, arguing once again that it was his "liberal agenda," not conservatism, that brought about his defeat: "Mr. Bush lost the election because he couldn't revive the ailing economy. He couldn't revive the economy because of the policies he's pursued. And the policies he's pursued are the same tax-spend-and-regulate policies that were the undoing of Jimmy Carter."[55] Such pronouncements, while undoubtedly put forward in good faith, were also meant to soothe the conservative faithful in that they situated "liberalism" as the problem rather than conservatism. None other than Milton Friedman responded excitedly to such a suggestion in a letter to Feulner after his *Wall Street Journal* op-ed was published. Friedman writes that the "op-ed piece was absolutely splendid" and "hit precisely the right mark." Even more interestingly, however, Friedman goes on to argue that he had "mixed feelings about Bush's defeat" as "I am not sure that for the long run it is not an advantage for us to be able to return fully to the opposition."[56] Such a sentiment was undoubtedly shared by many conservatives who undoubtedly felt more comfortable in opposition to federal legislation in general.

There was another factor at play as to why many at the Heritage Foundation were not particularly bothered by Clinton's election and Bush's defeat. Essentially, Republican-aligned conservative think tanks saw the "New Democrat" identity not so much as a repudiation of conservatism but as a victory. Heritage vice president Herb Berkowitz argued, shortly after Clinton's election, "To the extent Clinton embraces PPI's ideas, he'll be doing what we've been saying for 15 years."[57] Stuart Butler, the director of domestic studies at Heritage, argued that the PPI's *Mandate for Change* "neatly hijack[ed] a lot of ideas that are conservative in origin. . . . It's kind and gentle conservatism, everything that George Bush didn't do."[58] Indeed, one of the central problems that Heritage had with George Bush, in addition to raising taxes, was the fact that he did not work hard enough to enact NAFTA. In early 1991 Feulner argued that NAFTA was "an idea first offered by The Heritage Foundation a half a decade ago" and that Bush ignored it at his own peril.[59] In late 1991, Feulner again argued that Bush needed to mount a "vigorous defense of free trade and the North American Free Trade Agreement."[60] After Clinton's vigorous defense and passing of NAFTA it is not hard to see why Heritage would have viewed the "New Democrat" as anything but a victory for conservatism. However, in terms of the overall direction of Clinton's presidency, it would take another policy debate to firmly tilt the balance in favor of conservatism.

In the health care reform debate of 1993–94, think tanks in both parties played a key role in determining not only the outcome of the particular debate but also the trajectory of late twentieth-century American political culture. For the DLC, they would ultimately wholly win Clinton over to the New Democrat identity for the remainder of his presidency after the failure of his administration to pass any health care–related legislation. On the Republican side, the issue was used by a key think tank as a coalescing point to reassert conservative hostility to any expansion of the welfare state.

The DLC/PPI had long been ambivalent about the issue of health care reform and its centrality to the New Democrat identity. The necessity of heavy government involvement that any reform would likely entail was anathema to their project. Just before Clinton was elected in 1992, the PPI published an article by Jeremy Rosner entitled "Progressive Health Care Reform" that laid out their position on the issue. Explicitly shunning any single-payer program, the article opines that "reform should place most responsibility with the states," and that "reform must address not only financial incentives, but also the role of behavior, culture, and individual responsibility in shaping health costs and outcomes."[61] Rosner then further fleshes out this view in *Mandate for Change*, where he advocates universal coverage that "would require families to choose from new private health plans that emphasize competition and a sharing of risk, and that gives states flexibility to institute their own plans." Additionally, Rosner argues, "Government's primary role should be to improve the market's ground rules in order to decentralize decision making, spur innovation, reward efficiency and respect personal choice."[62] In all of these policy positions, the key problem of increasingly unaffordable health costs is subsumed to the imperatives of not disrupting the private health insurance market and the authority of states. Instead, the "New" of the New Democratic position is central through concepts such as individual state control, competition, private health plans, "flexibility," innovation, personal choice, and subservience to the market. A publically run health insurance option was simply not discussed. Unaffordability of health care is subsumed to questions of "values" such as the "behavior, culture, and individual responsibility" bound up in any health care policy decision making. This plan was also strikingly similar to the legislative parameters developed by the Heritage Foundation and that were put forth in response to Clinton's preferred legislation. Both Heritage and the DLC/PPI stressed the need for "individual choice" in a private health insurance marketplace as opposed to any government-run option.[63]

As time went on, the DLC's views and rhetoric shifted even more rightward. In July 1993, Al From wrote, "We are not willing to overrun the health-care system with government controls. Rather, we support a managed competition system that gives both patients and providers in-centives to exercise discipline in their own healthcare choices."[64] This type of language, devoid of much meaning, subsumed extensive policy discussion underneath worry that any program could put "at risk Clin-ton's pledge to be a 'different kind of Democrat,' by appearing to place him at odds with the public's abiding aversion to big government."[65] When Clinton's plan came out in late 1993, the DLC/PPI publicly aired its concern that "although the president has made the right diagnosis, we're somewhat leery of his prescription. . . . Health care reform needs to rely more on competition and less on bureaucracy if it is to be mean-ingful, affordable and lasting." According to the group, the "government should strive to fix broken markets, not supplant them."[66] In late 1993, with Clinton's introduction of his plan, it was not at all clear if those in the DLC/PPI world would support it. At the heart of the controversy, again, was how much to expand or contract the welfare state as well as concerns over how corporations would view Clinton's bill. As to this last point, the real sticking point of disagreement between the DLC/PPI and Clinton was that Clinton's proposed legislation asked employers to cover 80 percent of the cost of new coverage.[67]

While Democrats hashed out this internal debate, and the fundamen-tal questions they entailed, Republicans did the same—with conservative think tanks once again playing a key role in policy outcomes. Initially, Republicans in the House and Senate conceded that there was, in Senator Bob Dole's words, a "health care crisis" and they seemed to be willing to work with Clinton on a legislative solution—primarily using the Heritage Foundation's ideas on the subject as their preferred plan. This decision began to shift when Bill Kristol, son of Irving Kristol, directed all his energies toward harnessing Republican opposition to *any* health care reform whatsoever. Kristol started the Project for the Republican Future (which often claimed the mantle of a "think tank," even though it was more of a single-issue lobbying group) and used it to argue that it was a political necessity for Republicans to not cooperate with Clinton on health care reform. Kristol, unlike From and the DLC/PPI, saw the issue as one that had devastating potential to broaden Democratic sup-port within the middle class, *but only if a significant plan was passed*. In a memo to all Republicans, Kristol argues that the issue will "revive the reputation of . . . the Democrats . . . as the generous protector of middle class interests."[68] He then later took to the opinion page of the *Wall Street Journal*, where he contends that any "success would signal a rebirth of centralized welfare-state policy at the very moment that such policy is being perceived as a failure in other areas."[69] Kristol knew that the health care battle would be the primary arbiter over post–Cold War perceptions of the welfare state. He understood that if Clinton's plan, or any plan, passed that Clinton and the Democrats could eventually be looked at as the economic saviors of the middle class. What Kristol was most worried about was not that Clinton's policy would fail, but rather that it would *succeed*. As with his father's promotion of supply-side tax cuts, Kristol the younger gave primacy to the political/ideological implications of the policy as opposed to the material. The key question, indeed the only question, of concern for both Kristols is whether a policy's success or failure helps advance the conservative cause. According to Bill Kristol, the bill's "rejection by Congress and the public would be a monumental setback for the president, and an uncontestable piece of evidence that Democratic welfare-state liberalism remains firmly in retreat."[70] This, not access to health insurance, was what was important.

What was strange, however, was that the DLC/PPI thought precisely the opposite—that expanding the welfare state would *hurt* Clinton's chances among an amorphously defined middle class. This put Clinton in a bind from his right and his further right and created the same powerful "conventional wisdom" dynamic seen in the NAFTA debate. Now in the health care debate, multiple think tanks agreed with the basic premise that welfare state expansion was a mistake. In an article that flipped Kristol's logic, but nevertheless agreed with his basic view of the welfare state, Al From suggests that "Clinton must hold the middle class, but not with new entitlements." Not recognizing what conservatives like Kristol thought, From perceives that "Old Democrats believe the way to appeal to middle class voters is by creating universal entitlement programs that benefit the middle class as well as the poor. According to their theory, middle class voters don't hate government, they just don't like government programs that cut them out of the action." From argues instead for a program "stressing opportunity, responsibility and community as the pillars of a pragmatic, yet compassionate approach." He continues, arguing that the DLC/PPI believes "that middle class voters don't want government to be their caretaker, but rather wants it to give them the chance to help themselves."[71] As Republicans coalesced behind Kristol's plan and as DLCers in the House and Senate got behind their own bills with rhetoric similar to From's, Clinton was left with too little support for his own plan both inside and outside Congress. The DLC/PPI, of course, did not see the issue this way, arguing instead that the "interest groups" or the "guardians of the status quo" were "undermining President Clinton's reform agenda."[72] Whatever the diagnosis, Clinton's failure on health care, combined with a disastrous showing for Democrats in the 1994 midterm elections, portended a further DLC/PPI realignment of the Democratic Party. For the rest of Clinton's presidency, the parameters of policy debate and possibility moved decisively rightward.

IT WOULD BE HARD to overstate the psychological effect of the 1994 midterm elections on Bill Clinton, the Democratic Party, and the DLC/PPI. Democrats lost control of the House of Representatives for the first time in forty years and lost control of the Senate for the first time in eight years. For the first time since 1946, Republicans won a majority of votes cast for Congress. Most importantly, the election was read as a victory for the conservatism of Newt Gingrich's "Contract with America," on which many Republican candidates ran that year. This reading is tenuous given that the percentage of eligible voters who voted for a Republican House candidate was 18 percent. Nevertheless, this dominant narrative of the election took hold by the end of the election night, and Republicans were certainly able to better mobilize their voters in an off-year cycle.[73] This dominant narrative also greatly benefited the Heritage Foundation as much of the contract was born out of their "Issues '94" handbook and out of their shift toward influencing Congress as well as the presidency. The 1994 Republican victory brought a new wave of publicity for the leading conservative think tank.[74]

As for the DLC/PPI, although they were stung by the election, the results were nonetheless useful for their New Democrat brand in the marketplace of ideas. So while the think tank was certainly not happy with the Democratic loss, it nevertheless accurately sensed that the midterm election results gave them an opening to push their identity in a new way. In the special postelection issue of the *New Democrat*, Al From and Will Marshall argue that "if the Democrats' defeat was shattering it also was liberating. Like Humpty-Dumpty, the venerable New Deal coalition—which cracked in the 1968 Presidential election—cannot be put back together again."[75] From argued to the press soon after the election, "Hopefully, 1994 will have a big effect in terms of teaching our party that we can't stick with the old regime much longer."[76] Despite the Democratic losses suffered, the 1994 midterm elections were viewed positively by the New Democrats because they could be used as a disciplinary device within the party. The elections could now be used as a bludgeon against "liberal fundamentalists" to show the supposed disastrous results of their way of thinking. The election was also positive for New Democrats because it brought to power a more explicitly hard-right Republican Party—one that could now define a new pole in the left/right political dichotomy employed by the DLC to define their own "Third Way." The DLC's "political center" could now move more to the right because the entire political spectrum itself had shifted.

In light of this loss, New Democrats immediately revived their identity, and their own think tank, as the answer to the Democrats' defeat. They argued that Democrats needed to bring back "a third choice" that adhered "to the New Democrat formula of Progressive ideas, mainstream values, and innovative, nonbureaucratic ways of governing."[77] Initially, those at the DLC/PPI were skeptical as to whether Clinton would occupy this position, given that they felt betrayed by some of his actions in his first two years. Just before the midterms, Al From wrote that in order to change perceptions of his faltering presidency, Clinton needed "to govern forcefully as a New Democrat." He concluded that while it was "probably too late for Democrats up for election in November to adjust their ways," it was "not too late for the President to save his Presidency by reasserting his leadership of his party and governing decidedly as a New Democrat."[78] After the election, when the nature of the defeat was clear, From and others were not so open with their invitations to Clinton and sought to shift the perception of their think tank. From "offered the White House [a] cold shoulder, declaring that his organization is an independent think tank, 'not an adjunct of the Clinton administration.'"[79] Even more pointedly, Representative Dave Mc-Curdy of Oklahoma, then DLC chair, argued in a speech shortly after the election, "While Bill Clinton has the mind of a new Democrat, he retains the heart of an old Democrat. The result is an administration that has pursued elements of a moderate and liberal agenda at the same time, to the great confusion of the American people."[80] This quote is significant not only for its rebuke of Clinton, but also for the way it implicitly questioned Clinton's masculinity—that is, Clinton is following his heart and not his head. In this rendering, liberalism is rendered feminine, overly emotional, and nonrational while the New Democrat is masculine, tough-mined, thoughtful, and serious. Such a trope would be very important in the coming two years as New Democrats sought to solidify the primacy of their identity. Often invoked under the heading "credibility," such gendered overtones should not be overlooked as they contained enormous power for individuals seeking various political and policy goals.

Rhetoric aside, it was still unclear in the election's aftermath exactly how Democrats would be able to properly show their "credibility" as New Democrats. To showcase such credibility, those at the PPI turned to an old standby issue: "welfare reform."[81] The issue of welfare reform had long been central in defining conservative (and especially neoconservative) politics in the United States. With its ability to bind negative discourse of race, gender, sexuality, and taxes into one issue, by the mid-1990s the issue had been a conservative touchstone in elections from the 1960s onward. As other scholars have discussed, the very issue of "welfare reform" had emanated from conservative think tanks heading back to the 1970s, thus creating a powerful consensus issue when the DLC/PPI took it on.[82] Additionally, the issue had, since the DLC's inception, been invoked as the defining New Democrat issue—one that could be used to push off the party's base while at the same time representing "middle-class values." After the 1994 election, it was an easy choice as the issue that could reassert the "credibility" of Clinton and other Democrats as "New Democrats."[83] Al From recognized this even before the midterm elections were over. He argued that Clinton's lack of focus on the issue in his first two years denied him "a golden opportunity to prove to voters that he is a 'different kind of Democrat'" who would scale back the welfare state.[84] From argued that the view of Clinton as an Old Democrat was enhanced even more by his decision to concentrate on "a left-wing health-care reform plan" that expanded the welfare state.[85]

However, as From surely knew, and as others admitted in real time, the choice of health care reform over welfare reform in Clinton's first term was made for tangible reasons. Bruce Reed, a New Democrat to the core and the head of welfare policy in the Clinton administration, argues in a memo to the president that health care reform should come first largely to minimize the impact of welfare reform later on. Specifically, Reed argues that "health reform will move an estimated one million women and children off welfare. A recent survey of welfare recipients in Charleston and Nashville found that 83% would take a minimum wage job if it offered health coverage for them and their families. Another study found that only 8% of people who leave welfare for work get jobs that provide health insurance."[86] A December 1993 article by Will Marshall in the *New Democrat* agrees with Reed's memo, arguing that "we must assure universal access to health care" because "when welfare recipients take a job, they soon lose Medicaid benefits worth about $3,000 a year. The jobs they are most likely to take rarely offer health insurance or pay enough to let them buy their own policy. Health care reform must guarantee universal access and so remove a serious obstacle to work."[87] Finally, both men, in the internal memo and in the *New Democrat* article, also agree that the choice made sense politically as well given that liberal Democrats might be more inclined to support welfare reform if health care reform was passed first. After the 1994 midterms, such reasoning was forgotten or ignored as the DLC/PPI saw health care over welfare as showcasing Clinton's credentials as an Old Democrat welfare state expander.

The DLC also began to push welfare reform as a necessary policy for the coming of the supposed "New Economy" of the late 1990s. Such a "New Economy" was said to render much of the welfare state obsolete. A prime example of such theorizing is presented in the July–August issue of the *New Democrat* by author Michael Rothschild. In "Beyond Repair," Rothschild argues that "the politics of the Machine Age are hopelessly obsolete." Although standard for DLC/PPI writings, particularly to assert their politics as "New," Rothschild took this view to new heights. In his assessment, politics were changing merely because of new technology "such as one billion microchips flow[ing] from factories around the world." What does this have to do with politics? asks Rothschild. "Everything. Thanks to the near-miraculous capabilities of microelectronics, we are vanquishing scarcity . . . [thus] the venerable politics of class warfare . . . is dying, along with conventional economic thinking." Rothschild thought this new economic order would have losers, but this would be the fault of them and no one else as those who could not participate in the "Knowledge Age Economy" envisioned by Rothschild would "like illiterate peasants in the Age of Steam . . . [be] left behind by the new economy." According to Rothschild, "Everyone senses the promise of the new economy" and for those who do not all they need to know is "that there is no going back." Finally, the "New Economy" and its technologies created endless economic growth that made "the politics of scarcity obsolete."[88] Such theorizing was common among globalization proponents in the 1990s and naturalized their vision by removing all human agency involved in bringing this world about. By arguing that there "is no going back," Rothschild, and those like him, ignored governmental actions that were needed to bring this world about. Even more important, if such a vision of endless growth is accepted then there is little need for significant regulatory and/or welfare state intervention. If this brave new world really is coming into being, if "scarcity" will be a thing of the past, then why should the state try and intervene to alleviate inequality with "Machine Age" policies like Aid to Families with Dependent Children (AFDC)? Indeed, in the very next issue of the *New Democrat*, the supposed imperative of "Information Age Politics" is invoked as a reason to dismantle the welfare state: "for Democrats, the path back to power lies not in recreating the failures of the European welfare state but in finding new ways to make the party's traditional values of limited government and responsible individualism workable again."[89]

This focus on work, and the value of work, in a so-called New Economy became one of the key New Democrat ideas to sell welfare reform in the marketplace of ideas after the midterm elections. Will Marshall was plain about this after the elections when he argued that New Democrats "don't want to reform welfare, we want to replace it with work."[90] Marshall then clarifies this point in a lengthy article in the first issue of the *New Democrat* after the midterms. In the article, pointedly titled "Putting Work First," Marshall argues the following: "As our economy enters the Information Age, our social policy is stuck in the Industrial Era. The new rules of economic competition devalue manual skills and put a premium on mental skills, rewarding 'knowledge' workers capable of continuous learning. People trapped in the welfare economy, however, learn little of economic value. Information about the new economy's changing labor requirements are transmitted through work, but welfare pays people not to work." Now, "work" as a general and universal good is invoked as the *sole way* to bring welfare recipients into a new "Information Age" for its ability to "transmit information" regarding this new paradigm. In this way, education and job training programs are seen in a wholly negative light as they inhibit welfare recipients from "getting to work" and understanding "economic value" in "New Economy" labor markets. Marshall is plain about this. He argues that Clinton should shift "the focus of the current system from education and training to job development and placement." Marshall adds that this immediate job placement was needed as an *antipoverty* measure: "Last year, 1.3 million Americans joined the ranks of the poor, giving fresh urgency to President Clinton's promise to 'end welfare as we know it.'"[91] Again, in light of the way New Democrats were viewing the "New Economy," such a view made perfect sense given that scarcity "was being rendered obsolete" and downward redistribution of wealth was no longer needed.

While the DLC/PPI continued to promote the policy of welfare reform through "values" rhetoric like family, personal responsibility, and limited government, their focus on work in the New Economy as an end unto itself was strikingly new, even among conservative think tanks. This so-called work first policy, which became central to the New Democrat framing of welfare reform, had three enormous economic implications. First and foremost, this position would flood the low-wage labor market with millions of new workers, further suppressing the wages of those already there and those welfare recipients entering it. Such a position was beneficial to large companies that employed thousands of service-sector workers. This dynamic had always been clear to those in the DLC/PPI, even though it was not discussed publicly as a rationale for welfare reform. For instance, as far back as August 1993 in his work on the issue within the Clinton administration, Bruce Reed outlined the employer's view on the welfare reform issue in a handwritten note: "Employers view: ½ price worker, escape HC [healthcare] mandate, save up to $7,500 in labor costs."[92] This is *not* to say that this was the "real" reason for welfare reform that Democrats kept hidden from the public—only that those who were planning the policy recognized it would be viewed favorably by employers looking to keep labor costs low. The second economic implication was for a specific type of company: for-profit welfare-to-work firms. Such firms clearly supported such a policy, and the DLC's promotion of it, given that it presented them with a huge new pool of clients to try to put to work. Simply put, they would reap more profits with this new "work first" position as federal and state governments gave them money to place welfare recipients in jobs. The final economic implication was that welfare workers came to be used as a way to privatize higher-paying public employee jobs as many states would simply fire these workers and replace them with welfare-to-work workers.[93]

This new "work first" welfare reform also has to be considered in light of the material reality of who is funding the DLC/PPI. This is not to posit a "policy conspiracy," or to assert that policy planners and promoters in PPI did not believe in the policies they advocated, but rather to note the obviously pertinent fact that the think tank had corporate funders who were interested in obtaining more low-wage service-sector labor. Additionally, as just stated, for-profit welfare-to-work firms who funded the DLC/PPI were obviously supportive of the idea of "putting work first" as it gave them new clients to choose from in the states and municipalities that they served. America Works was one such company that used the DLC and PPI as bridges into the state in order to advocate their for-profit welfare-to-work services. As early as May 1993, the DLC and PPI were promoting America Works as a way to showcase their embrace of a "new kind of government." In the May 1993 issue of the *New Democrat*, an interview was conducted with Peter Cove, the founder of America Works. The interview is titled, "Welfare for Sale" and Cove knew the buzzwords to employ with the think tank: "In a true demonstration of reinventing government, we are saying to government, 'We will invest the money to recruit people who are on welfare, to train them, to place them in companies, to pay them a wage while they are at those companies, to give them a lot of support to help them move from dependency to independency. And only if the companies hire the people and they get off welfare do you pay us.' "[94] Again, in the December 1993 issue of the same journal, Cove's wife, and cofounder of America Works, wrote an article for the publication entitled "The Training Trap," wherein job training programs and education are dismissed in favor of putting people directly to work through firms like America Works. Shortly after both of these articles were put into print a 2,000-word damning report on America Works was published in the *New York Times*. In the report, city and state officials who dealt with America Works indicate that the group frequently received a vast majority of its placement fees as soon as a job was obtained for a welfare recipient—even if the recipient quit soon after. The group was also accused of "skimming," a process by which they only took clients who had the easiest possibility of placement.[95]

Despite these concerns, the PPI continued to promote America Works both inside and outside the government as a way to showcase their "work first" welfare reform and government–private sector partnerships. As early as May 1994, Bruce Reed wrote in a memo to President Clinton on the "Politics of Welfare Reform," that "communities will be encouraged to build strong links to the private sector, and can hire placement firms like America Works to help people find and keep jobs."[96] After the midterms, the think tank's promotion of America Works was ramped up even further as a way to articulate their "newness" and their faith in private enterprise and "the market" to work out any kinks in the system. Again, Will Marshall in his post-midterm article, wrote: "In true New Democrat fashion, the Clinton Administration should use public resources to create a competitive market for job placement and support services. America Works cofounder Peter Cove suggests that, by reinvesting savings when welfare recipients leave the rolls for work, government can create a growing pool of funds from which to pay private agencies a fee for job placement. Such an approach would lure private investment into welfare-to-work ventures, since they could make a profit. And it would pay only for success; projects that failed to place people in jobs would go out of business."[97] After the midterms, the pressure by New Democrats inside of the government was ramped up as well. In March of 1995, Reed wrote to the chief of staff, suggesting, "The President should have a luncheon with . . . representatives from America Works, a well-respected work program in New York."[98] Later, Cove and Bowes would show their full influence as they were invited to the signing ceremony when the final welfare reform legislation was signed into law in 1996.[99]

This turn toward showcasing "work first" welfare reform as a key element of a New Economy did not mean that the DLC/PPI abandoned the issue as a way to showcase the other elements of the New Democrat position. They still used the issue to distance themselves from social welfare liberalism and to further showcase their support of "middle-class values." Indeed, what is important to understand is the way in which the economy itself is a cultural construction bound up in certain normative conceptions of race, gender, sexuality, and family. Issues like welfare reform, and in particular the 1995–96 "welfare to work" version of the policy, were used to show that New Democrats were for "middle-class values" such as "work, family, personal responsibility, and self-reliance" precisely because of the economic implications of the bill just described.[100] The "economic" and the "cultural" elements of the New Democrat identity cannot, and should not, be separated from one another.

At the end of 1995, the welfare reform bill sent to Clinton's desk was mainly written by the Republican House of Representatives, leading even DLCers to denounce the bill not only for its harshness but also for its inability to live up to the New Democrat "work first" position. Thus, for Clinton, the decision to veto the bill on 9 January 1996 was made easier. His veto was interesting in that the language used was straight out of the DLC/PPI playbook. He (or mostly likely Bruce Reed) notes the following: "I am returning herewith without my approval H.R. 4, the 'Personal Responsibility and Work Opportunity Act of 1995.' In disapproving H.R. 4, I am nevertheless determined to keep working with the Congress to enact real, bipartisan welfare reform. The current welfare system is broken and must be replaced, for the sake of the taxpayers who pay for it and the people who are trapped by it. But H.R. 4 does too little to move people from welfare to work. It is burdened with deep budget cuts and structural changes that fall short of real reform. I urge the Congress to work with me in good faith to produce a bipartisan welfare reform agreement that is tough on work and responsibility, but not tough on children and on parents who are responsible and who want to work."[101] The Republicans in the House, in attempting to use the bill to cut $60 billion in services such as food stamps and school lunch programs, had allowed Clinton and the DLC/PPI to define themselves in a new "center" with these cuts representing the Far Right, liberals as the "do nothing" position, and their focus on getting "tough on work and responsibility" as the center. New Democrats were relatively content with the veto and with the overall way the policy debate was being constructed in the marketplace of ideas.

Moreover, Clinton's State of the Union Address on 23 January 1996 convinced New Democrats that he was firmly in their camp. The speech is now mainly remembered for the following lines: "We know big government does not have all the answers. We know there's not a program for every problem. We have worked to give the American people a smaller, less bureaucratic government in Washington. And we have to give the American people one that lives within its means. The era of big government is over. But we cannot go back to the time when our citizens were left to fend for themselves. Instead, we must go forward as one America, one nation working together to meet the challenges we face together. Self-reliance and teamwork are not opposing virtues; we must have both."[102] Al From immediately responded to the overall message of the speech in a *New Democrat* article entitled "More Than a Good Speech?" From argued that the speech "redefined the election year debate on New Democrat terms" and that "the question now is whether it will live up to its promise and be remembered as a historic turning point for the Democratic Party and our country." But what most excited From was the line for which the speech is remembered: "With one simple statement, 'the era of big government is over,' the President boldly declared an end to his party's *raison d'être* for the past six decades. Liberal Democrats in Congress had no choice but to applaud as their party leader said their time had passed."[103] Clearly From agreed with the agenda of the speech, but what really excited him was reading the speech as a poke in the eye to the "liberal fundamentalists" his group and think tank had spent the last decade decrying.

Clinton clearly agreed with the import the DLC attached to the speech as he immediately used it as a launching point for his reelection campaign and for what would be the final push for work first welfare reform. The PPI released a plan in June 1996 that would become the basis for the Clinton plan. Aptly titled "Work First," the policy focused on time limits for those on welfare as well as entrance into the job market as soon as any job became available.[104] It was with the release of this plan that many on the left began to notice this would create fundamental problems in the low-wage labor market. Hugh Price, president of the National Urban League, wrote President Clinton the following: "When David Ellwood originally advanced the idea of ending welfare as we know it, he called for time limits coupled with guaranteed public jobs (to replace the welfare entitlement) for former welfare recipients who could not find private employment. We implore you to insist that any welfare reform emerging from Congress embody these twin principles. Accepting the former without the latter would place poor people and the cities they inhabit at unconscionable risk."[105] But this is precisely the vision of the "Work First" plan Clinton was now advocating: flooding the private sector with low-wage labor and no backup public sector jobs. Lawrence Mishel and John Schmitt at EPI outline the consequences of such a policy: "Even if the private sector could find work for a huge inflow of welfare recipients without displacing those currently in work, it can do so only at a wage that is considerably below the already depressed earnings levels prevailing in the low-wage labor market. Moreover, the required wage declines will not be limited to former welfare recipients. The vast body of low-wage workers, already earning low and falling wages, will also see their wages pushed down. The working poor will thus pay an enormous price for so-called 'reform.' "[106] As the legislation was debated in the House and Senate, Republicans again loaded the bill with cuts in other social programs. In July 1996, Bob Greenstein of the Center on Budget and Policy Priorities wrote the president with an analysis of the pending legislation—in particular noting that the $28 billion in food stamp cuts "throws 700,000 people off the food stamp program after just 120 days without offering them an opportunity to work." Moreover, "its legal immigrant cuts are even deeper than in the bill you vetoed." Clinton seemed moved by the letter, and in a handwritten note to Bruce Reed wrote, "This is very troubling."[107]

With the emerging bill both the DLC/PPI and groups on the left began organizing for their respective positions. For instance, the following letter from the vice president of the Service Employees International Union typifies the tone of the letters Clinton was receiving: "If you do not VETO the above referenced bills which will make deep cuts in food programs, cuts in SSI for severely disabled children, and eliminate the right to cash assistance (AFDC) for families and children, I *will not* work for your re-election! I will urge our membership to *not* work for your re-election. We will not do phone banks, voter registration, or literature distribution on behalf of your re-election."[108] The final legislation, with all of the aforementioned elements, then passed both houses and came to Clinton's desk with everyone wondering what he would do. The DLC/ PPI advocated supporting the legislation despite its similarity to the earlier vetoed version. The think tank blamed liberals for the current form of the legislation, arguing, "Democrats have only themselves to blame for the current situation after missing the chance to dictate the terms of reform on our watch. Had liberals been willing to join in the acknowledgment of the system's failures and craft real reform when Democrats controlled Congress, we wouldn't face this predicament."[109]

The reality, however, was that many on the left had been criticizing AFDC since its inception but were nevertheless put into the position of defending the program as there emerged a consensus to cut AFDC entirely in the name of work, family and personal responsibility. This defense proved to not be enough as the New Democrat position hardened in agreement with Republicans. After years of stigmatization by conservative politicians, the media, and conservative intellectuals, among others, those defending the program had simply lost the "war of position" necessary to even maintain the status quo. The use of the issue by New Democrats continued that stigmatization and also sought to remove many of the program's remaining advocates within the Democratic Party itself. Additionally, New Democrats were interested with placing the issue solely under the purview of their expertise as opposed to involving those who were actually on the program itself. Their model of politics, in effect, worked to displace grassroots support for the issue. This point was crystallized by none other than Daniel Patrick Moynihan— the sometimes New Democrat and longtime neoconservative politician/ intellectual—who had been stirring the ire of welfare rights advocates since the 1960s. Moynihan, despite decades spent advocating for welfare reform, was firmly against the final version of the bill that went to Clinton's desk in late 1996. On Moynihan's side was Democratic Senator Paul Wellstone, who wrote the following in his autobiography: "At one point during the debate, Daniel Patrick Moynihan, the one acknowledged expert on welfare policy in the Senate, asked where the people were who would be hurt by this legislation. He was dismayed that there was so little organized opposition. Moynihan looked toward the front of the Capitol and asked why there were not thousands of protestors lined up all the way to the Supreme Court."[110] But Moynihan should not have been surprised as he helped create the stigmatization of the welfare program that inhibited recipients from getting out in the streets and demanding the program not be cut. After him came Republican politicians and think tankers and then finally DLC "New Democrats" within the Democratic Party itself who saw the issue as a perfect fit to show their love of "middle-class values," their antipathy to so-called special interests, and their subservience to the value of work in the "New Economy." This consensus, which think tanks like the DLC did so much to create, stigmatized the program and thus sapped the grassroots energy necessary to defend it.

At the crucial moment when the bill came to Clinton's desk it is almost impossible to overstate the enormous power that the New Democrat identity played in his decision to sign the bill into law. Returning to the "credibility" issue discussed earlier, there was enormous pressure on Clinton to sign the legislation so that he could fully occupy the "New Democrat" position just two and a half months before the 1996 election. As a CBS news reporter put the issue to a Republican Senator: "You've got him over a barrel here; he has to maintain credibility."[111] This trope proliferated in the media and exercised enormous power over Clinton's decision to sign the legislation. Al From recognized this more than anyone as Clinton decided at the end of July 1996 to sign the legislation. From wrote the following in a news release: "President Clinton's decision to sign welfare reform legislation should put to rest questions about whether he is willing to govern as a New Democrat."[112] In the end, Clinton showed "credibility" by signing the legislation, ignoring critics on his left, and fully occupying the position of "New Democrat."

After the signing of the Personal Responsibility and Work Opportunity Reconciliation Act on 22 August 1996, news reports proliferated describing the DLC's glee. One reported that DLC/PPI leaders hailed the signing "as an epochal event for Democrats, a signal that the party is moving away from its traditional image as the booster of big government."

Al From "cited four specific events in Clinton's presidency as evidence he has put his party on a 'New Democratic' path: his support for the North American Free Trade Agreement, his ultimate embrace of the goal of a balanced budget; his State of the Union declaration that the 'era of big government is over'; and his decision to sign the welfare bill."[113] In both chambers of Congress, slightly more than half of Democrats voted for the bill, thus accepting the New Democrat position on the subject and creating a powerful consensus around the issue as nearly all Republicans signed on to the legislation.[114] Additionally, the think tank's moment of party continued at the 1996 Democratic National Convention: "The 1996 party platform was written by Bruce Reed and Elaine Kamarck, two former DLC principals who are now White House aids. Reed is helping write Clinton's convention speech. And Indiana Gov. Evan Bayh, the keynote speaker Tuesday, is described by From as 'a New Democrat poster boy.'"[115] In many ways, the signing of welfare reform, combined with Clinton's reelection, proved Al From correct when he stated, "The ideological battle in our party is over."[116] At the end of 1996, New Democrats were at the pinnacle of the party, and when combined with Republican conservatism supported by a firmly entrenched think tank establishment, produced a market shift to the right in the parameters of policy debate as Clinton headed into his second term in office. In essence, the second-term victory of Bill Clinton was the final victory for the New Democrat position and the group would use it to continually exercise power within the party leading all the way up to the 2000 election. With the late 1990s dot-com boom, the DLC/PPI ramped up their millennialist pop-futuristic political narrative to new degrees—as did President Clinton and other elected New Democrats. Moreover, as a new grassroots social movement came into being in the late 1990s around the overall theme of anticorporate globalization, the New Democrat position once again provided a bludgeon through which to deride such a political project. Within the national Democratic Party, the DLC/PPI political project would not come up for true contestation again until the 2000 presidential election and a third-party challenge by Ralph Nader.

Before leaving the 1990s, however, it would be incomplete to not note other think-tank-related dynamics that contributed to the rightward shift of public policy at the end of the twentieth century. First and foremost, the development of new conservative media outlets in the late 1990s—including talk radio, the Internet, and Fox News—gave conservatives within traditional conservative think tanks like the Heritage

Foundation many new media venues from which to propagate their worldview. As a narrative of "liberal media bias" became firmly entrenched, media outlets continued to turn to conservative think tanks for sources in the name of "balance" as they had since the development of the marketplace of ideas. Moreover, the power of traditional conservative think tanks continued to grow throughout the 1990s. For instance, in 1996, the Heritage Foundation had an annual budget of $28.7 million and the American Enterprise Institute had recovered nicely from its mid-1980s near implosion with an annual budget of $13 million. The Hoover Institution had also grown enormously by 1996 with an annual budget of $19.5 million.[117] Additionally, the think tanks Republicans turned to were not only at the national level but also at the local level, as the 1990s brought about the formation of a state-based network of conservative think tanks. These state-based institutions, like their national counterparts, worked to advance conservatism in state governments and within local media outlets. Such think tanks used Heritage as their model and formed into two "networks" of state-based think tanks.[118]

All of these dynamics—new state-based think tanks, new media, committed and well-funded Republican national think tanks, and the development of the DLC/PPI "New Democrat" identity—converged in the 1990s to further move the parameters of political and policy debate rightward. Despite the occupation of the White House by a Democratic president, conservative advancement in an ideological "war" within the marketplace of ideas continued. Such a dynamic would continue into the twenty-first century.

5

Think Tanks, Foreign Policy, and the Marketplace of Ideas in the 2000s

The decade of the aughts saw a continuation of the role of think tanks in pushing American political culture rightward. In particular, the decade was characterized by three think-tank-related dynamics—two old and one new. First, the 2000s were a time when think tanks helped bring about the continued rightward drift of the parameters of public policy debates in the United States.[1] This was particularly true in the area of foreign policy. In the wake of the terrorist attacks of 11 September 2001, the think tank was one of the key institutions involved in pushing a reinvigorated militarized U.S. foreign policy. Conservative think tanks like AEI and "liberal" think tanks like Brookings and PPI helped create an elite consensus around a militarized response to 9/11, including an invasion of Iraq. The promotion and implementation of this foreign policy was made possible, in part, by the further entrenchment of the marketplace of ideas model of policy debate—the second think-tank-related dynamic of the decade. Within the public sphere of the media, the 2000s were a time where the marketplace of ideas became the central way in which policy was communicated to the American public. Claims to empirical expertise were largely subsumed or replaced by the need to present a supposedly "balanced debate." The 2000s also saw an explosion of media outlets on television, in print, and on the Internet, and the marketplace model made intuitive sense for news organizations looking to generate content at low cost. Think tank representatives filled such a void as an easy outlet for "expertise." However, given that the parameters of policy debates had moved so far to the right, it was very often the case that the marketplace of ideas was not at all balanced. Rather, as will be seen in the example of the foreign policy response to 9/11, the debate was often "balanced" between conservative voices like AEI and "liberal" voices like Brookings—despite the fact that these institutional voices tended to agree on the necessity of military action abroad. Finally, the 2000s also brought about a new think-tank-related dynamic as the decade was a time when the rejection of empirical expertise inherent in the marketplace of ideas seeped into the state itself. With think tanks appointees from the Heritage Foundation leading the way within the Bush administration, the administration accepted the idea that technocratic policy planning by "experts" was impossible as such a model was inherently biased toward liberalism. In its place, Heritage and the administration offered an almost nineteenth-century model for the state whereby political appointees dominated all realms of the executive branch.[2]

EVEN THOUGH THIS BOOK has been largely focused on domestic policy, think tanks have been no stranger to creating a climate within the marketplace of ideas more conducive to selling a militarized American foreign policy. The Cold War, in particular, saw the rise of think tanks dedicated to the increasing militarization of that war. Started in 1948, the RAND Corporation was one of the first such efforts. While it is not correct to argue that RAND was a movement conservative think tank, it nevertheless developed policies of aggressive confrontation with the Soviet Union that came to be associated with conservatism in the later decades of the Cold War. In the beginning of RAND's existence, it was thought of as a key institution within the liberal consensus—containing what one book terms "soldiers of reason" dedicated to fighting Cold War battles.[3] Along with the Council on Foreign Relations, which was established even earlier in 1921, these two think tanks helped to staff key foreign policy positions that would set the agenda of nearly every Cold War presidency.[4] More explicitly conservative think tanks dedicated to foreign policy entered the picture in the 1960s. Bill Baroody at AEI and Glenn Campbell at Hoover teamed up to create a new think tank in 1962 called the Center for Strategic and International Studies (CSIS). As Baroody puts it in one letter at the time, the think tank was founded to address the "inability of our Executive leadership since World War II to develop any sort of grand strategy to meet the Communist spectrum of aggression on all levels."[5] CSIS is still in existence today. By the 1970s, AEI itself, seeking to cultivate a neoconservative foreign policy, developed such a worldview largely in response to President Carter's foreign policy.[6] Finally, the Heritage Foundation took the lead in the Reagan administration advocating a hardline stance against revolutionary movements in Central America and the creation of a space-based Strategic Defense Initiative. The think tank was also critical of Reagan for his negotiations with the Soviet Union over nuclear arms limitation in his second term.

A think-tank-led consensus around a militarily aggressive foreign policy did not begin to congeal until after the Cold War ended in the 1990s. Cold War "hot wars" in Southeast Asia and Central America had chastened most Democrats in the use of military power. However, with the end of the Cold War and the rapidity of the first Gulf War, neoconservatives and "New Democrats" were instrumental in using the think tank apparatus to push a new foreign policy. For neoconservatives and New Democrats, the general point of agreement was that the relationship of the United States with the outside world would be defined by military hegemony. For neoconservative think tanks such as AEI, who were instrumental in advancing the argument within Republican policymaking circles, this meant that the United States must forthrightly declare its dominance on the world stage as the "sole superpower" after the end of the Cold War. For neoconservatives, it was essential that Americans fully embrace their new role in the post–Cold War world as a "benevolent hegemony." Think tanks such as the DLC/PPI advanced similar (although not the same) arguments within Democratic circles. Although concerned with maintaining unipolarity as well, the DLC/PPI generally advanced the notion of "liberal humanitarianism" much more often than their neoconservative counterparts. Under this rationale, American military might was seen as a force for good when intervening in failed states or sectarian conflicts that turned genocidal or had the potential to do so. In addition, the DLC/PPI also invoked such a foreign policy in order to criticize those "liberal fundamentalists" in the Democratic Party who were skeptical to such uses of military force after Vietnam. Despite their differing rationales and sometimes differing levels of intervention for which they advocated, the two sides coalesced so that, as International Relations scholar Andrew Bacevich argues, "In the aftermath of the Cold War, the principle that the United States required great military strength commanded universal assent in Washington. To dissent from that position was to place oneself beyond the bounds of respectable opinion."[7] Such a consensus had real-world consequences. From the end of the Cold War to 1999 "the United States embarked upon nearly four dozen military interventions . . . as opposed to only 16 during the entire period of the Cold War."[8]

Such an extensive use of American military power in the 1990s under a Democratic president did much to further a consensus around the need for military strength in the post–Cold War world. Even so, it would be a mistake to see the Republican Party after the end of the Cold War and before 9/11 as monolithic on such matters. On the contrary, conservative think tanks and their intellectuals were at the forefront in debating where conservatives should take their foreign policy in the 1990s. Representing the hardline neoconservative position was Bill Kristol. From his father, and from his own work defeating health care reform, Kristol was already intimately familiar with the use of the think tank as an ideological base of action. By the mid-1990s, after his victory over the Clinton health care plan, Kristol turned to the project of advancing the neoconservative foreign policy vision within the Republican Party. To do so, Kristol turned to the journal *Foreign Affairs*—arguably the premier foreign policy journal and one published by the think tank the Council on Foreign Relations. In 1996, Kristol and other conservatives were invited by the think tank to debate the future of foreign policy on the right. He, along with neoconservative Robert Kagan, laid out the post–Cold War neoconservative vision entitled "Toward a Neo-Reaganite Foreign Policy." In this article, Kristol and Kagan seek to clearly differentiate their foreign policy not only from Bill Clinton's but also from other strands of conservatism. As to the latter, they argue in the essay that conservatives are "adrift" in current foreign policy thought: "They disdain the Wilsonian multilateralism of the Clinton administration; they are tempted by, but so far have resisted, the neoisolationism of Patrick Buchanan; for now, they lean uncertainly on some version of the conservative 'realism' of Henry Kissinger and his disciples." The descriptive terms used in this opening paragraph were loaded and questionable, but Kagan and Kristol quickly turn to the primary purpose of the essay— lamenting the lack of a clear conservative post–Cold War foreign policy doctrine.

Kristol and Kagan wanted a post–Cold War American foreign policy as clear and as Manichean as the Cold War years under Ronald Reagan. According to Kristol and Kagan, Reagan had correctly "called for an end to complacency in the face of the Soviet threat" and advocated "large increases in defense spending, resistance to communist advances in the Third World, and greater moral clarity and purpose in U.S. foreign policy." Additionally, Reagan "championed American exceptionalism when it was deeply unfashionable" and "perhaps most significant, he refused to accept the limits on American power imposed by the domestic political realities that others assumed were fixed." For Kristol and Kagan, a similar "neo-Reaganite" moral clarity was needed once more, only now in the service of a "benevolent global hegemony" with its first objective being to secure America's status as the world's sole super-power. Such an "American hegemony is the only reliable defense against a breakdown of peace and international order. The appropriate goal of American foreign policy, therefore, is to preserve that hegemony as far into the future as possible." Such a hegemony would be secured through increased military spending—as much as $60–$80 billion more each year—and the willingness to use the military power such funds provided. Additionally, American citizens would need to become more martial given that "weak political leadership and a poor job of educating the citizenry to the responsibilities of global hegemony have created an increasingly distinct and alienated military culture." Finally, according to the authors, hegemony must "be informed with a clear moral purpose, based on the understanding that its moral goals and its fundamental na-tional interests are almost always in harmony." Ultimately, all of this would restore "national greatness . . . and restore a sense of the heroic, which has been sorely lacking in American foreign policy—and American conserva-tism in recent years."[9] A clearer expression of the neoconservative foreign policy mind-set could not be found.

Before 9/11, such a neoconservative position was not yet dominant within the Republican Party. In the 1990s, Kristol and neoconservatives were able to create a foreign policy consensus with Clintonian New Democrats much more easily than with many in their own party. As evi-dence for this fact, in the very next issue of *Foreign Affairs*, conserva-tives Kim Holmes and John Hillen presented a pointed rebuttal to Kristol and Kagan's piece. Both were leading foreign and military policy analysts at the Heritage Foundation, and their disagreement with Kristol shows even further how think tanks were at the heart of a conservative foreign policy debate in the 1990s. Although both would come around to Kristol's and Kagan's views after 9/11, Holmes and Hillen's response in 1996 was most interesting because it attacked Kristol's and Kagan's views as *un-conservative*. They argued that "Kristol and Kagan's vision of American foreign policy is without limits or constraints." Where Kris-tol and Kagan would be the first to advocate limited government domes-tically, when the lens shifts abroad Holmes and Hillen assert that there seems to be no limit on their "global democratic enterprise—one that ultimately would have the U.S. government engineering the domestic transformation of nations around the globe." For Holmes and Hillen, such a view represents "pure escapism" in that it pretends "America need not be selective in its engagements" when the federal government is committed to "spending a lot more money on defense." In the end, Holmes and Hillen argue for a "prudent approach" in foreign policy as the "essence of conservatism" rather than "Kagan and Kristol's call for a hegemonic crusade," which "does little beyond assuaging their desire for moral clarity."[10]

Given this initial reception, Kristol knew that he had a long way to go in order to convince conservatives to come on board with his neoconservative vision. So, in the spring of 1997, in the aftermath of another Republican presidential loss, Kristol started the Project for the New American Century (PNAC)—a group devoted to organizing conservatives around the foreign policy view he and Kagan articulated in their *Foreign Affairs* article. Although often thought of and referred to as a think tank, PNAC does not fit the mold of the conservative think tank articulated in this book. The organization was much more akin to the DLC in that it was an explicitly political organization that tried to organize elites in political parties—mostly the Republican Party. However, as we will see, just as the DLC used PPI as its more formal think tank policy center, PNAC would use AEI in much the same way.[11] The very name of PNAC shows how much Kristol's neoconservative foreign policy project centered on defining a new national narrative that would give Americans the same "sense of purpose" once offered by the Cold War. The group went to work immediately organizing Republican luminaries around their vision. For instance, PNAC's initial "Statement of Principles" was signed by politicians such as Jeb Bush (reflecting that he, and not his brother, was seen as a possible Republican presidential candidate at the time), Dick Cheney, Steve Forbes, Dan Quayle, and Donald Rumsfeld. These people were joined by well-known neoconservatives such as Bill Bennett, Francis Fukuyama, Donald Kagan, Norman Podhoretz, and Paul Wolfowitz. The document was a restatement of the earlier Kristol/Kagan vision of "Reaganite" hegemony in a post–Cold War world—although the word "hegemony" is now dropped most likely because of its imperial overtones. Again, the main policy prescription offered is that "we need to increase defense spending significantly if we are to carry out our global responsibilities today and modernize our armed forces for the future." However, one new element is added to the document—the need for preventive military action to preserve American hegemony. The document is quite plain on this matter: "The history of the 20th century should have taught us that it is important to shape circumstances before crises emerge, and to meet threats before they become dire."[12] This language would, of course, proliferate in the aftermath of 9/11. However, in 1997 PNAC members were interested only in bringing around members of the Republican Party to their view.

Although PNAC would be used to promote the neoconservative foreign policy vision among Republican Party elites in the late 1990s, AEI would do so within the wider public sphere. Such a project became even easier for conservatives given the development of new forms of conservative media in the late 1990s. Most obviously, the founding of the twenty-four-hour news channel Fox News in 1996 by Rupert Murdoch gave conservatives at think tanks and elsewhere a direct line into the homes of 14 million cable subscribers. A year previous Murdoch had also given Kristol $3 million to start and edit the opinion magazine the *Weekly Standard*—a more high-brow endeavor than Fox that would be dedicated to advancing the neoconservative cause among elite Washingtonians. As told by former neoconservative Scott McConnell, Murdoch's hefty grant meant that "the *Standard* not only passed out thousands of complimentary issues around Washington, it had them personally delivered to Beltway influentials as soon as they were printed." In this same analysis, McConnell also hones in on the "synergistic triangle" created by the *Standard*, Fox News, and neoconservative think tanks, arguing that the *Standard* "provided employment for a small coterie of neoconservative essayists and a ready place to publish for dozens . . . who held posts at the American Enterprise Institute and other neocon-friendly think tanks. With the fledgling Fox News network, the *Standard* soon emerged as the key leg in a synergistic triangle of neoconservative argumentation: you could write a piece for the magazine, talk about your ideas on Fox, pick up a paycheck from Kristol or from AEI."[13] This "synergistic triangle" described by McConnell was powerful indeed and in many ways was one of the key dynamics that allowed think tanks to take on a whole new kind of power and accessibility within the marketplace of ideas.

However, it is incorrect that conservative think tanks and think tank intellectuals were given new power in the marketplace of ideas solely by new conservative media outlets of the late 1990s. Equally as important, if not more so, was the way in which traditional news outlets had come to give conservative think tanks much more exposure than either their liberal or "centrist" counterparts. As evidence for this fact, the media monitoring group Fairness and Accuracy in Reporting (FAIR) began studying the use of think tanks in the media beginning in the year 1995 and continuing into the twenty-first century. Using a LexisNexis database search of major newspaper, radio, and TV transcripts, the group quantified how often think tanks or think tank intellectuals were used as sources. What they found was an overwhelming tilt toward the use of conservative think tanks. For instance, in 1995, conservatives not only received more references than both centrist and liberal think tanks but their outnumbering of liberal think tanks was more than sevenfold. In addition, in this first year of the study, the Heritage Foundation was the single most-cited think tank within the traditional media. This was a huge jump for Heritage as "in 1990, Heritage got about 44 percent of the coverage Brookings got; in 1995, for the first time, Heritage surpassed its centrist rival."[14] As we will continue to see with these FAIR studies throughout this chapter, this trend would only be exacerbated throughout the late 1990s and 2000s. Through these studies, by the mid-1990s we see just how successful think tank conservatives had become in inserting their institutional voices in the marketplace of ideas in the name of "balance." As these studies suggest, places like Heritage and AEI had now become the go-to sources to "get the conservative side" in any policy debate. Additionally, and unsurprisingly, this new think tank media exposure also coincided with new corporatization of the media brought about by the 1996 Telecommunications Act. This act, another point of policy consensus in the late 1990s between conservatives and New Democrats, broke down regulatory barriers to media ownership that fueled corporate investment in the media. This investment led to profit-seeking, cost-cutting measures—one of which saw think tank intellectuals as cheap go-to "experts" for any policy debate.

In addition to this imbalance in the marketplace of ideas, conservative think tanks were often not identified ideologically—giving them more power as many news consumers undoubtedly perceived them as neutral arbiters. In the FAIR study of think tank references in the media in 1997, this lack of proper labeling of think tank sources is examined by looking at a random 10 percent of the citations of the top four think tanks in the study—Brookings, Heritage, AEI, and Cato. The study concludes, "Surprisingly, all four institutions were not identified at all in a majority of their respective citations." Specifically, the Heritage Foundation "was not identified in 68 percent of 182 cases; in a further 8 percent, only its location in Washington was noted. Its political orientation was noted only 24 percent of the time." Additionally, "Seventy-two percent of the time, the American Enterprise Institute appeared with no qualifying label. In only 14 percent of the 132 stories sampled was it identified as conservative" or similar.[15] For the specific purposes of this chapter, the lack of a label for AEI in almost three-quarters of all citations is of immense importance. For the uninitiated member of the American public, such a lack of labeling undoubtedly gave AEI much more power given that such news consumers would assume a certain level of ideological impartiality that did not exist for the think tank.

Neoconservatives at think tanks and elsewhere were able to use this new position in the marketplace of ideas media landscape to move forward their foreign policy agenda. Late in the 1990s such an agenda came into focus with a direct call for military action against Saddam Hussein and Iraq as opposed to a generalized call for "American hegemony." The opening salvo in this new phase of promotion was a November 1997 *Weekly Standard* piece entitled, "Saddam Must Go." In the piece, Bill Kristol argued that a U.S. attack was needed immediately and that an attack "that leaves Saddam in charge of Iraq . . . might serve only to expose the futility of American power." Later in the same essay, Kristol is even clearer in his desire for a full-scale ground assault given that such an assault is "the only sure way to take Saddam out." He argues that while such a ground invasion "seems unthinkable," we nevertheless have "to start thinking the unthinkable." In this essay, in 1997, Kristol is clearly previewing and laying the groundwork for making such a policy "thinkable." Specifically, he discusses the ease with which such a policy could be implemented as the job "would take fewer than the half-million troops deployed in Desert Storm to roll into Baghdad today, especially after an air campaign scattered or destroyed whatever resistance Saddam might be able to throw up." Additionally, Iraqi soldiers would simply not put up a fight because of "their last experience against American forces and weapons." Finally, making this new policy thinkable involved frightening the American public. Inaction, according to Kristol, meant continuing along the present course and getting "ready for the day when Saddam has biological and chemical weapons at the tips of missiles aimed at Israel and at American forces in the Gulf." According to Kristol, "That day may not be far off."[16]

After the *Weekly Standard* piece, Kristol once again returned to PNAC for the next round of selling his new foreign policy product in the marketplace of ideas. In early 1998, Kristol organized a PNAC letter writing campaign targeted at elite lawmakers—including President Clinton. Again designed to showcase the variety of political elites who backed "regime change" in Iraq, the first letter was sent directly to President Clinton. The names who signed this letter would become commonplace in the media landscape leading up the 2003 Iraq invasion. These include: Richard Armitage (he would become deputy secretary of state in George W. Bush's first term); Bill Bennett (a former Reagan official who worked for CNN during the run-up to the war); John Bolton (an AEI analyst who would become undersecretary of state for arms control and international security); Zalmay Khalilzad (at various points George W. Bush's ambassador to Afghanistan, Iraq, and the United Nations); Bill Kristol; Richard Perle (an AEI fellow who worked in multiple venues to advance the invasion both within the administration and without); Donald Rumsfeld (Bush's secretary of defense during the Iraq War); Paul Wolfowitz (Bush's deputy secretary of defense); and James Woolsey (former CIA director who was constantly on CNN in the run-up to the Iraq War). This 1998 letter frames the situation in Iraq in the most apocalyptic terms and situates the threat in relationship to the end of the Cold War: "We are writing you because we are convinced that current American policy toward Iraq is not succeeding, and that we may soon face a threat in the Middle East more serious than any we have known since the end of the Cold War." The letter then calls for a "removal of Saddam Hussein's regime from power."[17] A similar letter was then sent in May 1998 to Speaker of the House Newt Gingrich and Senate Majority Leader Trent Lott.[18] Letters like these and the continued advocacy of an Iraq invasion helped move policy in the late 1990s. For instance, the Iraq Liberation Act was signed into law in October 1998 by Bill Clinton. It declares, "It should be the policy of the United States to support efforts to remove the regime headed by Saddam Hussein from power in Iraq and to promote the emergence of a democratic government to replace that regime." The act was passed with an overwhelming majority in the House and unanimously in the Senate.[19] Additionally, December 1998 saw the launch by President Clinton of Operation Desert Fox in Iraq, which, "over the course of four days ... blasted ninety-seven targets, among them weapons research facilities, barracks housing the Republican Guard, an oil refinery, and seven of Saddam's palaces."[20]

In the late 1990s, another think-tank-affiliated academic was also key in the selling of this new foreign policy agenda in the marketplace of ideas. Laurie Mylroie, an academic affiliated with AEI, pushed the outer limits of debate as it related to foreign policy. In many ways, she shows the expansiveness of the marketplace of ideas at the end of the twentieth century as literally any policy, regardless of how fantastical, is given an airing in the name of a diversity of viewpoints or "balancing" an already right-leaning marketplace. At first blush, Mylroie's credentials convey academic expertise on Iraq: "She has held faculty positions at Harvard and the U.S. Naval War College and worked at the Washington Institute for Near East Policy, as well as serving as an advisor on Iraq to the 1992 Clinton presidential campaign." However, her career took a strange turn in 1993 when she started to write papers and eventually a book (*The Study of Revenge*, published by AEI in 2000), which worked to advance "a unified field theory of terrorism" around the nexus of Saddam Hussein. *The Study of Revenge* argues that Hussein was behind "every anti-American terrorist incident of the past decade," including the 1993 World Trade Center attack, the bombing of U.S. embassies in Kenya and Tanzania, the 1995 Oklahoma City bombing, the 1996 bombing of a U.S. military facility in Saudi Arabia, and the crash of TWA Flight 800 in 1996. Later, she would add the bombing of the USS *Cole* in 2000, the attacks of 9/11, and the post-9/11 anthrax attacks. As veteran foreign policy reporter Peter Bergen correctly notes, all of this thinking should have correctly situated her as an intellectual "crackpot," but with AEI's assistance, she was anything but.[21] Thanks to AEI, Mylroie was embraced at the upper echelons of conservative intelligentsia and thanks to the marketplace of ideas her views were given hearing across the media landscape in the twenty-first century. Iraqi historian Juan Cole correctly identifies the think tank as the central institution in how fringe views such as Mylroie's have been mainstreamed. Cole notes that AEI, at the turn of the century, published "anything Mylroie handed into them, no matter how fantastic" and without being refereed by any expert in any relevant field. Then the mere fact of her work's "existence can become a reference-point in political debate."[22]

As the 1990s came to a close and another presidential election loomed, it was unclear if the neoconservative foreign policy vision and such fantastical views like Mylroie's were going to gain additional traction within a new presidential administration or within the marketplace of ideas. In the 2000 Republican presidential primary, Bill Kristol endorsed John McCain over George W. Bush—thinking (accurately) that McCain was more fully committed to the neoconservative foreign policy project. However, McCain lost the nomination and Kristol's vision seemed to be on the outs as Bush came to articulate a relatively noninterventionist foreign policy in the 2000 campaign. Moreover, the sway of conservative think tanks, particularly those devoted to foreign policy, was being challenged as domestic concerns were largely at the forefront of the presidential campaign. The 2000 FAIR study of think tank media visibility reflects this shift. While conservative think tanks still received half of all media citations, liberal think tanks received 20 percent—the highest ever and a 79 percent gain over 1999. Moreover, liberal think tanks who dealt with the economy, such as EPI, saw big gains in the amount of times they were cited. Finally, foreign policy was clearly being put on the back burner as "internationally oriented think tanks, or those devoted to military issues . . . either suffered declines or did not increase at all." At the same time, the same study notes that "overall, media citations of think tanks grew 29 percent in 2000." This included an increase of only 5 percent in newspapers, but a 65 percent increase in radio and television transcripts. The study attributes this shift to "the proliferation of pundit-oriented shows" in the twenty-four-hour news environment.[23] Such a shift was important for the neoconservative foreign policy project, which was best sold through a fast-paced, sound-bite-driven format like cable news.

At the same time, think tank neoconservatives could also take some solace that their foreign policy project was gaining traction in the marketplace of ideas at the end of the twentieth century. In polling conducted by Gallup "the percentage of Americans persuaded that the United States was spending *too little* on defense grew steadily in the decade following the end of the Cold War, from 9 percent in 1990 to 40 percent in August 2000." The percentage who said "too much" to the same question in the same period of time declined from 50 percent to 20 percent.[24] As PNAC produced their final document before the events of 11 September there was considerable evidence that their view was gaining traction in the government and among the public. Their final pre-9/11 document was entitled "Rebuilding America's Defenses" and was targeted at whatever administration would assume the new presidency. Reasserting their arguments for hegemony, the document argues, "At present the United States faces no global rival. America's grand strategy should aim to preserve and extend this advantageous position as far into the future as possible." The authors declare that they will not let their vision of hegemony be contained by "pre-ordained constraints that followed from assumptions about what the country might or might not be willing to expend on its defenses." They argue that not only were such constraints built on de-militarized post–Cold War assumptions but also that "the surplus expected in federal revenues over the next decade . . . removes any need to hold defense spending to some preconceived low level."[25] With the incoming Bush presidency, these surpluses, but not the neo-conservative vision, would vanish. Instead, their vision was fully mainstreamed as policy and within the marketplace of ideas in the aftermath of the attacks of 11 September.

IN ADDITION TO such a foreign policy vision, conservative think tanks also had a new administrative model to sell to the Bush administration upon entering office. The impetus for this model was a paper written for the administration by the Heritage Foundation. This paper immediately set the tone on the matter of expertise and empirical analysis in policy planning within the administration. Cowritten by Robert E. Moffit, the paper is entitled "Taking Charge of the Federal Personnel." In it, Moffit and his coauthors are explicit that the administration should move toward what he terms a "political administration model." Such a model meant that "political appointees must be in charge of policy." This model was counterposed against "the public administration model" in which career civil servants were charged with implementing policy and studying policy effectiveness in "a value-free 'scientific' program of government administration." The problem with the public administration model, as Moffit saw it, was that "the civil servant . . . had been empowered" to too great a degree to enact his or her preferences under the guise of being value-free expertise. This meant that the president would have these "barriers" in his way when trying to make policy. Moffit argues that the closeness of the 2000 election should not hamper Bush from implementing the political administration model. Rather, the election circumstances only meant that Bush "has lost precious time in making the transition" to this model. According to Moffit, Bush should not "be tempted to name fewer political appointees to various positions within the agencies and departments." What was being attacked in this memo was the very idea of a detached technocratic expertise within the state itself. Whereas previously conservatives in think tanks and elsewhere worked to undermine such an idea in institutions outside of the state, now that relativistic model was being moved within the state itself. Moffit and his coauthors are very explicit in suggesting that what they are rejecting is the "Progressive ideal" of government from the early twentieth century in favor of a nineteenth-century model where political appointees dominated all aspects of policymaking.[26] Such a model, if accepted by the incoming administration, would be an obvious boon to Heritage given that they would supply many of the political appointees for such positions. Indeed, by March 2001, Ed Feulner, still Heritage's president at the time, was glowing about all the "familiar faces" in the administration. This was largely due to the fact that Heritage had "passed on 1,200 to 1,300 names and resumes" for hiring purposes during the transition period.[27]

Besides the abundance of Heritage staffers within the administration, there is ample evidence from early in Bush's term that his administration chose to take Heritage's advice and reject the very notion of detached expertise in policy planning. Reports from that period show that those in the administration who were interested in empirical policy analysis found very few allies. For instance, John DiIulio, who was picked to be the head of the White House Office of Faith-Based and Community Initiatives, told reporter Ron Suskind, "There is no precedent in any modern White House for what is going on in this one: a complete lack of a policy apparatus.... What you've got is everything—and I mean everything—being run by the political arm." DiIulio reported that he never saw "actual policy white papers on domestic issues" and that there were "only a couple of people in the West Wing who worried at all about policy substance and analysis."[28] In addition to DiIulio's description, Suskind chronicled the story of Paul O'Neill as treasury secretary, which highlighted the same devaluation of policy-planning expertise within the administration.[29]

With this devaluation of expertise in place within the state, and the marketplace of ideas in place within the wider culture, neoconservatives were in a uniquely opportune position to sell their foreign policy vision. Such a project was made even more possible with the fear engendered by the attacks of 11 September. Americans and policymakers were grasping for responsive foreign policy solutions that were easily accessible and understandable. Think tank neoconservatives were ready to provide such policies. Like no other force, think tank neoconservatives from AEI and through PNAC, both inside and outside the administration, were ready to use the events of that day to implement their foreign policy vision. This vision meant widening the war beyond the al Qaeda network that had attacked the United States and instead toward a broader "war on terror" under whose rubric many ideologically disparate groups could be linked. Given the pre-9/11 writings of these think tanks, the primary shift in focus they hoped to make was from al Qaeda and Osama bin Laden to Iraq and Saddam Hussein.

From the moment of the attacks this goal of shifting the focus among those affiliated with neoconservative institutions became apparent. On CNN the very next day, former CIA director and PNAC signatory James Woolsey was the first person in the public record who attempted to connect Hussein's Iraq to the events of 9/11. He was invited on CNN at least three times on 12 September 2001 to air this view. The first two times, he is only identified as a former CIA director and was allowed to state a connection between 9/11 and Saddam Hussein without rebuttal. In the first instance, he cited the president's speech in which he says the United States will fight all those who "harbor" terrorists. In response to this, Woolsey argues, "A harbor for terrorists might be, say, the Taliban regime in Afghanistan. But there may be more involved than harbors here, there may be a government other than a harbor, such as the Iraqi government, that is orchestrating this to some extent, funding it, working closely on it behind bin Laden or some other terrorist group." He continued saying, "It really need [sic] to look carefully at the possibility there may be state sponsorship here, and I think the most likely, certainly not the only possibility is Iraq."[30] In a different interview that same day, Woolsey goes even further and says that Hussein might be behind the operation since it was "a very complex operation" that would need a "state-sponsor behind or working with bin Laden, such as possibly Iraq." At this point, Woolsey even cites Mylroie's work as "evidence" for such assertions; she believed Hussein to be behind the 1993 World Trade Center bombing. Unfortunately, the AEI scholar's work had "been pooh-poohed to some extent by the Clinton administration" but still needed to be taken seriously.[31] It was only during Woolsey's third appearance that day on CNN that his claims of an Iraqi connection to 9/11 were finally challenged by Larry Johnson—a former State Department counterterrorism official. Woolsey once again makes similar claims to those aired earlier in the day: "My suspicion—it's no more than that at this point—is that there could be some government action involved together with Bin Laden or a major terrorist group. And one strong suspect there I think would be the government of Iraq." To this, Johnson responds that such a move would be "highly unlikely for several reasons," including the fact that such a move would turn the entire world against Hussein at a time he was making progress "in the United Nations in getting sanctions lifted." Given this, and other factors, Johnson argues that "we should not ascribe to him—that kind of idiocy."[32] Nevertheless, it was this message that Woolsey and other think tankers continued to push in the days, weeks, and months ahead. Sometimes the claims would go unchallenged, and sometimes they would be challenged—as these examples show. Nevertheless, the rhetorical link was always made between Hussein and the attacks—which was enough in a twenty-four-hour news environment. Within the marketplace of ideas, such a position merely became another position to be debated—being no more or less open to scrutiny than any other.

As was the case in the 1990s, think tank neoconservatives were also making their case for a broader militarized foreign policy in more elite political environments. On 20 September 2001, PNAC sent a letter to President Bush that focused on a broad-based "war on terror" as opposed to a war only against bin Laden and al Qaeda. In an interesting twist, much of the letter sought to attribute the policies they were advocating to Secretary of State Colin Powell—the person in the administration most likely to be against their idea of a wider war. The letter states, "We agree with the Secretary of State that U.S. policy must aim not only at finding the people responsible for this incident, but must also target those 'other groups out there that mean us no good' and 'that have conducted attacks previously against U.S. personnel, U.S. interests and our allies.'" The letter also states, "We agree with Secretary of State Powell's recent statement that Saddam Hussein 'is one of the leading terrorists on the face of the Earth.'" Powell's words are used to argue for a "comprehensive strategy" in which a "key goal, but by no means the only goal" would be to "capture or kill Osama bin Laden." Another goal would obviously be attacking Iraq, "even if evidence does not link Iraq directly to the attack" because "any strategy aiming at the eradication of terrorism and its sponsors must include a determined effort to remove Saddam Hussein from power in Iraq." According to the authors, anything less than Hussein's removal would represent a "decisive surrender in the war on international terrorism." As had always been the case with PNAC letters, its signatories were a who's who of neoconservative intellectuals—giving the document massive weight with policymaking circles.[33]

In addition to this letter, and once again as in the 1990s, the *Weekly Standard* was used by PNAC and AEI members and intellectuals to further target Washington's conservative elite. The first such article after the attacks was by Gary Schmitt and Thomas Donnelly. Both were employed by AEI and were part of PNAC (Schmitt as executive director). The article, entitled "What Our Enemies Want," makes the case for a broader militaristic foreign policy in the wake of the attacks of

11 September. What is most surprising about the piece was that the authors do little to conceal the fact that they find a limited engagement with Osama bin Laden and al Qaeda to be trivial. Going after bin Laden is downplayed throughout the piece, and bin Laden is never mentioned without also mentioning Saddam Hussein. For instance, the authors argue that while "Usama bin Laden and his organization should be a prime target of this campaign . . . the larger campaign also must go after Saddam Hussein." Bin Laden is downplayed to such an extent that the men even argue that war with Afghanistan "is probably not necessary." Rather, the focus for Donnelly and Schmitt is gaining a foothold in the Middle East through Iraq—Afghanistan and bin Laden are peripheral to such a goal. As the title of the piece suggests, the focus should be on "what our enemies want" and then doing the exact opposite. So, the authors argue, "Our adversaries want to push the United States out of the Middle East. Our response must be to prevent that." These adversaries are bin Laden and Saddam Hussein, who don't care "much about America's role in Europe or East Asia. They want us out of their region." Again they are explicit that it is about gaining a foothold in the region when they argue that what bin Laden and Hussein "hate most is that America and its allies prevent them from seizing control of Saudi Arabia and the surrounding region, whether to rule in triumph or fundamentalist glory." Given this, Americans must "reassert U.S. preeminence in the region," including the ability to "preempt and to strike first" against Saddam to gain a hegemonic foothold.[34]

Inside the administration this same message was being pushed by former PNAC signatories Secretary of Defense Donald Rumsfeld and Deputy Secretary of Defense Paul Wolfowitz. The most vivid account of their actions in the days after the attack was provided by counterterrorism official Richard Clarke in his book *Against All Enemies*. Clarke writes about how he came into the first response-planning meetings after the 11 September attacks to find out that people were talking about entities other than al Qaeda. He writes, "Then I realized with almost a sharp physical pain that Rumsfeld and Wolfowitz were going to try to take advantage of this national tragedy to promote their agenda about Iraq. Since the beginning of the administration, indeed well before, they had been pressing for a war with Iraq." This Iraq agenda was being pushed even after the CIA had determined that al Qaeda was behind the attacks. According to Clarke, Wolfowitz was not persuaded and said the attacks were "too sophisticated and complicated an operation . . . for a

terrorist group to have pulled off by itself without a state sponsor—
Iraq must have been helping them."[35] Then, in what was perhaps the
most bizarre revelation in Clarke's book, he writes that later on 12 September, "Secretary Rumsfeld complained that there were no decent
targets for bombing in Afghanistan and that we should consider bombing Iraq, which, he said had better targets. At first I thought Rumsfeld
was joking. But he was serious and the President did not reject out of
hand the idea of attacking Iraq."[36]

Despite these efforts inside and outside of the administration, in the
months after 11 September it was not yet clear whether the wider militarized response advocated by think tank neoconservatives would gain
traction with the public. According to the 2001 FAIR think tank study,
conservative think tank operatives who might advocate such a foreign
policy actually declined in media exposure in the four months after the
attacks. Reliably liberal think tanks went down as well, with "bipartisan" think tanks like Brookings picking up all the slack. The one good
piece of news, as far as think tank neoconservatives were concerned, was
that in the 2001 post-9/11 environment the media clearly began turning
its focus away from domestic politics. The same FAIR study shows that
"the think tanks whose visibility declined most after September 11 were
the Family Research Council, the Urban Institute, the Center for Public
Integrity and the Competitive Enterprise Institute." All of these think
tanks focused primarily on domestic issues. Even after an economic recession was announced in November, it "did not seem to produce a particularly large number of mentions of economic think tanks."[37] The
pre-9/11 neoconservative goal of getting the nation and media to de-
emphasize domestic concerns was clearly taking place.

By early 2002, with foreign policy still focused on the war in Afghanistan, think tank neoconservatives were working to re-center Iraq and
Saddam Hussein—a war they now felt might not come into being. In
April 2002, PNAC members once again sent a letter to President Bush
urging action against Iraq. The letter cites Hussein's supposed "chemical, biological, or nuclear weapons," which he might give to terrorists;
his support for "terrorism against Israel"; his harboring of terrorists; and
his supposed "links to the Al Qaeda network." According to the letter,
if the United States didn't act against Hussein, "the damage our Israeli
friends and we have suffered until now may someday appear but a
prelude to much greater horrors." Such action would ultimately show
"a renewed commitment on our part ... to the birth of freedom and

democratic government in the Islamic world."[38] This letter was striking in its attempt to connect Hussein with anything that could possibly be a rationale for war, regardless of the evidence. On the point of evidence, think tank neoconservatives also had some of their people on the inside of the administration working on two different "intelligence" units that sought to connect Hussein and Iraq to al Qaeda and bin Laden. Both were led by Undersecretary of Defense Douglas Feith and had numerous think tank connections. The first, the Counter Terrorism Evaluation Group (CTEG), involved David Wurmser of AEI and Michael Maloof, a journalist, working with Feith to look at "raw intelligence" from the CIA on Iraq. Their findings were then presented to several administration officials. James Risen, a *New York Times* reporter who uncovered the existence of this group, argued that "the unit played a role in the administration's evolving effort to define the threat of Iraq—and sell it to the public."[39] Feith also worked with many other think tank affiliated individuals in the Pentagon's Office of Special Plans on a similar "raw intelligence" project looking for connections between Hussein and bin Laden.[40] The combination of outside pressure and intelligence manipulation led to an overt shift by the administration to sell a war with Iraq to the American public by the summer of 2002. Many of the dubious Iraq–al Qaeda "connections" found by CTEG and the Office of Special Plans were cited by administration officials during that summer. The biggest ideological victory for think tank neoconservatives came in September 2002 with the administration's "National Security Strategy of the United States of America," or, as it was referred to in the media, "The Bush Doctrine." The document clearly articulated the neoconservative militaristic foreign policy vision.

The Bush Doctrine was released to coincide with the request by the administration for a force authorization against Iraq from the Congress. It was at this point that New Democratic, bipartisan, and centrist think tanks helped create a consensus around an invasion of Iraq. The DLC/ PPI, in their earliest dispatch on the upcoming resolution, singled out for praise Democratic Senators Joseph Lieberman, John Kerry, and John Edwards, all of whom were staking out a pro-war stance. In particular, the group endorsed a John Edwards *Washington Post* op-ed on the subject that argues that "the point of the resolution should be to 'clearly endorse the use of all necessary means to eliminate the threat posed by Saddam Hussein's weapons of mass destruction,' preferably by Security Council–sanctioned multilateral action, but if necessary by the United

States with 'whatever allies will join us.' "[41] The think tank would later have qualms about how the debate played out in September and October of 2002. They focused on the issue of WMDs as the proper rationale and decried both the idea that "Saddam Hussein may directly attack the United States with weapons of mass destruction" and the "right of preemption" contained in the Bush Doctrine.[42] The think tank also critiqued Bush's timing of the vote for maximum electoral gain in the 2002 midterm elections.[43] Nevertheless, none of these reservations made the group question supporting the resolutions eventually voted on in both houses. As the debate proceeded, the DLC even urged Democrats to reject an alternative resolution by Senator Carl Levin (D-Mich.) "that would require specific U.N. approval before U.S. troops could be committed to a military action."[44] When the eventual resolution was passed, the think tank declared it the "right thing" despite sympathizing "with those Democrats who express concerns about the Administration's reckless disdain for multilateral cooperation and world opinion in the past, and its motives for focusing on Iraq at this particular moment." Nevertheless, "George W. Bush is the only President we have, and he needs both the support and the legal authority to bring Saddam Hussein to heel. And for the foreseeable future, Democrats need to get used to the post-9/11 reality that war and rumors of war will never be completely off the nation's political radar screen."[45]

In addition to this type of advocacy by the DLC/PPI, so-called bipartisan think tanks were also essential in creating a consensus around the need to attack Hussein. In particular, the Brookings Institution and the Council on Foreign Relations made war with Iraq seem immensely more reasonable with the publication of Kenneth Pollack's book *Threatening Storm: The Case for Invading Iraq*. Pollack, a former CIA operative in Iraq turned Brookings analyst, published the book with the CFR and became the face of the reasonable "liberal hawk" within media circles. After being published in September 2002, the book became an immediate bestseller and Pollack's presence was inescapable across all media platforms. Moreover, Pollack's and Brookings's positioning as a "reasonable," non-neoconservative voice for war meant that such a position could reach the most mainstream of media outlets in the marketplace of ideas.[46] *Threatening Storm*, and Pollack's advocacy with Brookings's authority behind him, arguably did more to sell the war than any other think tank produced product. Taken together with the advocacy of think tanks like the DLC, Brookings and Pollack helped create a consensus around the invasion of Iraq. Their motives were certainly different than AEI and PNAC, but the policy result would be the same. The idea of invading Iraq had now taken on the air of a bipartisan consensus, rather than a far-right neoconservative pet project, in part because of the actions taken by think tanks like the DLC/PPI and Brookings.

In early 2003, this new elite consensus hardened as it became increasingly likely that the invasion of Iraq was going to take place. Neoconservatives were emboldened and energized by this. PNAC members sent off another letter to the president that acknowledged that the United States was now "ready to end the threat of Saddam Hussein's regime in Iraq."[47] In February 2003, President Bush gave a primetime televised speech from AEI's offices in Washington where he declared that "a liberated Iraq can show the power of freedom to transform that vital region, by bringing hope and progress into the lives of millions. America's interests and security, and America's belief in liberty, both lead in the same direction, to a free and peaceful Iraq."[48] Finally, on the same day President Bush declared war, 19 March 2003, PNAC members sent another letter to the president in which they declared that it was "time to act to remove Saddam Hussein and his regime from power" without a "fixation on exit strategies and departure deadlines."[49]

The occupation of Iraq became a think tank project in itself. As Naomi Klein and others have documented, the American occupying forces sought to make the country "a gleaming showroom for laissez-faire economics, a utopia such as the world had never seen." Paul Bremer, head of the Coalition Provisional Authority (CPA), would implement a "Baghdad Year Zero" plan whereby "500,000 state workers, most of them soldiers, but also doctors, nurses, teachers, publishers, and printers" would be immediately fired. Then Bremer and his allies "flung open the country's borders to absolutely unrestricted imports: no tariffs, no duties, no inspections, no taxes." Continuing the Bush administration's preference for the political administration model that devalued technocratic expertise within the state, the staffers of the CPA were "straight out of the Heritage Foundation, all of them given responsibility they could never have dreamed of receiving at home."[50] Klein's reporting was not an exaggeration. Jim O'Beirne, who screened candidates for jobs in postwar Iraq at the Pentagon, was primarily concerned with whether his candidates were ideological conservatives, not with their expertise in postwar reconstruction. O'Beirne was a political appointee of Bush's in the political administration model, so his job was to make sure all his appointments were conservative ideologues. Rajiv Chandrasekaran, who has written extensively on the occupation of Iraq, reported on this subject. According to Chandrasekaran, "To recruit the people he wanted, O'Beirne sought résumés from the offices of Republican congressmen, conservative think tanks and GOP activists. He discarded applications from those his staff deemed ideologically suspect, even if the applicants possessed Arabic language skills or postwar rebuilding experience."[51] Journalist Ariana Eunjung Cha provides an even more detailed report of how the process worked through an account of Simone Ledeen, "the 28-year-old daughter of [AEI] neoconservative pundit Michael Ledeen." She, and others like her, had been hired to perform low-level tasks in Iraq, but as more senior staffers left, these low-level staffers "found themselves managing the country's $13 billion budget, making decisions affecting millions of Iraqis." Soon nearly everyone who worked in the CPA had never "worked in the Middle East, [did not speak] Arabic, and few could tell a balance sheet from an accounts receivable statement." According to Cha, "For months they wondered what they had in common, how their names had come to the attention of the Pentagon, until one day they figured it out: They had all posted their resumes at the Heritage Foundation."[52]

Such a project of putting low-level nonexperts from conservative think tanks in charge of a postwar occupation had obvious disastrous consequences. Under even the best circumstances the occupation would have been a near-impossible task. However, the actions taken by the CPA to institute dubious economic experiments under the guidance of conservative ideologues gave fuel to the Iraqi insurgency and added immensely to the chaos of the postwar period. The full consequences of these actions, however, were not apparent until after President Bush had been elected to a second term in office in 2004. Thus, during much of late 2003 and 2004, the administration was still emboldened with hubris regarding the supposed success of their foreign policy. Such hubris led to one of the more famous quotes by an unnamed Bush staffer from this period in time when he told Ron Suskind that members of the administration were not "part of the reality-based community." By this, the staffer meant that "community" that believes "that solutions emerge from [the] judicious study of discernible reality." Instead, according to the staffer, "That's not the way the world really works anymore. . . . We're an empire now, and when we act, we create our own reality. And while you're studying that reality—judiciously, as you will—we'll act again, creating other new realities, which you can study too, and that's how things will sort out. We're history's actors . . . and you, all of you, will be left to just study what we do."[53] A more explicit rejection of the idea of administrative technocratic expertise could not be found. Such an attitude was undoubtedly emboldened even further as President Bush was reelected to a second term in office just three weeks later.

With Bush's second-term victory, narratives of conservative ascendancy were everywhere in the media. However, things began to unravel very quickly for the Bush presidency in its second term. Much of this unraveling had to do with the combination of the failure of neoconservative foreign policy and Bush's commitment to the political administration model. Emboldened by think tanks like the Cato Institute and political appointees within the administration in charge of economic policy, the Bush administration made an immediate second-term push for the privatization of Social Security. Much of the administration's campaign against the central pillar of New Deal liberalism was built on an obfuscation of the solvency of the program and an ideological push for untested private accounts invested in the stock market. The public and congressional reaction against this policy proposal was swift.[54] Additionally, in 2005, real-world catastrophic events showed the need for technocratic expertise in government and also the dangers of imperial overstretch inherent in the neoconservative foreign policy vision. Chaos in Iraq continued unabated and, in September 2005, Hurricane Katrina laid bare the need for competent civil servants—as opposed to political appointees—running government agencies such as Federal Emergency Management Agency.[55]

The 2006 midterm election victories by Democrats seemed to be a repudiation of neoconservative foreign policy and Bush's political administration model. However, in his final two years in the presidency, Bush's move away from these was not at all straightforward. In particular, the election did not bring respite from further neoconservative foreign policies as longtime AEI scholar Frederick Kagan advocated and sold an escalation of the Iraq War to the Bush administration. This escalation (or "surge," in popular parlance) came as a response to the report by the Baker-Hamilton Iraq Study Group report, which advocated a shift away from the neoconservative foreign policy vision. Think tank neoconservatives immediately attacked the Baker-Hamilton report, calling it "preposterous," "a monumental disappointment," and "wrong or of no consequence."[56] In an effort to offer their own counterplan, neoconservatives used AEI as a base from which to offer their own response. Kagan was the point man in this regard as it was he who appeared in numerous media outlets to promote the "surge." Although Kagan's doctorate was as a historian of Russian and Soviet military history, he was the primary voice in the marketplace of ideas advocating an escalation of the Iraq War.[57] His lack of expertise in the region and his support for the launch of the Iraq War in 2003 did little to diminish his voice in the marketplace. Thus, despite the 2006 election, the balance in the foreign policy marketplace of ideas was still clearly tilted rightward as the Kagan-AEI plan was ultimately implemented as policy. The high-profile nature of AEI in promoting the Iraq escalation in 2006 and 2007 reflected the larger continued imbalance in the marketplace of ideas when it came to think tanks. Of the 14,790 think tank citations in the media in 2007, bipartisan and conservative think tanks predominated. Brookings and the Council on Foreign Relations—both still heavily committed to the militaristic foreign policy consensus—were cited the first and second most in the media respectively. AEI, Heritage, and CSIS came in third, fourth, and fifth, respectively.[58] The marketplace of ideas, far from being balanced or diverse, was heavily tilted in a rightward direction.

As the Bush administration came to a close in 2008 and was enveloped by the worst financial catastrophe since the Great Depression, there were some signs that the political administration model was coming to an end. As David Greenberg notes, top appointments in the Justice Department, Federal Reserve, and Treasury Department all focused on professionalism over ideological bona fides during this period of crisis.[59] Moreover, the financial crisis itself seemed to call into question conservative fixed economic ideas regarding deregulation and "free markets." As Barack Obama entered the presidency in 2009, it seemed possible that there would be a move away from the right-wing parameters of debate that had dominated for so long—both in foreign and domestic policymaking. Moreover, with the political administration model in disrepute and the marketplace of ideas seemingly becoming larger and larger with changes to the media landscape brought about by the Internet, the role of the think tank in American political culture seemed unstable and unclear heading into Obama's presidency.

Conclusion

Policy as Identity Politics

As a way of debating policy, the marketplace of ideas model is now thoroughly entrenched. For all Americans, elite and otherwise, the idea that policy debates should center primarily around questions of expertise, empiricism, and "workability" seems quaint. Instead, to the extent that Americans are concerned with policy and policy debates, they are concerned primarily with the question of the subjectivity of the participants involved—their biases and whether such biases are "balanced" in the debate. This book has argued that think tanks, and particularly conservative think tanks, were integral in the shift to this model. In the late 1960s and 1970s, conservative think tanks were one of the only conservative institutions able to effectively argue for a shift to this new model. As one of the few institutional creators of conservative public policies, the people in these institutions could convincingly argue that they had been shut out of policy debates beholden to the liberal technocratic ideal. Men like William Baroody at AEI and Edwin Feulner at the Heritage Foundation effectively argued that their conservative policy products were being ignored in the face of a liberal intellectual monopoly. This new model of policy debate could have created a liberated policy environment where all sorts of political subjectivities were heard in a way they had not been during the postwar period where the liberal technocratic ideal held. A truly diverse marketplace of ideas from the 1970s onward could have included a wide variety of political identities from across the American ideological landscape. As this book has shown, this is not what occurred. Instead of creating an ideologically diverse marketplace of ideas, conservatives wielded this new model in a much more limited way—focusing instead on the obsessive need for "balance" in policy debates. In a balanced marketplace of ideas, what was really important was having only two positions: "liberal" and "conservative." In such a debating world, conservative policies could be heard simply by being identified as "conservative." While the policies identified in such a way could be rigorously thought through and planned out, they did not have to be. As I showed in the case of supply-side tax-cutting policies, rigor was certainly not required to enter the balanced marketplace of ideas. Finally, the balanced marketplace of ideas created even more rightward movement in political debates given that liberal think tanks and institutions (including the Democratic Party) so thoroughly internalized this understanding of policy debate within their own institutions. Rather than committing to be the liberal voices in the balanced marketplace of ideas, these liberal institutions decided to discipline themselves and internally balance their own sites. Brookings became bipartisan, and the Democratic Party, at the behest of the DLC/PPI, began to police itself against all signs of strident liberalism. Taken together, this shifted the whole plane of political debate rightward—foreclosing nearly any policy possibility to the left of the "New Democrat" position on a whole host of issues.

Although some would undoubtedly argue that such a policy debating world has diminished in power in the age of the Obama presidency, I think this view is mistaken. The Obama administration's signature policy achievement provides evidence for the continuation of the balanced marketplace of ideas and the overall rightward field of policy debate. The Affordable Care Act (ACA), the Obama administration's signature legislation that was designed to move the United States toward universal health care coverage while containing health care costs, is similar in structure to the type of healthcare reform long advocated by the Heritage Foundation.[1] As passed, the ACA has four integral components. First, health insurance companies are not allowed to deny coverage on the basis of a previous health care condition. Second, individuals would be compelled to buy insurance as they would other types of insurance (such as car insurance). Third, for those who couldn't afford coverage, subsidies from the federal government would be given for purchase. Finally, such insurance would be purchased through online "exchanges" where health care providers would sell their various insurance products. The first three of these components had been advocated by Heritage as far back as the late 1980s and early 1990s as a response to Democratic proposals. At that time, Heritage health care policy writers envisioned their proposals as balancing Democrats' more statist alternatives in the marketplace of ideas. Where the Democrats were said to be advocating something more akin to a national "single payer" system, conservatives through Heritage advocated making private health care markets work more efficiently.[2] Even when Clinton's efforts were defeated, Heritage never abandoned the first three components and in the 2000s added the idea of a health insurance exchange where consumers could purchase private health insurance.[3] All four of these components were trumpeted by Heritage after they seemed to work as public policy when enacted by a Democratic legislature and a Republican governor (Mitt Romney) in Massachusetts.

However, in 2009–10, with a Democratic president trumpeting many of the specifics of the Heritage reforms, the think tank promptly abandoned the policy. This is somewhat shocking but nonetheless shows the power of the balanced marketplace of ideas to continually shift political debates rightward. In the early 1990s, Heritage advanced these proposals as the conservative, market-based solution to Clintonian health care reforms. Less than twenty years later, a Democratic president and Congress had embraced much of the Heritage model while abandoning anything that smacked of a public insurance option not controlled by private health insurance companies. Rather than declare success, Heritage used the Democrats' new position to declare a new right-wing pole in a "balanced" health care debate—thus moving the entire spectrum of debate even further to the right. If the Democrats embraced their reforms, then the reforms must be too liberal. As a result, Heritage came out as one of the primary institutional opponents of the ACA both before and after its passage. The think tank used its opposition to the ACA to rekindle its vibrancy and grassroots identity after its moribund standing at the end of the Bush administration. In opposition to the ACA, they became the think tank of the conservative "Tea Party" movement. Feulner, while still president of Heritage in 2010, established a new offshoot organization, "Heritage Action," to capitalize on this new standing.[4] Heritage Action would mobilize the grassroots conservative movement into political action against the ACA and other Democratic initiatives. Such a dynamic was ratcheted up even further in 2012 when Feulner resigned as president in favor of Jim DeMint—the Tea Party Republican senator from South Carolina. DeMint, Heritage, and Heritage Action were widely credited with precipitating a Republican shutdown of the federal government in an attempt to defund the ACA.[5]

In the end analysis, then, we are left to wonder how far into the future the balanced marketplace of ideas, and its ability to create a rightward plane of debate, can last. With Democrats now manning the barricades for a healthcare policy developed by the Heritage Foundation and with the Heritage Foundation aggressively advocating against that policy, one has to think we have reached the endpoint in how far to the right the debate parameters can move. In the near future, however, the dynamics that brought this about seem unlikely to change. Heritage is growing financially and organizationally as the grassroots Tea Party think tank. AEI is taking advantage of this by soliciting corporate donations from elite conservatives uncomfortable with Heritage's grassroots positioning.[6] Cato still positions itself as the libertarian alternative in the marketplace of ideas even though this is somewhat unstable. As for Brookings, it still works its identity as a bipartisan, balanced arbiter in the policy-debating world. The DLC disbanded in 2011, largely because it won the argument within the Democratic Party.[7] It leaves behind PPI, but that think tank is a shell of its former self without the DLC umbrella. A powerful new Democratically aligned think tank, the Center for American Progress, seems destined to pick up where the DLC left off. While the new think tank sometimes advocates positions outside the New Democrat model, it is largely in tune with such an identity.[8] When you combine all of this with a traditional media landscape still well versed in the marketplace of ideas metaphors of balance, I see no reason why policy debates that occur on a rightward playing field would cease. Policy will continue to be a matter of identity politics where Americans are largely disinterested in policy specifics or the workability of policies and instead use policies as tribal markers to easily declare allegiances. The best Americans can probably hope for, then, is that the marketplace of policy ideas actually becomes truly diverse as opposed to "balanced" between various conservative positions. The Internet and media fragmentation may make such diversity possible heading into the future. An exposure to a wider spectrum of ideas through such a fragmentation would undoubtedly make for a healthier democracy than the one we have now.

Notes

Abbreviations

AFB   Arthur F. Burns Files, Gerald R. Ford Presidential Library,
      Ann Arbor, Mich.
BEHP B. Edwin Hutchinson Papers, Hoover Institution Archives,
      Stanford, Calif.
BGP   The Personal and Political Papers of Senator Barry M. Goldwater,
      Arizona Historical Foundation, Tempe, Ariz.
BP   William J. Baroody Papers, Library of Congress, Washington, D.C.
BRF   Bruce Reed Files, William J. Clinton Presidential Library,
      Little Rock, Ark.
CBL   Clare Boothe Luce Papers, Library of Congress, Washington, D.C.
DKP   Denison Kitchel Papers, Hoover Institution Archives, Stanford, Calif.
FSAP Free Society Association Records, Hoover Institution Archives,
      Stanford, Calif.
GRFP President Gerald R. Ford Papers—White House Central Subject Files,
      Gerald R. Ford Presidential Library, Ann Arbor, Mich.
HP   Friedrich A. von Hayek Papers, Hoover Institution Archives,
      Stanford, Calif.
LEF   Lee Edwards Papers, Hoover Institution Archives, Stanford, Calif.
MFP   Milton Friedman Papers, Hoover Institution Archives, Stanford, Calif.
MLF   Melvin R. Laird Files, Gerald R. Ford Presidential Library,
      Ann Arbor, Mich.
PWP   Paul M. Weyrich Scrapbooks, Library of Congress, Washington, D.C.
RFP   Roger A. Freeman Papers, Hoover Institution Archives, Stanford, Calif.
TEP   Thomas Byrne Edsall Papers, Hoover Institution Archives,
      Stanford, Calif.

Introduction

1. William Baroody to Karl Hess, 30 November 1962, folder 7, box 13, BP. Emphasis in original.

2. William J. Baroody, "The Corporate Role in the Decade Ahead," delivered at the Business Council meeting, Hot Springs, Virginia, 20 October 1972, folder 6, box 86, BP.

3. *Right Moves* contributes to the emergent historiography of the 1970s that stresses the time as both uncertain and filled with ascendant conservative forces. See, for instance, Borstelmann, *The 1970s*; Cowie, *Stayin' Alive*; Kalman, *Right Star Rising*; Perlstein, *Nixonland*; Rodgers, *Age of Fracture*; Schulman, *The Seventies*;

Schulman and Zelizer, *Rightward Bound*; Self, *All in the Family*; Stein, *Pivotal Decade*; Zaretsky, *No Direction Home*. In thinking about a shift to the marketplace of ideas model of policy debate, my thinking is heavily in debt to Daniel Rodgers's unifying concept of fracture to describe the intellectual climate from the 1970s to the present. The marketplace of ideas was, at its very core, about fracturing intellectual and policy debates in such a way so as to allow more "voices," especially conservative ones, into the debate. It did so while at the same time relativizing those debates in a way that had not been seen before.

4. This is not to say that nothing has been written about think tanks and their conservative variants by nonhistorians. Such studies can be divided into two categories: popular trade press publications and nonhistorical academic studies. In the popular press, two authors have sought to delineate the history of think tanks for a wider audience. The first, and most well-known, work is James Allen Smith's *The Idea Brokers: Think Tanks and the Rise of the New Policy Elite*, and the second is Sidney Blumenthal's *The Rise of the Counter-Establishment: From Conservative Ideology to Political Power*. Both are useful primers into the think tank and its development but have enormous inadequacies and different focuses from *Right Moves*. First and foremost, both are more than two decades old and do not have the benefit of the last two decades through which to examine think tank power and accessible archives. Second, Smith's book is enormously wide-ranging, seeking to cover all sorts of think tanks and think tanks projects, thus the centrality of the think tank as an institution of conservative political power is lost. Blumenthal is much more concerned with the institution as a conservative one, but think tanks occupy one of many sites of conservative power in his wide-ranging journalistic account. And again, his book is almost three decades old and was written in the midst of Ronald Reagan's terms in office, thus the benefit of historical distance and historical archival research is absent. As for academic studies, political scientists and sociologists have produced the most studies to date. Most employ some measure of historical research, but their aim is largely to discuss how best to understand the think tank's place as an institution in the present-day political process. Three studies stand out in this regard: Tom Medvetz's *Think Tanks in America*, David Ricci's *The Transformation of American Politics*, and Andrew Rich's *Think Tanks, Public Policy, and the Politics of Expertise*. Ricci and Rich come from the field of political science and, while they both employ historical methods at points in their books, the primary focus of their studies are in understanding the think tank as an institution, and its influence, in the present. While both discuss conservative think tanks, their primary purpose is not in understanding the history of the think tank as a central institution of conservative political organizing. Medvetz's work is similar to Ricci's and Rich's in that it tries to understand the place of the think tank as an institution of policymaking, albeit from the perspective of a sociologist. And while his study is more historical than Ricci's or Rich's, it is once again not interested first and foremost in the think tank's position within the history of American conservatism.

5. Andrew, *The Other Side*; Bailey, *Sex in the Heartland*; Brennan, *Turning Right*; Carter, *The Politics of Rage*; Critchlow, *Phyllis Schlafly*; Edsall and Edsall, *Chain*

Reaction; Farber and Roche, *The Conservative Sixties*; Formisano, *Boston against Busing*; Freedman, *The Inheritance*; Himmelstein, *To the Right*; Klatch, *A Generation Divided*; Klatch, *Women of the New Right*; McGirr, *Suburban Warriors*; Nickerson, *Mothers of Conservatism*; Perlstein, *Before the Storm*; Schneider, *Cadres for Conservatism*; and Sugrue, *The Origins of the Urban Crisis*. Finally, for even more citations and analysis of the social history of the American Right, see McGirr, "A History"; Moore, "Good Old-Fashioned New Social History"; and Ribuffo, "Why Is There So Much Conservatism?"

6. Burgin, *The Great Persuasion*; Burns, *Goddess of the Market*; Moreton, *To Serve God and Wal-Mart*; Phillips-Fein, *Invisible Hands*; Robin, *The Reactionary Mind*; Teles, *The Rise*. Recent dissertations include Hemmer, "Messengers of the Right"; Waterhouse, "A Lobby for Capital."

7. Phillips-Fein's *Invisible Hands* and Rodgers's *Age of Fracture* stand out in this regard.

8. Phillips-Fein, "Conservatism," 730.

9. In other words, in this project, I am ultimately concerned with what Stuart Hall has termed the "thought and language of everyday calculation" as they have related to the formation of conservative identities. While I am concerned with how think tanks altered the policy directions of the state and how they gained power and authority, I am at a fundamental level most concerned with how they helped alter the "commonsense assumptions" people use when articulating their politics and political identities. I am concerned with how think tanks helped in the process of getting Americans, elite and nonelite, to accept for themselves new conservative identities; see Hall, "The Toad in the Garden," 40.

Chapter 1

1. O'Connor, *Social Science for What?*, 2.
2. O'Connor, *Poverty Knowledge*, 8.
3. Critchlow, *The Brookings Institution*, 4.
4. Ibid., 9.
5. Ibid., 10.
6. Bernstein, *A Perilous Progress*, 15.
7. Ibid., 13.
8. Ibid., 42.
9. Critchlow, *The Brookings Institution*, 8.
10. Ibid., xi.
11. Ibid., 105.
12. Ibid., 11.
13. Ibid., 11–12.
14. Hodgson, *America in Our Time*, 67–98.
15. On economics as a field during the period, see Bender and Schorske, *American Academic Culture*, 57–122; Bernstein, *A Perilous Progress*. On political science, see Bender and Schorske, *American Academic Culture*, 243–308. On psychology, see Herman, *The Romance of American Psychology*; May, *Homeward Bound*.

16. Nils Gilman's work details the way in which the Center for International Studies was integral in promoting Cold War "modernization theory" as such institutions sought to "short-circuit the give-and-take of politics and instead substitute fact, knowledge, and indisputable authority of science" in foreign policymaking (*Mandarins of the Future*, 8). S. M. Amadae details the history of the RAND Corporation, a think tank that similarly influenced Cold War foreign policymaking through the development of rational choice theory (*Rationalizing Capitalist Democracy*).

17. O'Connor, *Social Science for What?*, 79. Also important to note is the way in which such a worldview relied heavily on gendered understandings of politics and policymaking whereby the liberal center was situated as "hardheaded," or simply "hard," as counterposed to the "soft Left" and the irrational Right. Historian K. A. Cuordileone describes it: "Liberal realism—a bulwark against fuzzy ideological thinking—was a contrivance of the cold war imperative to claim a view of the world that was unclouded by the uncontrollable vagaries of emotion and sentiment" (*Manhood and American Political Culture*, 34).

18. Critchlow, *The Brookings Institution*, 5.

19. Smith, *The Idea Brokers*, 175. Rick Perlstein also employs the "luncheon club" trope in his book on Barry Goldwater, *Before the Storm* (256).

20. Medvetz, *Think Tanks in America*, 81.

21. For AEA's early years in particular, see Phillips-Fein, *Invisible Hands*, 60–67.

22. DeMuth and Bowman, "The American Enterprise Institute," 6.

23. Certificate of Incorporation of American Enterprise Association, 12 January 1943, folder 3, box 44, BP.

24. For more on Roosevelt's "Four Freedoms" and the conservative addition of free enterprise as a "Fifth Freedom," see chapters 10 and 11 in Foner, *The Story of American Freedom*.

25. U.S. House, House Select Committee on Lobbying Activities, *American Enterprise Association*, 81st Cong., 2d sess., 28 December 1950 (Washington, D.C.: Government Printing Office, 1950), 1–2.

26. DeMuth and Bowman, "The American Enterprise Institute," 2.

27. Brown, "Using Private Business Agencies, to Achieve Public Goals in the Postwar Period," *The American Economic Review*, March 1943, 72.

28. Ibid., 77.

29. Ibid., 80. For a more specific articulation of Brown's antistatist views as they pertained to wartime price controls, see Lewis H. Brown, "How to Get the Country Back to Work," *Vital Speeches of the Day* 12 (no. 11): 342–45.

30. Critchlow, *Phyllis Schlafly*, 26. I should note here that Critchlow had unique access to Schlafly's personal papers as well as oral interviews. Thus, it was impossible to look at the primary sources myself, which is why I am so heavily reliant on Critchlow's work.

31. Ibid., 26–27.

32. Ibid., 27.

33. Ibid., 41.

34. Herman Gray, *Should State Unemployment Insurance Be Federalized?* (New York: American Enterprise Association, 1946); Henry Hazlitt, *The Full Employment Bill: An Analysis* (New York: American Enterprise Association, 1945); Earl E. Muntz, *The National Health Program Scheme: An Analysis of the Wagner-Murray Health Bill* (New York: American Enterprise Association, 1946).

35. John V. Van Sickle, *Industry-Wide Collective Bargaining and the Public Interest* (New York: American Enterprise Association, 1947), 6 and 11–17.

36. Ibid., 5.

37. Joseph H. Ball, *Where Does Statism Begin?: A Study of Pending Proposals to Expand Government Control of the Economy* (New York: American Enterprise Association, 1950), 7, 6.

38. Ibid., 5, 8.

39. DeMuth and Bowman, "The American Enterprise Institute," 4.

40. Letter cited in ibid., 5.

41. House Select Committee on Lobbying Activities, *American Enterprise Association*, 7.

42. Rick Perlstein, for instance, discusses the AEA analyses in the following way: "Washington was complex, and AEA made its name by making it simpler— providing legislators with a steady stream of issue guides that meticulously and fairly spelled out both sides of a pending bill, amendment, or policy question. Every word was vetted by an advisory council of professors" (*Before the Storm*, 256). Likewise, James Smith argues that AEA's pre-1953 writings were akin to a "lawyerly approach to legislative analysis" (*The Idea Brokers,* 175).

43. House Select Committee on Lobbying Activities, *American Enterprise Association*, 1.

44. Ibid., 3.

45. Ibid., 4.

46. Ibid., 5.

47. Ibid., 7.

48. Ibid., 8.

49. Ibid., 10.

50. Ibid., 7, 12, 17.

51. Ibid., 9.

52. Ibid., 10.

53. Ibid., 17–18.

54. Ibid., 19.

55. DeMuth and Bowman, "The American Enterprise Institute," 8–9.

56. Ibid., 9.

57. A. D. Marshall to B. E. Hutchinson, 5 April 1955, folder unmarked, box 38, BEHP.

58. William Baroody to Frederick S. Blackall Jr., 31 August 1955, folder unmarked, box 38, BEHP.

59. A. D. Marshall, Monthly Report to the AEA Executive Committee, 30 November 1955, folder unmarked, box 38, BEHP.

60. Henry Hazlitt, "States' Rights and Labor Law," *Newsweek*, 16 May 1955.

61. Roger A. Freeman, *Federal Aid to Education—Boon or Bane?* (Washington, D.C.: American Enterprise Association, 1955), 47.

62. Barry Goldwater to William Baroody, 30 April 1955, folder unmarked, box 38, BEHP.

63. Senator Thomas E. Martin to William Baroody, 25 June 1955, folder unmarked, box 38, BEHP.

64. B. E. Hutchinson to A. D. Marshall, 2 June 1955, folder unmarked, box 38, BEHP. Emphasis in original.

65. A. D. Marshall to B. E. Hutchinson, 6 June 1955, folder unmarked, box 38, BEHP. Emphasis in original.

66. A. D. Marshall to H. W. Prantis Jr., chairman of Armstrong Cork Company, 21 February 1956, folder D, box 2, BEHP.

67. American Enterprise Association, "Current Operations," May 1956, folder D, box 2, BEHP.

68. William Baroody to Milton Friedman, 6 August 1956, folder 2, box 11, BP.

69. For some of these AEA studies, see Philip D. Bradley, *Involuntary Participation in Unionism* (Washington, D.C.: American Enterprise Association, 1956); Edward H. Chamberlin, *The Economic Analysis of Labor Union Power* (Washington, D.C.: American Enterprise Association, 1958); Goetz Briefs, *Unionism Reappraised: From Classical Unionism to Union Establishment* (Washington, D.C.: American Enterprise Association, 1960). For an example of how such studies were promoted in the mass media, see William Henry Chamberlin, "Labor Monopoly," *Wall Street Journal*, 12 March 1958, 12.

70. Rita R. Campbell and W. Glenn Campbell, *Voluntary Health Insurance in the United States* (Washington, D.C.: American Enterprise Association, 1960).

71. George C. S. Benson and John M. Payne, *National Aid to Higher Education* (Washington, D.C.: American Enterprise Association, 1958); Jerrold G. Van Cise, *The Federal Antitrust Laws* (Washington, D.C.: American Enterprise Association, 1962).

72. DeMuth and Bowman, "The American Enterprise Institute," 8.

73. William Baroody to B. E. Hutchinson, 26 October 1956, folder D, box 2, BEHP.

74. B. E. Hutchinson to William Baroody, 26 October 1956, folder D, box 2, BEHP.

75. For AEA facts and Humphrey letter, see American Enterprise Association, "Minutes of Meeting of Board of Trustees, 29 March 1960," folder unmarked, box 29, BEHP. For the Richard Nixon letter, see Richard Nixon to William Baroody, 12 October 1961, folder 6, box 23, BP.

76. American Enterprise Association, "Minutes of Meeting of Board of Trustees, 29 March 1960," folder unmarked, box 29, BEHP.

77. William Baroody to B. E. Hutchinson, 21 October 1960, folder unmarked, box 29, BEHP. In 1960, James Smith cites the Earhart, Falk, Kresge, Pew, and Sloan Foundations as the only conservatively oriented foundations (*The Idea Brokers*, 176).

78. National Review Publisher (unnamed) to William Baroody, 11 May 1963, folder 10, box 73, BP.

79. William Baroody to Harvey Peters, 17 July 1959, folder 4, box 40, BP.

80. Office of Superintendent of Corporations of the District of Columbia, 1 June 1962, folder 3, box 44, BP.

81. William Baroody to Karl Hess, 30 November 1962, folder 7, box 13, BP. Emphasis in original.

82. Thomas Sowell, "W. Glenn Campbell (1924–2001)," *Hoover Digest* 1 (2002), http://www.hoover.org/publications/hoover-digest/article/7514 (23 July 2013).

83. W. Glenn Campbell to Richard M. Scaife, 3 December 1962, folder 11, box 90, BP.

84. For evidence of the 1964 grant, see E. M. Moore Executive Assistant to the Director at the Hoover Institution to William Baroody, 10 September 1964, folder 11, box 90, BP.

85. J. E. Wallace Sterling to W. Glenn Campbell, 27 December 1962, folder 11, box 90, BP.

86. R. Daniel McMichael to C. E. Ford, 16 August 1963, folder 11, box 90, BP.

87. Stephen Shadegg, *What Happened to Goldwater?: The Inside Story of the 1964 Republican Campaign* (New York: Holt, Rinehart, and Winston, 1965).

88. For instance, upon seeing the page proofs of Shadegg's book, Goldwater wrote him a letter saying, "I think on the whole it is well done and will provide people reading of this campaign in the future with an incite [sic] to it that is far more than casual." In the same letter, Goldwater then made a "for your eyes only" admission, saying that by the end of the campaign he "was well aware of the inadequacies of the speeches...that came to us from [Baroody and others] in Washington." Barry Goldwater to Mr. Stephen Shadegg, 23 June 1965, folder: "Correspondence, Goldwater, Barry, 1964–1970," box 2, DKP.

89. Barry M. Goldwater with Jack Casserly, *Goldwater* (New York: Doubleday, 1988), 147–48.

90. Shadegg, *What Happened to Goldwater?*, 120.

91. Ibid., 132, 165–66.

92. Goldwater and Casserly, *Goldwater*, 156, 190.

93. Shadegg, *What Happened to Goldwater?*, 190, 194.

94. Goldwater and Casserly, *Goldwater*, 188.

95. "Campaign Speech before the American Political Science Association, Chicago, Illinois," 11 September 1964, folder 8, box 133, Series 2: 1964 Campaign, BGP.

96. "Nationwide TV Address on 'The Free Society,'" 22 October 1964, folder 18, box 133, Series 2: 1964 Campaign, BGP. Emphasis in original.

97. Shadegg, *What Happened to Goldwater?*, 250, 253.

98. Barry M. Goldwater, *With No Apologies: The Personal and Political Memoirs of United States Senator Barry M. Goldwater* (New York: William Morrow, 1979), 163–64. For more on the development of "law and order conservatism" in the 1960s, see Flamm, *Law and Order*.

99. For a description of the formation of the Free Society Association idea in Jamaica, see Denison Kitchel to Mr. John J. Kennedy, 25 June 1965, folder "Americans for Conservative Education," box 1, FSAP.

100. Articles of Incorporation of the Free Society Association, Inc., Washington, D.C., 10 May 1965, folder "By-Laws and Articles of Incorporation," box 1, FSAP.

101. A Suggested Publications Program for the Free Society Association, undated, folder "FSA By-Laws," box 1, FSAP.

102. Ibid.

103. For more on JBS's role in the history of modern conservatism see Mulloy, *The World of the John Birch Society*; Schoenwald, *A Time for Choosing*, chap. 3.

104. Statement by Barry Goldwater on the Free Society Association, 17 June 1965, folder "Press Release—F.S.A. Announcement by Goldwater, 6/17/65," box 13, FSAP.

105. "Statement of Cash and Contributor Totals per month," 23 February 1966, folder "Financial Data," box 3, FSAP.

106. Barry Goldwater to Mr. Denison Kitchel, 23 June 1965, folder "Goldwater File (DK Personal)," box 5, FSAP.

107. David S. Broder, "Kitchel Reveals 1960 Birch Link," *New York Times*, 19 July 1965.

108. Burley T. Owen of Dallas, Texas, to Denison Kitchel, 21 July 1965, folder "Birch Society," box 7, FSAP.

109. R. P. Terrell of Claverack, New York, to Denison Kitchel, 25 July 1965, folder "Birch Society," box 7, FSAP.

110. "Statement of Income and Expense for the Month Ending December 31, 1965," folder "Audit Reports," box 1, FSAP. "Statement of Cash and Contributor Totals per Month," 23 February 1966, folder "Financial Data," box 3, FSAP.

111. "The New Student Left" Pamphlet (Washington, D.C.: Free Society Association, December 1965), folder "FSA Publications," box 14, FSAP. "Black Power!: It's Gonna Be a Long Hot Decade," *Free Society Association Newsletter* 1, no. 10 (July–August 1966), folder "FSA-," box 10, FSAP.

112. Barry Goldwater to Denison Kitchel, 2 February 1966, folder unmarked, box 10, FSAP.

113. In January 1967 a list was drawn up "in the event of tax-exemption." "List of Conservatively-Oriented Foundations and Corporations," 11 January 1967, folder "FSA Correspondence," box 2, FSAP.

114. See Barry Goldwater to William J. Baroody, March 13, 1967, folder 20, box 48, Series 1: Personal Papers, BGP.

115. Barry Goldwater to William J. Baroody, June 15, 1967, folder 20, box 48, Series 1: Personal Papers, BGP.

116. On acquisition of tax exemption, see "A New Look at The Free Society Association: A Reevaluation of Purpose and Program," December 1967, folder "FSA Correspondence," box 2, FSAP. For notice of closing, see Denison Kitchel to Members, 1 June 1969, folder "FSA-," box 10, FSAP.

117. Minutes of the annual meeting of the Board of Trustees, American Enterprise Institute for Public Policy Research, 30 December 1964, folder 5, box 39, BP.

118. "Rightist Group Lists Expenses of $421,088," *St. Louis Post-Dispatch*, 20 January 1965, 15A.

119. Smith, *The Idea Brokers*, 178.

Chapter 2

1. Ronald A. Buel, "Hoover Library Gathers Material to Shed Light on Events' Overseas," *New York Times*, 2 June 1967.

2. William Baroody to Orville E. Melby, Treasurer of the Bendix Corporation, 8 July 1968, folder 4, box 59, BP.

3. William Baroody to Richard Nixon, 27 November 1968, folder 6, box 23, BP.

4. H. R. Haldeman to Mr. Cole, 1 May 1969, in Bruce Oudes, ed., *From: The President: Richard Nixon's Secret Files* (New York: Harper and Row, 1989), 29.

5. Richard Harwood and Laurence Stern, "Congressmen Seek Experts' Advice as Self-Improvement Becomes a Fad," *Washington Post*, 18 June 1969.

6. William Baroody to Arthur F. Burns, Counselor to President Nixon, 18 June 1969, folder 5, box 86, BP.

7. Arthur F. Burns, Counselor to President Nixon to William Baroody, 23 June 1969, folder 5, box 86, BP.

8. L. Higby to Mr. Huston, 14 July 1970, in Oudes, *From: The President*, 146.

9. H. R. Haldeman to Mr. Huston, 16 July 1970, in ibid., 147–48. On the "firebombing" see Critchlow, "Think Tanks, Antistatism, and Democracy," fn. 21, 293. Another point of contention between the administration and Brookings was over Brookings receiving IRS data to conduct a study on one of Nixon's tax reform proposals. See Charles Colson to John Dean, 1 May 1972, in Oudes, *From: The President*, 435.

10. H. R. Haldeman to Mr. Huston, 16 July 1970, in Oudes, *From: The President*, 147–48.

11. William Baroody to Richard A. Ware, Earhart Foundation, 11 March 1970, folder 5, box 59, BP.

12. "The Brookings Institution," 12 August 1970, folder 1, box 62, BP.

13. John S. Lynn, General Manager, Lilly Endowment, to William Baroody, 27 October 1970, folder 11, box 60, BP.

14. Memorandum to the Secretary of Defense Melvin Laird from William Baroody, 23 January 1971, folder "American Enterprise Institute—General, 1971–72," box A52, MLF.

15. Dan Thomasson, "Laird Plans a Haven for Ex-GOPers," *Washington Daily News*, 2 August 1971. Baroody was also able to enlist fundraising help from the chairman of the Federal Reserve, Arthur Burns, around the same time. See Arthur F. Burns, Chairman of the Federal Reserve to Mr. D. K. Ludwig, Chairman and President, National Bulk Carriers, Inc., 22 November 1971, folder "Baroody, Jr. William J.," box K2, AFB.

16. William Baroody to Mr. John Swearingen, Chairman of the Board, Standard Oil Company, 16 November 1971, folder 7, box 56, BP. All emphasis in original.

17. Baroody had a personal meeting with Coors in August 1971 to discuss such matters. William Baroody to Mr. Joseph Coors, Executive Vice President, Adolph Coors Company, 30 August 1971, folder 6, box 7, BP.

18. For details on the Scaife funding during this period, see "Letter to the Commissioner of the IRS," 6 May 1974, folder 4, box 44, BP, and "AEI Attachment to Form 990 for Fiscal Year July 1, 1971 to June 30, 1972," folder 7, box 43, BP.

19. "AEI Attachment to Form 990 for Fiscal Year July 1, 1971 to June 30, 1972," folder 7, box 43, BP.

20. William R. Kintner to William Baroody, 31 May 1972, folder 9, box 36, BP.

21. William Baroody to William R. Kintner, 7 June 1972, folder 9, box 36, BP.

22. "American Enterprise," in *Ford Foundation Newsletter*, 1 March 1972, 3.

23. DeMuth and Bowman, "The American Enterprise Institute," 16–17.

24. "Confidential: Prepared for Speakers at Baroody 20th Anniversary Dinner," 7 February 1974, folder "American Enterprise Institute," box 7, RFP.

25. "AEI Attachment to Form 990 for Fiscal Year July 1, 1971 to June 30, 1972," folder 7, box 43, BP. "AEI New and Increased Contributions over Prior Year for Fiscal Year 1973," folder 7, box 43, BP. These documents only show donations from Olin in the amount of $10,000 in both of the fiscal years ending in 1972 and 1973.

26. John Merrill Olin to William Baroody, 12 April 1972, folder 8, box 60, BP.

27. William Baroody to John Merrill Olin, 24 April 1972, folder 8, box 60, BP.

28. John Merrill Olin to William Baroody, 27 April 1972, folder 8, box 60, BP.

29. "Hoover Center to Stress Domestic Problems, Too," *New York Times*, 30 July 1972.

30. W. Glenn Campbell to Mr. Richard M. Scaife, Chairman, the Carthage Foundation, 18 August 1972, folder 1, box 91, BP.

31. Jack Anderson, "Powell's Lesson to Business Aired," *Washington Post*, 28 September 1972. Jack Anderson, "FBI Missed Blueprint by Powell," *Washington Post*, 29 September 1972. The *New York Times* also covered the memo after Anderson's first column. Fred P. Graham, "Powell Proposed Business Defense," *New York Times*, 29 September 1972.

32. This background is taken from the archival introduction to the memo at the Powell archives. Introduction to Lewis F. Powell Jr., "Attack on American Free Enterprise System," http://law.wlu.edu/powellarchives/page.asp?pageid=1251 (13 September 2013).

33. Lewis F. Powell Jr., "Attack on American Free Enterprise System," 23 August 1971, http://law.wlu.edu/deptimages/Powell Archives/PowellMemorandum-Typescript.pdf (5 August 2013).

34. William J. Baroody, "The Corporate Role in the Decade Ahead," delivered at the Business Council meeting, Hot Springs, Virginia, 20 October 1972, folder 6, box 86, BP.

35. John Merrill Olin to William Baroody, 12 March 1973, folder 8, box 60, BP. John Merrill Olin to William Baroody, 22 March 1973, folder 8, box 60, BP.

36. Richard M. Larry, Scaife Family Charitable Trusts, to William Baroody, 19 December 1972, folder 6, box 86, BP. William Baroody to Richard M. Larry, Scaife Family Charitable Trusts, 27 December 1972, folder 6, box 86, BP.

37. William J. Baroody, "Towards Intellectual Competition," *National Association of Manufacturers Reports*, 16 April 1973, folder "Baroody, William J. Sr.," box 290, RFP.

38. "Energy Project Outline," 5 October 1973, folder 3, box 72, BP.

39. Ibid.

40. "Laird Will Head 2-Year AEI Energy Project," *AEI Memorandum*, Winter 1973, folder "American Enterprise Institute (2)," box A129, MLF.

41. "Energy Project Outline," 5 October 1973, folder 3, box 72, BP.

42. "Confidential: Prepared for Speakers at Baroody 20th Anniversary Dinner," 7 February 1974, folder "American Enterprise Institute," box 7, RFP.

43. "Baroody Is Honored at Anniversary Dinner," *AEI Memorandum*, Winter 1973, folder "American Enterprise Institute (2)," box A129, MLF.

44. Patrick Buchanan to President Richard Nixon, 10 November 1972, in Oudes, *From: The President*, 564.

45. Ibid., 564–65.

46. Ibid., 565.

47. Ibid., 564.

48. For factual matters regarding the Heritage Foundation, particularly in its early history, I rely on an internal history of the think tank commissioned and published by Heritage on its twenty-five-year anniversary. While I think such a text is extremely useful for such factual matters, I have largely shunned using the book's analysis and interpretative threads in my writing given its largely ha-giographic approach. Written by longtime conservative activist and writer Lee Edwards, the approach taken to the think tank in the text is almost uniformly heroic and thus of limited utility as a work of critical scholarship. Lee Edwards, *The Power of Ideas: The Heritage Foundation at 25 Years* (Ottawa, Ill.: Jameson Books, 1997).

49. Ibid., 4.

50. Feulner's background here is taken from Sidney Bluementhal, "Heritage Led by a True Believer," *Washington Post*, 24 September 1985.

51. Ibid., 2.

52. Ibid., 4.

53. Ibid., 5.

54. Medvetz, *Think Tanks in America*, 252n35.

55. Edwards, *The Power of Ideas*, 5.

56. Paul M. Weyrich, "The Most Important Legacy of Joe Coors," 24 March 2003, http://enterstageright.com/archive/articles/0303/0303coors.htm (22 August 2013).

57. Edwards, *The Power of Ideas*, 8.

58. Karen Rothmyer, "Citizen Scaife," *Columbia Journalism Review* 20, no. 2 (July–August 1981). The same article notes that in the 1970s Scaife gave a total of $4 million to Heritage.

59. Edwards, *The Power of Ideas*, 10.

60. Memorandum from Ed Feulner, Jerry James, and Paul Weyrich to Joe Co-ors, 29 June 1973, folder 2, box 5, PWP.

61. Edwards, *The Power of Ideas*, 11. Internal Revenue Service to the Heritage Foundation, 27 November 1973, folder "Heritage Foundation," box 8, RFP.

62. Niels Bjerre-Poulsen has termed this Heritage model a "Second-Generation Think Tank." According to Bjerre-Poulsen, such a new think tank model would integrate "research, the marketing of ideas, and the 'cultivation' of congressional staffers and legislators, as well as the recruitment of dedicated conservatives for

government positions" ("The Heritage Foundation," 154). Given that my work shows AEI's concern for such a model, I reject the "second-generation" framing taken by Bjerre-Poulsen. However, it is undeniable that Heritage perfected such an institutional mission.

63. "The Heritage Foundation, Inc.: Prospectus for 1974," folder "Heritage Foundation," box 8, RFP.

64. Edwin J. Feulner, "Ideas, Think-Tanks and Governments," *Quadrant* 29 (November 1985): 22–26.

65. Connaught Coyne Marshner, "Federal Child Development: What's Developing?" (Washington, D.C.: Heritage Foundation, 1974), folder "Heritage Foundation," box 8, RFP.

66. Roger A. Freeman to Mr. Jerry P. James, President of the Heritage Foundation, 18 September 1974, folder "Heritage Foundation," box 8, RFP.

67. Marshner, "Federal Child Development," 33.

68. Onalee McGraw, *Secular Humanism and the Schools: The Issue Whose Time Has Come* (Washington, D.C.: Heritage Foundation, 1976), 17.

69. Stephen Isaacs, "Coors' Capital Connection: Heritage Foundation Fuels His Conservative Drive," *Washington Post*, 7 May 1975.

70. In my discussion of the impulses of postwar conservatism, I borrow from George Nash's still relevant work regarding the makeup of the postwar conservative movement. After the 1970s, Nash argues that the movement encompassed five impulses: libertarianism, traditionalist, anticommunist, neoconservative, and the interfaith religious right. Nash, in much of his work, argues that there were central institutions, such as the *National Review*, which sought to "fuse" these seemingly disparate impulses. I argue here that the Heritage Foundation in the 1970s was attempting to be another fusionist institution and would solidify that status in the 1980s. For my more extensive take on Nash's argument over the totality of his career, see Jason Stahl, book review of George H. Nash, *Reappraising the Right: The Past & Future of American Conservatism*, H-1960s, H-Net Reviews (March 2011), http://www.h-net.org/reviews/showrev.php?id=31209 (17 October 2013).

71. Lawrence D. Pratt, Treasurer of the Heritage Foundation, to Roger A. Freeman, 25 October 1974, folder "Heritage Foundation," box 8, RFP.

72. Ann M. Reilly, "Reagan's Think Tank," *Dun's Review*, April 1981, 112.

73. Quote from part 1 of the series: Stephen Isaacs, "Coors Beer—and Politics—Move East," *Washing Post*, 4 May 1975.

74. Stephen Isaacs, "Coors Bucks Network 'Bias': Sets Up Alternative TV News to Offset Liberals," *Washington Post*, 5 May 1975. Stephen Isaacs, "Coors-Backed Unit Seeks Defeat of Hill 'Radicals,'" *Washington Post*, 6 May 1975. Stephen Isaacs, "Coors' Capital Connection: Heritage Foundation Fuels His Conservative Drive," *Washington Post*, 7 May 1975.

75. "Grants and Contributions Summary, 1975–76 FY," folder 7, box 43, BP.

76. "AEI Attachment to Form 990 for Fiscal Year July 1, 1976 to June 30, 1977," folder 7, box 43, BP.

77. Robert G. Wingerter, President Libbey-Owens-Ford Company to the Board of Trustees of AEI, 28 May 1974, folder 5, box 56, BP.

78. "Hoover Institution Gifts, 1 September 1973 to 30 June 1974," folder "Hoover Institution: General," box 8, RFP.

79. "Status Report: Domestic Studies Program at the Hoover Institution, Stanford University," April 1974, folder "Hoover Institution: General," box 8, RFP.

80. Steven Rattner, "A Think Tank for Conservatives," *New York Times*, 23 March 1975.

81. Max R. Grossman, "Washington's Mostly Conservative Think Tank," *Finance Magazine*, December 1975.

82. David Pauly and Jeff B. Copeland, "Cerebration on the Right," *Newsweek*, 17 May 1976.

83. Presidential background information for meeting with William J. Baroody Sr. and Dr. Paul W. McCracken, 11 April 1975, folder "PR 7–1 4/10/75–4/14/75," box 55, GRFP. Presidential background information for meeting with Board of Trustees of American Enterprise Institute, 7 May 1975, folder "PR 7–1 5/3/75–5/7/75," box 56, GRFP.

84. Background information, President's drop-by at American Enterprise Institute's Dinner, May 19, 1976, folder TR1, 5/19/76–5/20/76 Executive, box 9, GRFP.

85. Pauly and Copeland, "Cerebration on the Right."

86. William Baroody to Mr. Irving Kristol, 13 November 1974, folder 4, box 17, BP. In this letter Baroody suggests that Kristol proposed the very idea of *Regulation* as well as making an entreaty to the Sloan Foundation.

87. Canedo, "The Rise of the Deregulation Movement"; Murphy, "On Our Own."

88. William Baroody to Mr. Arthur Singer of the Alfred P. Sloan Foundation, 22 August 1975, folder 2, box 56, BP.

89. William Baroody to Mr. Arthur Singer of the Alfred P. Sloan Foundation, 19 December 1975, folder 2, box 56, BP.

90. "AEI Attachment to Form 990 for Fiscal Year July 1, 1976 to June 30, 1977," folder 7, box 43, BP.

91. DeMuth and Bowman, "The American Enterprise Institute," 23.

92. Canedo, "The Rise of the Deregulation Movement"; Murphy, "On Our Own."

93. Letter from William Baroody to *Regulation* readers, undated, folder 11, box 43, BP.

94. "The Conservative's Think Tank," *Businessweek*, 2 May 1977.

95. Eileen Shanahan, "Casting Begins for the Next 'Shadow Cabinet,'" *New York Times*, 21 November 1976.

96. Smith, *Brookings at Seventy-Five*, 110.

97. Ibid., 111.

98. Ibid.

99. Warren M. Shapleigh, President Ralston Purina Company to John Merrill Olin, 9 May 1973, folder 8, box 60, BP.

100. "Brookings Needs Help," *Los Angeles Times*, undated, folder 5, box 86, BP.

101. "Two 'Think Tanks' with Growing Impact," *U.S. News and World Report*, 25 September 1978.

102. Critchlow, "Think Tanks, Antistatism, and Democracy," 294–95. Critchlow argues in the same article, and I concur, that this shift represents "a widespread acceptance of relativism, embodied institutionally in the think tanks, [which] has irrevocably altered the process of social investigation and the uses of social knowledge" (322).

103. Mr. Thomas P. Pike, Honorary Vice Chairman of the Board, Fluor Corporation to Mr. W. Glenn Campbell, 26 February 1976, folder 2, box 91, BP.

104. Robert A. Hornby to William Baroody, 4 October 1977, folder 3, box 37, BP.

105. William Baroody to Robert A. Hornby, 18 October 1977, folder 3, box 37, BP.

106. Morton Kondrake, "The Heritage Model," *New Republic*, 20 December 1980. Reilly, "Reagan's Think Tank."

107. Reilly, "Reagan's Think Tank."

108. Feulner, "Ideas, Think-Tanks and Governments," 22–26.

109. Kondrake, "The Heritage Model."

110. Feulner, "Ideas, Think-Tanks and Governments."

111. Rothmyer, "Citizen Scaife."

112. Reilly, "Reagan's Think Tank."

113. Ibid.

114. Doherty, *Radicals for Capitalism*, 410–11.

115. Ralph Raico, Senior Editor, *Inquiry*, to Professor F. A. Hayek, 7 April 1977, folder 20, box 14, HP.

116. "*Inquiry*: Announcing a New Political Affairs Magazine," folder 20, box 14, HP.

117. Letter from Edward H. Crane III, President of the Cato Institute, to supporters, undated, folder 20, box 14, HP.

118. *Cato's Letters*, vol. 1, no. 2, Spring 1979, folder 20, box 14, HP.

119. Irving Kristol, "On Corporate Philanthropy," *Wall Street Journal*, 21 March 1977.

120. *Cato's Letters*, vol. 1, no. 2, Spring 1979, folder 20, box 14, HP.

121. Robert A. Nisbet, "The Dilemma of Conservatives in a Populist Society," *Policy Review* (Spring 1978), 102.

122. Max M. Kampelman, "The Power of the Press: A Problem for Our Democracy," *Policy Review* (Fall 1978), 19.

123. "The Conservative's Think Tank," *Businessweek*, 2 May 1977. "The Other Think Tank," *Time*, 19 September 1977. Richard Burt, "Foreign Policy 'Counterestablishment,' Critical of Carter Policies, Emerging in Capital," *New York Times*, 27 March 1978. John Herbers, "Thunder on the Right Has Turned into an Insistent Rumble," *New York Times*, 4 June 1978. Ann Crittenden, "The Economic Wind's Blowing toward the Right—for Now," *New York Times*, 16 July 1978. Kenneth Lamott, "Right-Thinking Think Tank," *New York Times*, 23 July 1978. "Two

'Think Tanks' with Growing Impact," *U.S. News and World Report*, 25 September 1978. Peter Steinfels, "The Reasonable Right," *Esquire*, 13 February 1979.

124. "American Enterprise Institute Names President," *Wall Street Journal*, 22 March 1978.

125. Reilly, "Reagan's Think Tank."

Chapter 3

1. My background of the development of the relationship between Kristol and Wanniski is largely taken from Geoffrey Norman, "The Godfather of Neoconservatism (and His Family)," *Esquire* (13 February 1979): 37–42.

2. Ibid., 37.

3. Jude Wanniski, "It's Time to Cut Taxes," *Wall Street Journal*, 11 December 1974.

4. Norman, "The Godfather of Neoconservatism," 37.

5. Jude Wanniski, "The Mundell-Laffer Hypothesis—A New View of the World Economy," *Public Interest* (Spring 1975): footnote on page 32.

6. Ibid., 32–33.

7. Ibid., 31, 32.

8. Ibid., 49, italics in original, 51.

9. Ibid., footnote on page 49–50.

10. Norman, "The Godfather of Neoconservatism," 37.

11. Jude Wanniski, "Taxes, Revenues, and the 'Laffer Curve,'" *Public Interest* (Winter 1978): 3, drawing of the curve found on page 4.

12. Ibid., 7.

13. Ibid., 12, 13.

14. Ibid., 16. Kennedy's former economic advisers vehemently dissented from Wanniski's interpretation of the Kennedy tax cuts using the Laffer Curve. For instance, see Walter W. Heller, "The Kemp-Roth-Laffer Free Lunch," *Wall Street Journal*, 12 July 1978.

15. Jude Wanniski to William Baroody, 22 October 1976, folder 7, box 78, BP.

16. William Baroody to Jude Wanniski, 3 November 1976, folder 7, box 78, BP.

17. William Baroody to Mr. Leslie Lenkowsky, Director of Research, Smith Richardson Foundation, Inc., 24 November 1976, folder 7, box 78, BP. William Baroody to Jude Wanniski, 7 January 1977, folder 7, box 78, BP.

18. Jude Wanniski, *The Way the World Works: How Economies Fail and Succeed* (New York: Basic Books, 1978).

19. Sidney Blumenthal, "A Well-Connected Conservative: Scalia Was a Think Tank Scholar in 1977," *Washington Post*, 22 June 1986.

20. Benjamin J. Cohen, "Book Review of *The Way the World Works: How Economies Fail—And Succeed* by Jude Wanniski," *Journal of Interdisciplinary History* 10 (Autumn 1979): 358–60.

21. Norman, "The Godfather of Neoconservatism," 38.

22. Ibid., 37–38.

23. Irving Kristol, "The Meaning of Proposition 13," *Wall Street Journal*, 28 June 1978.

24. Milton Friedman, "The Limitations of Tax Limitation," *Policy Review* (Summer 1978): 7.

25. Ibid., 11.

26. Quoted in Heller, "The Kemp-Roth-Laffer Free Lunch."

27. Irving Kristol, "Will 'Conservative' Economics Work?," *Wall Street Journal*, 22 October 1979.

28. Paul Craig Roberts, "The Economic Case for Kemp-Roth," *Wall Street Journal*, 1 August 1978.

29. Jude Wanniski, "The No. 1 Problem," *New York Times*, 27 February 1980.

30. Irving Kristol, "The Battle for Reagan's Soul," *Wall Street Journal*, 16 May 1980.

31. Irving Kristol, "The New Republican Party," *Wall Street Journal*, 17 July 1980.

32. Bernard Weinraub, "Conservatives Aid Transition Plans behind the Scenes," *New York Times*, 5 December 1980.

33. Ann M. Reilly, "Reagan's Think Tank," *Dun's Review*, April 1981.

34. Phil McCombs, "Building a Heritage in the War of Ideas: The Tigers in the Think Tank Celebrate 10 Years," *Washington Post*, 3 October 1983.

35. Reilly, "Reagan's Think Tank."

36. Morton Kondrake, "The Heritage Model," *New Republic*, 20 December 1980.

37. Weinraub, "Conservatives Aid Transition Plans."

38. Kondrake, "The Heritage Model."

39. McCombs, "Building a Heritage in the War of Ideas."

40. Bernard Weinraub, "Hoover Institution Gains Entree to White House," *New York Times*, 22 December 1980. Art Pine, "Think Tanks Ponder Their Post-Electoral Political Future," *Washington Post*, 8 December 1980.

41. Pine, "Think Tanks."

42. Reilly, "Reagan's Think Tank."

43. Weinraub, "Conservatives Aid Transition Plans."

44. Kondrake, "The Heritage Model."

45. Reilly, "Reagan's Think Tank."

46. Edwin J. Feulner, "Ideas, Think-Tanks and Governments," *Quadrant* 29 (November 1985).

47. Charles L. Heatherly, ed., *Mandate for Leadership: Policy Management in a Conservative Administration* (Washington, D.C.: Heritage Foundation, 1981), 655–56.

48. George Gilder online profile at the Discover Institute, www.discovery.org /p/10 (1 December 2013).

49. For more on Fisher's efforts worldwide, see Cockett, *Thinking the Unthinkable*.

50. George Gilder, *Wealth and Poverty* (New York: Basic Books, 1981), ix–x.

51. Ibid., 179–80.

52. Ibid., 181.

53. Ibid., 188.

54. I borrow this phrase from Murphy, "On Our Own." Murphy's work is part of an emergent trend, particularly in the field of American Studies, to see "eco-

nomic conservatism" and "social conservatism" as not being inherently contradictory. See also Duggan, *Twilight of Equality*; Self, *All in the Family*.

55. Gilder, *Wealth and Poverty*, 72.

56. Ibid., 73.

57. Ibid., 74.

58. Ibid., xi–xii.

59. Ibid., 69.

60. Ibid., 87.

61. Ibid., 96.

62. Ibid., 98.

63. Carl F. Christ and Alan A. Walters, "The Mythology of Tax Cuts," *Policy Review* (Spring 1981): 73.

64. Ibid., 86, 85.

65. Ibid., 86.

66. Paul Craig Roberts, "Supply-Side Myths?," *Policy Review* (Summer 1981): 3.

67. Ibid., 3–4.

68. Jude Wanniski, "A Job Only Gold Can Do," *New York Times*, 27 August 1981.

69. Irving Kristol, "Economic Policy: Trouble on the Supply Side," *Wall Street Journal*, 27 October 1981.

70. Irving Kristol, "The Truth about 'Reaganomics,'" *Wall Street Journal*, 20 November 1981.

71. Tim Congdon, "What's Wrong with Supply-Side Economics," *Policy Review* (Summer 1982): 9.

72. Ibid., 10, 9.

73. Ibid., 14–15.

74. Ibid., 9.

75. All statistics taken from Jerry Tempalski, assistant secretary for tax policy, U.S. Department of the Treasury, "Revenue Effects of Major Tax Bills," Office of Tax Analysis, Working Paper 81, Revised September 2006, http://www.treasury.gov/resource-center/tax-policy/tax-analysis/Documents/ota81.pdf (1 December 2013). All figures in 2006 dollars.

76. Feulner, "Ideas, Think-Tanks and Governments."

77. Edwin J. Feulner Jr., "Foreword," in *Essays in Supply Side Economics*, ed. David G. Raboy (Washington, D.C.: Institute for Research on the Economics of Taxation, 1982): 1.

78. David G. Raboy, "The Theoretical Heritage of Supply Side Economics" in Raboy, *Essays in Supply Side Economics*, 31. It should be noted that Raboy's essay is not particularly rigorous as well and, ironically, reads much like Wanniski's writings—attempting to use the past two centuries of economic theory to support his position.

79. Bernard Weinraub, "Heritage Foundation 10 Years Later," *New York Times*, 30 September 1983.

80. Edward H. Crane, "A Conservative Isn't an Ideologue," *Wall Street Journal*, 25 November 1983.

81. Adam Meyerson, "What Conservatives Think of Reagan: A Symposium," *Policy Review* (Winter 1984): 13.

82. Paul M. Weyrich, "What Conservatives Think of Reagan: A Symposium," *Policy Review* (Winter 1984): 19.

83. Weinraub, "Heritage Foundation 10 Years Later."

84. McCombs, "Building a Heritage in the War of Ideas."

85. Ibid.

86. Martin Tolchin, "Brookings Thinks about Its Future," *New York Times*, 14 December 1983.

87. Critchlow's discussion on Brookings in the 1980s is taken from Critchlow, "Think Tanks, Antistatism, and Democracy," 293–95.

88. Financial details of Heritage's activities over the period from 1985 to 1989 are taken from the following sources: Sidney Bluementhal, "Heritage Led by a True Believer," *Washington Post*, 24 September 1985. "The Heritage Foundation 1986 Proposed Budget," folder 5, box 720, CBL. Heritage Foundation Tax Return for 1987, folder "Heritage/Fundraising," box 132, LEF. Heritage Foundation 1989 Annual Report, folder "Heritage/Fundraising," box 132, LEF. Heritage Foundation Tax Return for 1989, folder "Heritage/Finances," box 135, LEF.

89. "A Proposal to The Honorable Clare Boothe Luce (1986)," folder 6, box 720, CBL.

90. Thank-you letter from Edwin J. Feulner Jr. to Clare Booth Luce, 31 January 1986, folder 6, box 720, CBL.

91. Philip M. Boffey, "Heritage Foundation: Success in Obscurity," *New York Times*, 17 November 1985.

92. Benjamin Hart, "Abbie Hoffman's Nightmare: The New Generation of Conservative Activists," *Policy Review* (Fall 1987).

93. Margaret Shapiro, "Republican Think Tank Faces Funding Problem: American Enterprise Institute Orders Cuts," *Washington Post*, 28 December 1985.

94. Sidney Blumenthal, "Hard Times at the Think Tank: For American Enterprise Institute, a Crisis of Money and Conservatism," *Washington Post*, 26 June 1986.

95. Paul W. McCracken, President of AEI, to Professor F. A. Hayek, 23 October 1986, folder 4, box 10, HP.

96. Christopher C. DeMuth, President of AEI, to Clare Booth Luce, 15 September 1987, folder 10, box 719, CBL.

97. Warren Weaver Jr., "Cato Institute Marks 10 Years," *New York Times*, 19 May 1987.

98. Paul M. Weyrich, "The Reagan Revolution That Wasn't: Why Conservatives Have Achieved So Little," *Policy Review* (Summer 1987).

Chapter 4

1. Thomas Medvetz calls this a "double marginalization." He argues that academic disciplines marginalized themselves by being "less likely to reward those who dedicate their work to the goal of enlightening public debate" and that aca-

demics were also marginalized by think tanks who "played a pivotal role in undermining the relevance of autonomously produced social scientific knowledge in the United States by fortifying a system of social relations that relegates its producers to the margins of public debate" (*Think Tanks in America*, 225).

2. The DLC/PPI is a good example of what Thomas Medvetz describes as the "problem of demarcation" for scholars seeking to define a "think tank," or for the purposes of this book, a "conservative think tank." While I don't fully subscribe to Medvetz's anti-definitional stance, he is nevertheless correct that we cannot let definitions get in the way of including think tanks like Hoover and PPI in such a category given that they are "widely agreed-upon examples from the think tank category" (*Think Tanks in America*, 31). For PPI, I would take this stance even further and in some ways include the DLC itself since many in the media cited the organization as a think tank.

3. "Arena Profile: Al From" http://www.politico.com/arena/bio/al_from.html (28 September 2015).

4. Phil Gailey, "Dissidents Defy Top Democrats; Council Formed," *New York Times*, 1 March 1985.

5. Ibid.

6. Robin Toner, "Reporter's Notebook: Democrats Savoring Plans," *New York Times*, 15 December 1986.

7. Paul A. Gigot, "Democrat Heretic Wants Party's Soul at Center," *Wall Street Journal*, 22 April 1988.

8. Robert Lindsey, "Democratic Group Stumps California for Recruits," *New York Times*, 19 August 1985.

9. Ibid.

10. Peter T. Kilborn, "Democrats' Ideas on Economy Shift," *New York Times*, 12 August 1986. Paul Taylor, "Democrats' New Centrists Preen for '88," *Washington Post*, 10 November 1985. Phil Gailey, "Democrats Call Trade Top Issue," *New York Times*, 3 October 1985.

11. Gailey, "Dissidents Defy Top Democrats."

12. Gailey, "Democratic Group Seeks Mainstream," *New York Times*, 19 May 1985.

13. Gailey, "Dissidents Defy Top Democrats."

14. Jane Seaberry, "Conservative Democrats Set New Agenda," *Washington Post*, 9 November 1986.

15. Charles R. Babcock, "Democratic Conference Bankrolled," *Washington Post*, 9 March 1989.

16. E. J. Dionne Jr., "Party Told to Win Middle-Class Vote," *New York Times*, 12 March 1989.

17. Robin Toner, "Jackson Urges Support for 'Special Interest'" *New York Times*, 23 June 1987.

18. Thomas Oliphant, "Democratic Leadership Council, Chapter Two," *Boston Globe*, 21 March 1990.

19. William Galston and Elaine Ciulla Kamarck, "The Politics of Evasion: Democrats and the Presidency," *Progressive Policy Institute* (September 1989). Found in folder 9, box 104, TEP.

20. Senator Charles S. Robb, "Toward a Mainstream Agenda," *Mainstream Democrat* 1 (December 1989).

21. Senator Daniel Patrick Moynihan, "The Tax on Working People," *Mainstream Democrat* 2 (March 1990).

22. Paul Taylor and Maralee Schwartz, "Jackson's Unity Address Baffles, Irks Some Moderate Democrats," *Washington Post*, 25 March 1990.

23. Ibid.

24. Ibid.

25. Al From, "The New Politics," *Mainstream Democrat* 3 (March 1991).

26. Michael K. Frisby, "Jackson Counters Slight with Challenge," *Boston Globe*, 17 April 1991.

27. A. L. May, "Jackson Lashes Out at Council; He Says Moderates Dividing Democrats," *Atlanta Journal and Constitution*, 29 April 1991.

28. "Introducing the New Democrat," *New Democrat* 3 (May 1991).

29. David Osborne and Ted Gaebler, "Reinventing Government," *New Democrat* 4 (March 1992). For more in this genre, see the entire May 1992 issue of the *New Democrat* entitled "The New Economic World."

30. John D. Donahue, "Privatization and Its Discontents," *New Democrat* 4 (March 1992).

31. See John Milne, "Arkansas Governor, in N.H., Urges Party to Woo Middle Class," *Boston Globe*, 6 August 1991.

32. Larry Tye, "Democratic Group Says Party Must Target 'Ordinary People,'" *Boston Globe*, 27 June 1991.

33. Michael K. Frisby, "Jubilant Clinton Pushes Message," *Boston Globe*, 11 March 1992.

34. E. J. Dionne Jr., "Clinton Strives to Regain the Mantle of Innovator," *Washington Post*, 3 May 1992.

35. All quotes of Clinton's speech taken from Governor Bill Clinton, "Acceptance Speech to the Democratic National Convention," 16 July 1992, http://www.4president.org/speeches/billclinton1992acceptance.htm (14 December 2013).

36. Lloyd Grove, "Al From, the Life of the Party," *Washington Post*, 24 July 1992. Political scientist Stephen A. Borrelli disagrees with Jackson's assessment here. Borrelli argues that the DLC, and specifically Al From, was able to impose its "New Democrat" agenda on the 1992 platform. Borrelli, "Finding the Third Way."

37. Adam Nagourney, "Democratic Council to Play Key Role in Administration," *USA Today*, 4 December 1992.

38. Jonathan Marshall, "Moderate Demo Think Tank Guiding Clinton's Reform Plans," *San Francisco Chronicle*, 11 December 1992.

39. Dan Balz, "The Economic Buzzes in President-Elect Clinton's Ear," *Washington Post*, 8 December 1992.

40. David Von Drehle, "With Friends in High Places, Democratic Think Tank Bids for Glory," *Washington Post*, 7 December 1992.

41. Will Marshall, "Mandate for Change," *New Democrat* 5 (January 1993): 3.

42. Michael Kelly, "'New Democrats' Say Clinton Has Veered Left and Left Them," *New York Times*, 23 May 1993.

43. Al From, "Hey, Mom—What's a New Democrat?," *Washington Post*, 6 June 1993.

44. "Reinventing government" encompassed, among other measures, privatization of government services. Bruce Reed and Al Gore took the lead in the area within the administration. For information on Reed's role, see Stephen Barr, "Linking Politics and Policy; Reed Is at Center of Clinton Initiative," *Washington Post*, 17 May 1993. Gore's report on the subject, "From Red Tape to Results" strongly reflected DLC ideology about bringing a "business model" of "competition" and "customers" to the federal government. See the report at http://govinfo .library.unt.edu/npr/library/nprrpt/annrpt/redtpe93/index.html.

45. From, "Hey, Mom—What's a New Democrat?"

46. Thomas B. Edsall, "NAFTA Debate Reopens Wounds in the Body of the Democratic Party," *Washington Post*, 24 October 1993.

47. Ibid.

48. NAFTA and the National Interest," *New Democrat* 5 (November 1993): 5.

49. Debra J. Saunders, "Lemmings on the Right Enjoy a Following," *San Francisco Chronicle*, 23 December 1992.

50. Jill Lawrence, "GOP Moderates Form New PAC," *Chicago Sun-Times*, 16 December 1992.

51. Ibid.

52. "Forum: Who Should Succeed Reagan?," *Policy Review* 37 (Summer 1986).

53. Edwin J. Feulner Jr., "Fashionably out of Fashion Again," found in folder 27, box 98, HP.

54. "Key Conservative Plans Speech Critical of Bush," *Wall Street Journal*, 23 January 1992.

55. Edwin Feulner, "The Blame Game Begins," *Wall Street Journal*, 5 November 1992.

56. Milton Friedman to Edwin Feulner, 12 November 1992, folder 2, box 147, MFP.

57. Von Drehle, "With Friends in High Places."

58. Jonathan Marshall, "Moderate Demo Think Tank," *San Francisco Chronicle*, 11 December 1992.

59. Feulner, "Fashionably out of Fashion Again."

60. "Key Conservative Plans Speech Critical of Bush."

61. Jeremy Rosner, "Progressive Health Care Reform," *New Democrat* 4 (October 1992): 14.

62. Quoted in Balz, "The Economic Buzzes."

63. Stuart Butler, *A National Health System for America* (Washington, D.C.: Heritage Foundation, 1989).

64. Al From, "The Ruling Class," *New Democrat* 5 (July–August 1993): 2.

65. Al From and Will Marshall, "The First 100 Days," *New Democrat* 5 (May 1993): 5.

66. "The Prescription Is Competition," *New Democrat* 5 (December 1993): 4.

67. Carolyn Lochhead, "Clinton Courts 'New Democrats,'" *San Francisco Chronicle*, 4 December 1993.

68. William Kristol, "Memorandum to Republican Leaders: Defeating President Clinton's Health Care Proposal" (Washington, D.C.: Project for the Republican Future, December 2, 1993, typescript), 2. As quoted in Skocpol, *Boomerang*, 145. Skocpol's book offers the best discussion by far of the health care reform battle and Kristol's mobilization of the Republicans against the act. See also Rich, *Think Tanks*, chapters 4 and 5.

69. William Kristol, "How to Oppose the Health Plan—and Why," *Wall Street Journal*, 11 January 1994.

70. William Kristol, "Memorandum to Republican Leaders: Defeating President Clinton's Health Care Proposal" (Washington, D.C.: Project for the Republican Future, December 2, 1993, typescript), 4. As quoted in Skocpol, *Boomerang*, 146.

71. Al From, "The Mother Lode," *New Democrat* 5 (December 1993): 21.

72. Al From, "Carter Redux?," *New Democrat* 6 (July–August 1994): 28.

73. Center for Voting and Democracy, "Voting and Democracy Index: 1995," http://archive.fairvote.org/reports/1995/chp6/vdi05.html (28 September 2015).

74. For more information about the contract, and Heritage's role in its production, see Jeffrey B. Gayner, "The Contract with America: Implementing New Ideas in the U.S," 12 October 1995, http://www.heritage.org/research/lecture/the-contract-with-america-implementing new ideas in the us (12 July 2014).

75. Al From and Will Marshall, "A Fresh Start," *New Democrat* 7 (January–February 1995): 5.

76. Bennett Roth, "Searching for the New Democrat" *Houston Chronicle*, 8 December 1995.

77. From and Marshall, "A Fresh Start," 6.

78. Al From, "Happy Days Are Here . . . and Gone," *New Democrat* 6 (November 1994): 32.

79. Dan Balz, "Centrist Group Offers Reply to GOP 'Contract,'" *Washington Post*, 6 December 1994.

80. Remarks reported in John King, "Clinton Fires Back at Democratic Critics," *Chicago Sun-Times*, 6 December 1994.

81. Note that the very term "welfare reform" is one created by anti-welfare advocates who wish to end the Aid to Families with Dependent Children welfare program. I want to note this at the outset of my writing in order to distance myself from the position and its implications. I choose this avenue rather than the use of "scare quotes" throughout the chapter.

82. See, in particular, Medvetz, *Think Tanks in America*, chap. 5.

83. For just a few examples of writings outside the DLC linking welfare reform with the "credibility" of the New Democrat position, see Jodie Allen, "CBO's Necessary Operation: The Price of Doctoring the Health Numbers," *Washington Post*, 13 February 1994; Mona Charen, "Beware of Small Print in Welfare Reform," *Washington Times*, 7 February 1994; Mona Charen, "Does Clinton Have the Guts for Welfare Reform?," *Chicago Tribune*, 18 August 1993.

84. From, "Happy Days."

85. George Embrey, "Clinton Is Urged to Resurrect 'New Democrat' Label," *Columbus Post-Dispatch*, 3 November 1994.

86. "Memorandum for the President from Bruce Reed," 30 May 1994, folder 9, box 21, BRF.

87. Will Marshall, "Under Indictment: Americans Want to Change, but Not Demolish, the Welfare System," *New Democrat* 5 (December 1993): 8.

88. Michael Rothschild, "Beyond Repair: The Politics of the Machine Age Are Hopelessly Obsolete," *New Democrat* 7 (July–August 1995): 8–11.

89. Fred Siegel and Will Marshall, "Liberalism's Lost Tradition," *New Democrat* 7 (September–October 1995): 8.

90. Balz, "Centrist Group Offers Reply."

91. Will Marshall, "Putting Work First," *New Democrat* 7 (January–February 1995): 43.

92. Handwritten note by Bruce Reed, 12 August 1993, folder 1, box 54, BRF.

93. Once again, as this book has sought to point out, too often in the literature on conservative/neoliberal policy, there is a false binary invoked between "social/cultural" issues and "economic" issues. In this vein, "welfare reform" as an issue is often invoked solely in terms of its political value as "social/cultural issue"—one that showcases so-called middle-class values like family and personal responsibility. However, as with so many issues that animate American conservatism, this paradigm inhibits understanding of the multifaceted ways in which an issue can operate. In attempting to undermine this often false binary as it pertains to welfare reform, my hope is to show that the issue can operate simultaneously as a "social/cultural" issue and an "economic" one—it can speak to cultural "values" as well as economic "value" at the same time. For a more detailed discussion of this false binary, see Collins and Mayer, *Both Hands Tied*; Duggan, *Twilight of Equality*, 14–17; Fox Piven, "Welfare Reform."

94. "Welfare for Sale: An Interview with Peter Cove," *New Democrat* 5 (May 1993): 21.

95. Esther B. Fein, "For Job-Finding Concern, a Troubled Past," *New York Times*, 1 March 1994.

96. "Memorandum for the President from Bruce Reed," 30 May 1994, folder 9, box 21, BRF.

97. Marshall, "Putting Work First," 46.

98. Memorandum for the Chief of Staff from Rahm Emanuel and Bruce Reed, 30 March 1995, folder 6, box 37, BRF.

99. "21 August 1996 Singing Event Invite List," folder 3, box 35, BRF.

100. Marshall, "Putting Work First," 44.

101. Presidential Veto of Presidential Welfare Reform Bill HR 4, 9 January 1996, http://www.lectlaw.com/files/leg21.htm (3 January 2014).

102. President William Jefferson Clinton, "State of the Union Address," 23 January 1996, http://clinton4.nara.gov/WH/New/other/sotu.html (3 January 2014).

103. Al From, "More Than a Good Speech?," *New Democrat* 8 (March–April 1996): 36.

104. Lyn A. Hogan, "Work First: A Progressive Strategy to Replace Welfare with a Competitive Employment System," *Democratic Leadership Council Blueprint for Change*, June 1996.

105. Hugh B. Price, President of National Urban League, to President Clinton, 7 March 1996, folder 8, box 26, BRF.

106. Lawrence Mishel and John Schmitt, "Cutting Wages by Cutting Welfare: The Impact of Reform on the Low-Wage Labor Market," *Economic Policy Institute Briefing Paper*, September 1995, 5.

107. Bob Greenstein at Center on Budget and Policy Priorities to President Clinton, 15 July 1996, folder 2, box 35, BRF.

108. Vice President, Service Employees International Union, to President Clinton, 19 July 1996, folder 3, box 35, BRF. All emphasis in original.

109. "The DLC Update: Democrats Should Support Conference Report on Welfare," 30 July 1996 fax, folder 4, box 35, BRF.

110. Paul Wellstone, *The Conscience of a Liberal: Reclaiming the Compassionate Agenda* (New York: Random House, 2001), 101.

111. Transcript of CBS "This Morning" interview with Senator Don Nickles (R-Okla.), Senator Paul Wellstone (D-Minn.), 24 July 1996, folder 5, box 19, BRF.

112. DLC News Release from Al From, 31 July 1996, folder 4, box 35, BRF.

113. Craig Gilbert, "New Democrats' Claim Credit for Shift away from Liberal Focus," *Milwaukee Journal Sentinel*, 27 August 1996.

114. For final vote tallies, see Social Security Administration, "Vote Tallies on 1996 Welfare Reform Legislation," http://www.ssa.gov/history/tally1996.html (5 January 2014).

115. Jill Lawrence, "Clinton Back in Step with 'New Democrats,'" *USA Today*, 26 August 1996.

116. Gilbert, "New Democrats' Claim."

117. David Callahan, "$1 Billion for Conservative Ideas," *Nation*, 26 April 1999.

118. For more on this movement in the 1990s, see Clarkson, "Takin' it to the States"; Stahl, "Selling Conservatism," 197–205.

Chapter 5

1. This chapter attempts to write a history of the present despite the pitfalls often associated with such an endeavor. I do so as I am in agreement with Renee Romano that "even if we cannot write [recent] histories as well as we might like, and even if our versions of the recent past are sure to be revised as time passes, it is important that we try" in order to "shed light and historical understanding on the world we live in today." See Renee C. Romano, "Not Dead Yet: My Identity Crisis as a Historian of the Recent Past," in Potter and Romano, *Doing Recent History*, 42.

2. There is only now emerging a historiography of the Bush years, and it is very underdeveloped given our proximity to those years. However, my interpretation here of the administrative state under George W. Bush largely syncs with some of the first histories of these years. For instance, David Greenberg characterizes the Right in the Bush years as "promoting a radical epistemological relativism: the idea that established experts' claims lacked empirical foundation and represented simply a political choice." See David Greenberg, "Creating Their Own

Reality: The Bush Administration and Expertise in a Polarized Age," in Zelizer, *The Presidency of George W. Bush*, 203–4. Commentators during the 2000s were also obviously in tune with this dynamic as well. For instance, see Joshua Micah Marshall, "The Post-Modern President," *Washington Monthly*, September 2003; Ron Suskind, "Without a Doubt," *New York Times Magazine*, 17 October 2004.

3. Abella, *Soldiers of Reason*.

4. For more on the Council on Foreign Relations, see Grose, *Continuing the Inquiry*; Shoup and Minter, *Imperial Brain Trust*.

5. Draft Letter for Mr. Charles Stewart Mott, The Charles Stewart Mott Foundation, undated, folder 7, box 87, BP.

6. Richard Burt, "Foreign Policy 'Counterestablishment,' Critical of Carter Policies, Emerging in Capital," *New York Times*, 27 March 1978. Such a neoconservative position was also deeply concerned with overcoming a so-called Vietnam Syndrome, whereby Americans were reluctant to exercise military force around the world. For more, see McAlister, *Epic Encounters*, chap. 4.

7. Bacevich, *American Empire*, 125.

8. From the U.S. Commission on National Security/21st Century, *New World Coming: the United States Commission on National Security/21st Century* (Washington, D.C., 1999), 128. As quoted in Bacevich, *American Empire*, 142–43.

9. William Kristol and Robert Kagan, "Toward a Neo-Reaganite Foreign Policy," *Foreign Affairs* 75 (July–August 1996).

10. Kim R. Holmes and John Hillen, "Misreading Reagan's Legacy," *Foreign Affairs* 75 (September–October 1996).

11. Most think tank scholars with looser definitions of "think tanks," argue that PNAC should be recognized as one. See, for example, Medvetz, *Think Tanks in America*, 172.

12. Elliott Abrams, Gary Bauer, William J. Bennett, Jeb Bush, Dick Cheney, Eliot A. Cohen, Midge Decter, Paula Dobriansky, Steve Forbes, Aaron Friedberg, Francis Fukuyama, Frank Gaffney, Fred C. Ikle, Donald Kagan, Zalmay Khalilzad, I. Lewis Libby, Norman Podhoretz, Dan Quayle, Peter W. Rodman, Stephen P. Rosen, Henry S. Rowen, Donald Rumsfeld, Vin Weber, George Weigel, and Paul Wolfowitz, "Statement of Principles," Project for the New American Century, 3 June 1997, http://www.newamericancentury.org/statementofprinciples.htm (15 March 2007).

13. Scott McConnell, "The Weekly Standard's War," *American Conservative*, 21 November 2005.

14. Michael Dolny, "The Think Tank Spectrum," Fairness and Accuracy in Reporting, 1 May 1996, http://www.fair.org/index.php?page=1357 (7 September 2014). For the FAIR study of think tank references in 1996, see Michael Dolny, "New Survey on Think Tanks," Fairness and Accuracy in Reporting, 1 July 1997, http://www.fair.org/index.php?page=1391 (7 September 2014).

15. Michael Dolny, "What's in a Label?," Fairness and Accuracy in Reporting, 1 May 1998, http://www.fair.org/index.php?page=1425 (7 September 2014). For the 1998 and 1999 think tank citation numbers, see Michael Dolny, "New Study: Center/Right Think Tanks Dominate News," Fairness and Accuracy in

Reporting, 13 June 2000, http://fair.org/press-release/new-study-centerright
-think-tanks-dominate-news (7 November 2014).

16. "Saddam Must Go," *Weekly Standard*, 17 November 1997.

17. Elliott Abrams, Richard L. Armitage, William J. Bennett, Jeffrey Bergner, John Bolton, Paula Dobriansky, Francis Fukuyama, Robert Kagan, Zalmay Khalilzad, William Kristol, Richard Perle, Peter W. Rodman, Donald Rumsfeld, William Schneider Jr., Vin Weber, Paul Wolfowitz, R. James Woolsey, and Robert B. Zoellick, "Letter to President Clinton on Iraq," Project for the New American Century, 26 January 1998, http://www.newamericancentury.org/iraqclintonlet ter.htm (15 March 2007).

18. Elliott Abrams, William J. Bennett, Jeffrey Bergner, John Bolton, Paula Dobriansky, Francis Fukuyama, Robert Kagan, Zalmay Khalilzad, William Kristol, Richard Perle, Peter W. Rodman, Donald Rumsfeld, William Schneider Jr., Vin Weber, Paul Wolfowitz, R. James Woolsey, and Robert B. Zoellick, "Letter to Gingrich and Lott on Iraq," Project for the New American Century, 29 May 1998, http://www.newamericancentury.org/iraqletter1998.htm (15 March 2007).

19. Thomas Library of Congress Catalogue, "Iraq Liberation Act of 1998," HR 4655 as passed by both Houses, http://thomas.loc.gov/cgi-bin/query/z?c105:H.R .4655.ENR: (11 November 2014).

20. Bacevich, *American Empire*, 151.

21. Peter Bergen, "Armchair Provocateur," *Washington Monthly*, December 2003. Much of my profile of Mylroie is drawn from this Bergen profile.

22. Juan Cole, "Mylroie as Bush Rasputine," *Informed Comment*, 7 July 2004, http://www.juancole.com/2004/07/mylroie-as-bush-rasputine-peter-bergen .html (11 November 2014).

23. Michael Dolny, "Think Tanks Y2K," Fairness and Accuracy in Reporting, 1 August 2001, http://fair.org/extra-online-articles/think-tanks-y2k/ (11 November 2014).

24. Bacevich, *American Empire*, 139, 269n65. Emphasis in original.

25. Thomas Donnelly (principal author), "Rebuilding America's Defenses: Strategy, Forces and Resources for a New Century," *Project for the New American Century*, September 2000, http://www.newamericancentury.org/RebuildingAmericasDe fenses.pdf (15 March 2007) and in author's possession.

26. Robert E. Moffit, George Nesterczuk, and Donald J. Devine, "Taking Charge of Federal Personnel," Heritage Foundation Backgrounder #1404, 10 January 2001, http://www.heritage.org/Research/GovernmentReform/BG1404.cfm (3 November 2014).

27. Robin Toner, "Conservatives Savor Their Role as Insiders at the White House," *New York Times*, 19 March 2001.

28. Ron Suskind, "Why Are These Men Laughing?," *Esquire*, January 2003.

29. Suskind, *The Price of Loyalty*.

30. *CNN Live This Morning*, "America under Attack: Former CIA Director Asserts Iraq May Be behind Terrorist Attacks," first broadcast on 12 September 2001 by CNN. Transcript #091213CN.V74. News, LexisNexis Academic.

31. Ibid.

32. CNN Live Event/Special, "America under Attack: How Could It Happen?," first broadcast on 12 September 2001 by CNN. Transcript #091260CN.V54. News, LexisNexis Academic.

33. William Kristol, Richard V. Allen, Gary Bauer, Jeffrey Bell, William J. Bennett, Rudy Boshwitz, Jeffrey Bergner, Eliot A. Cohen, Seth Cropsey, Midge Decter, Thomas Donnelly, Nicholas Eberstadt, Hillel Fradkin, Aaron Friedberg, Francis Fukuyama, Frank Gaffney, Jeffrey Gedmin, Reuel Marc Gerecht, Charles Hill, Bruce P. Jackson, Eli S. Jacobs, Michael Joyce, Donald Kagan, Robert Kagan, Jeane Kirkpatrick, Charles Krauthammer, John Lehman, Clifford May, Martin Peretz, Richard Perle, Norman Podhoretz, Stephen P. Rosen, Randy Scheunemann, Gary Schmitt, William Schneider Jr., Richard H. Shultz, Henry Sokolski, Stephen J. Solarz, Vin Weber, Leon Wieseltier, and Marshall Wittmann, "Letter to President Bush on the War on Terrorism," Project for the New American Century, 20 September 2001, http://www.newamericancentury.org/Bushletter .htm (15 March 2007).

34. Gary Schmitt and Tom Donnelly, "What Our Enemies Want," *Weekly Standard*, 24 September 2001.

35. Clarke, *Against All Enemies*, 30.

36. Ibid., 31.

37. Michael Dolny, "Think Tanks in a Time of Crisis," Fairness and Accuracy in Reporting, 1 March 2002, http://fair.org/extra-online-articles/think-tanks -in-a-time-of-crisis/ (1 November 2014). This trend would continue in 2002, leading Dolny (the author of the FAIR studies) to conclude that after 9/11 there was (and would continue to be) "a decline in visibility of domestic policy think tanks, an increase in exposure for foreign policy think tanks, and an increasing focus on centrist to conservative voices, leaving progressives out of the debate." See Michael Dolny, "Spectrum Narrows Further in 2002," Fairness and Accuracy in Reporting, 1 July 2003, http://fair.org/extra-online-articles/spectrum-narrows -further-in-2002/ (1 November 2014).

38. Ken Adelman, Gary Bauer, Jeffrey Bell, William J. Bennett, Ellen Bork, Linda Chavez, Eliot Cohen, Midge Decter, Thomas Donnelly, Nicholas Eberstadt, Hillel Fradkin, Frank Gaffney, Jeffrey Gedmin, Reuel Marc Gerecht, Charles Hill, Bruce P. Jackson, Donald Kagan, Robert Kagan, William Kristol, John Lehman, Tod Lindberg, Rich Lowry, Clifford May, Joshua Muravchik, Martin Peretz, Richard Perle, Daniel Pipes, Norman Podhoretz, Stephen P. Rosen, Randy Scheunemann, Gary Schmitt, William Schneider Jr., Marshall Wittmann, and R. James Woolsey, "Letter to President Bush on Israel, Arafat and the War on Terrorism," Project for the New American Century, 3 April 2002, http://www .newamericancentury.org/Bushletter-040302.htm (15 March 2007).

39. James Risen, "How Pair's Finding on Terror Led to Clash on Shaping Intelligence," *New York Times*, 28 April 2004.

40. For more on the Office of Special Plans, see Seymour Hersh, "Selective Intelligence," *New Yorker*, 12 May 2003.

41. "How to Craft a Congressional Resolution on Iraq," *DLC New Dem Daily*, 19 September 2002, http://www.dlc.org/ndol_ci.cfm?kaid=131&subid=192&contentid =250854 (15 April 2004).

42. "A Tough, Clear Resolution, Not a Rubber Stamp," *DLC New Dem Daily*, 23 September 2002, http://www.dlc.org/ndol_ci.cfm?kaid=131&subid=192&contentid =250886 (15 April 2004).

43. "Change the Tone, Mr. President," *DLC New Dem Daily*, 26 September 2002, http://www.ndol.org/ndol_ci.cfm?kaid=131&subid=192&contentid=250900 (15 April 2004).

44. "A Time for Resolve," *DLC New Dem Daily*, 3 October 2002, http://www .dlc.org/ndol_ci.cfm?kaid=131&subid=192&contentid=250924 (15 April 2004).

45. "Democrats and Iraq," *DLC New Dem Daily*, 15 October 2002, http://www .dlc.org/ndol_ci.cfm?kaid=131&subid=192&contentid=250948 (15 April 2004).

46. Kenneth M. Pollack, *The Threatening Storm: The Case for Invading Iraq* (New York: Random House, 2002). For instance, Pollack appeared on the *Oprah Winfrey Show* to advocate for war. See Bill Moyers Journal, "Buying the War," http:// www.pbs.org/moyers/journal/btw/watch.html (1 November 2014).

47. William Kristol, Gary Bauer, Max Boot, Frank Carlucci, Eliot Cohen, Midge Decter, Thomas Donnelly, Frank Gaffney, Daniel Goure, Bruce P. Jackson, Donald Kagan, Robert Kagan, Lewis E. Lehrman, Tod Lindberg, Rich Lowry, Daniel McKivergan, Joshua Muravchik, Danielle Pletka, Norman Podhoretz, Stephen P. Rosen, Randy Scheunemann, Gary Schmitt, William Schneider Jr., Richard Shultz, Henry Sokolski, Chris Williams, and R. James Woolsey, "Letter to President Bush," Project for the New American Century, 23 January 2003, http://www .newamericancentury.org/defense-20030123.htm (15 March 2007).

48. Peter Jennings, "Specials and Breaking News," 26 February 2003, ABC News, LexisNexis Academic Transcripts.

49. Ronald Asmus, Max Boot, Frank Carlucci, Eliot Cohen, Ivo H. Daalder, Thomas Donnelly, Peter Galbraith, Jeffrey Gedmin, Robert S. Gelbard, Reuel Marc Gerecht, Charles Hill, Martin S. Indyk, Bruce P. Jackson, Robert Kagan, Craig Kennedy, William Kristol, Tod Lindberg, Rich Lowry, Will Marshall, Joshua Muravchik, Danielle Pletka, Dennis Ross, Randy Scheunemann, Gary Schmitt, Walter Slocombe, James B. Steinberg, and R. James Woolsey, "Statement on Post-War Iraq," Project for the New American Century, 19 March 2003, http:// www.newamericancentury.org/iraq-20030319.htm (15 March 2007).

50. Naomi Klein, "Baghdad Year Zero: Pillaging Iraq in Pursuit of a Neocon Utopia," *Harper's Magazine*, September 2004.

51. Rajiv Chandrasekaran, "Best-Connected Were Sent to Rebuild Iraq," *Washington Post*, 16 September 2006.

52. Ariana Eunjung Cha, "In Iraq, the Job Opportunity of a Lifetime," *Washington Post*, 23 May 2004. For more on conservative political economy and think tank staffing in Iraq, see "Let's All Go to the Yard Sale," *Economist*, 25 September 2003. Chandrasekaran, *Imperial Life in the Emerald City*. Daphne Eviatar, "Free-Market Iraq? Not So Fast," *New York Times*, 10 January 2004. Matthew Harwood, "Pinkertons at the CPA," *Washington Monthly*, April 2005. Klein, *The Shock*

Doctrine. Naomi Klein, "The Rise of Disaster Capitalism," *Nation*, 2 May 2005. Paul Krugman, "Battlefield of Dreams," *New York Times*, 4 May 2004. Paul Krugman, "Who Lost Iraq?," *New York Times*, 29 June 2004.

53. Ron Suskind, "Without a Doubt," *New York Times Magazine*, 17 October 2004.

54. For a more detailed account of think tanks and their role in social security privatization, see the conclusion of Stahl, "Selling Conservatism."

55. This did not stop many at conservative think tanks from using the chaos of Katrina to impose conservative economic policies on New Orleans. For more, see John R. Wilke and Brody Mullins, "After Katrina, Republicans Back a Sea of Conservative Ideas," *Wall Street Journal*, 15 September 2005.

56. Michael Abramowitz and Glenn Kessler, "Hawks Bolster Skeptical President," *Washington Post*, 10 December 2006.

57. "Online Biography Frederick W. Kagan," American Enterprise Institute, http://www.aei.org/author/frederick-w-kagan/ (1 November 2014).

58. Michael Dolny, "The Incredible Shrinking Think Tank," Fairness and Accuracy in Reporting, 1 March 2008, http://fair.org/extra-online-articles/The-Incredible-Shrinking-Think-Tank/ (15 November 2014).

59. Greenberg, "Creating Their Own Reality," 222–23.

Conclusion

1. For a good analysis of the extent to which the ACA is similar to Heritage proposals, see: "Obama Says Heritage Foundation is Source of Health Exchange Idea," Politifact, 1 April 2010, http://www.politifact.com/truth-o-meter/statements/2010/apr/01/barack-obama/obama-says-heritage-foundation-source-health-excha/ (21 November 2014).

2. Stuart M. Butler and Edmund F. Haislmaier, *A National Health System for America* (Washington, D.C.: Heritage Foundation, 1989).

3. For instance, see Robert E. Moffit, "The Rationale for a Statewide Health insurance Exchange," Heritage Foundation Web Memo, 5 October 2006, http://www.heritage.org/research/reports/2006/10/the-rationale-for-a-statewide-health-insurance-exchange (21 November 2014).

4. For more on Feulner's articulation of the goals of Heritage Action, see Edwin J. Feulner and Michael A. Needham, "New Fangs for the Conservative 'Beast,'" *Wall Street Journal*, 12 April 2010.

5. Many pundits and reporters wrote of these changes at Heritage as if they were fundamental alterations in the think tank's goals and methods. See, for instance, Molly Ball, "The Fall of the Heritage Foundation and the Death of Republican Ideas," *Atlantic*, September 2013. Julia Ioffe, "A 31-Year-Old Is Tearing Apart the Heritage Foundation," *New Republic*, 24 November 2013. Zeke J. Miller, "Hidden Hand: How Heritage Action Drove D.C. to Shut Down," *Time*, 30 September 2013. Jennifer Steinhauer and Jonathan Weisman, "In the DeMint Era at Heritage, a Shift from Policy to Politics," *New York Times*, 23 February 2014. I lay out in detail why I think those claims are false here: Jason Stahl, "The Heritage Foundation

Has Always Been Full of Hacks," *Salon.com*, 20 October 2013, http://www.salon.com/2013/10/20/the_heritage_foundation_has_always_been_full_of_hacks/ (21 November 2013).

6. Zachary A. Goldfarb, "Exclusive: One of Washington's Wealthiest Is Giving $20 Million to a Top Conservative Think Tank," *Washington Post Wonkblog*, 24 February 2014, http://www.washingtonpost.com/blogs/wonkblog/wp/2014/02/24/exclusive-one-of-washingtons-wealthiest-is-giving-20-million-to-a-top-conservative-think-tank/ (21 November 2014). Pema Levy, "Arthur Brooks's Push to Make the American Enterprise Institute—and Republicans—Relevant Again," *Newsweek*, 1 April 2014.

7. Ben Smith, "Democratic Leadership Council Will Fold," *Politico.com*, 7 February 2011, http://www.politico.com/blogs/bensmith/0211/Democratic_Leadership_Council_will_fold.html (21 November 2014).

8. Michael Scherer, "Inside Obama's Idea Factory in Washington," *Time*, 21 November 2008, http://content.time.com/time/politics/article/0,8599,1861305,00.html (21 November 2014).

Selected Bibliography

Manuscript Collections

Ann Arbor, Mich.
   Gerald R. Ford Presidential Library
      Arthur F. Burns Files
      President Gerald R. Ford Papers—White House Central Subject Files
      Melvin R. Laird Files
Little Rock, Ark.
   William J. Clinton Presidential Library
      Bruce Reed Files
Stanford, Calif.
   Hoover Institution Archives
      Thomas Byrne Edsall Papers
      Lee Edwards Papers
      Free Society Association Records
      Roger A. Freeman Papers
      Milton Friedman Papers
      Friedrich A. von Hayek Papers
      B. Edwin Hutchinson Papers
      Denison Kitchel Papers
Tempe, Ariz.
   Arizona Historical Foundation
      The Personal and Political Papers of Senator Barry M. Goldwater
Washington, D.C.
   Library of Congress
      William J. Baroody Papers
      Clare Boothe Luce Papers
      Paul M. Weyrich Scrapbooks

Secondary Sources

Abella, Alex. *Soldiers of Reason: The RAND Corporation and the Rise of the American Empire.* New York: Mariner Books, 2009.

Akin, William E. *Technocracy and the American Dream: The Technocrat Movement, 1900–1941.* Berkeley: University of California Press, 1977.

Amadae, S. M. *Rationalizing Capitalist Democracy: The Cold War Origins of Rational Choice Liberalism.* Chicago: University of Chicago Press, 2003.

Andrew, John A. *The Other Side of the Sixties Young Americans for Freedom and the Rise of Conservative Politics.* New Brunswick, N.J.: Rutgers University Press, 1997.

Bacevich, Andrew J. *American Empire: The Realities and Consequences of U.S. Diplomacy*. Cambridge, Mass.: Harvard University Press, 2002.

Bailey, Beth. *Sex in the Heartland*. Cambridge, Mass.: Harvard University Press, 1999.

Bender, Thomas, and Carl E. Schorske, eds. *American Academic Culture in Transformation*. Princeton, N.J.: Princeton University Press, 1998.

Bernstein, Michael A. *A Perilous Progress: Economists and Public Purpose in Twentieth-Century America*. Princeton: Princeton University Press, 2004.

Bjerre-Poulsen, Niels. "The Heritage Foundation: A Second-Generation Think Tank." *Journal of Policy History* 3, no. 2 (1991): 152–72.

Blumenthal, Sidney. *The Rise of the Counter-Establishment: From Conservative Ideology to Political Power*. New York: Crown, 1986.

Borrelli, Stephen A. "Finding the Third Way: Bill Clinton, the DLC, and the Democratic Platform of 1992." *Journal of Policy History* 13, no. 4 (October 2001): 429–62.

Borstelmann, Thomas. *The 1970s: A New Global History from Civil Rights to Economic Inequality*. Princeton, N.J.: Princeton University Press, 2011.

Brennan, Mary C. *Turning Right in the Sixties: The Conservative Capture of the GOP*. Chapel Hill: University of North Carolina Press, 2007.

Burgin, Angus. *The Great Persuasion: Reinventing Free Markets since the Depression*. Cambridge, Mass.: Harvard University Press, 2012.

Burns, Jennifer. *Goddess of the Market: Ayn Rand and the American Right*. Cambridge: Oxford University Press, 2009.

Canedo, Eduardo Federico. "The Rise of the Deregulation Movement in Modern America, 1957–1980." Ph.D. diss., Columbia University, 2008.

Carter, Dan T. *The Politics of Rage: George Wallace, the Origins of the New Conservatism, and the Transformation of American Politics*. Baton Rouge: Louisiana State University Press, 2001.

Chandrasekaran, Rajiv. *Imperial Life in the Emerald City: Inside Iraq's Green Zone*. New York: Vintage Books, 2007.

Clarke, Richard A. *Against All Enemies: Inside America's War on Terror*. New York: Free Press, 2004.

Clarkson, Frederick. "Takin' It to the States: The Rise of Conservative State-Level Think Tanks." *Public Eye* 13, nos. 2–3 (1999).

Cockett, Richard. *Thinking the Unthinkable: Think-Tanks and the Economic Counter-Revolution, 1931–83*. London: Fontana Press, 1995.

Collins, Jane Lou, and Victoria Mayer. *Both Hands Tied: Welfare Reform and the Race to the Bottom of the Low-Wage Labor Market*. Chicago: University of Chicago Press, 2010.

Cowie, Jefferson. *Stayin' Alive: The 1970s and the Last Days of the Working Class*. New York: The New Press, 2010.

Critchlow, Donald T. *The Brookings Institution, 1916–1952: Expertise and the Public Interest in a Democratic Society*. DeKalb: Northern Illinois University Press, 1985.

———. *The Conservative Ascendancy: How the Republican Right Rose to Power in Modern America*. Lawrence: University Press of Kansas, 2011.

———. *Phyllis Schlafly and Grassroots Conservatism: A Woman's Crusade*. Princeton, N.J.: Princeton University Press, 2005.

———. "Think Tanks, Antistatism, and Democracy: The Nonpartisan Ideal and Policy Research in the United States, 1913–1987," in *The State and Social Investigation in Britain and the United States*, edited by Mary Furner and Michael J. Lacy, 279–322. Cambridge: Cambridge University Press, 1993.

Cuordileone, K. A. *Manhood and American Political Culture in the Cold War*. New York: Routledge, 2004.

DeMuth, Christopher C., and Karlyn Bowman. "The American Enterprise Institute: A Brief History." Unpublished manuscript in author's possession.

Doherty, Brian. *Radicals for Capitalism: A Freewheeling History of the Modern American Libertarian Movement*. New York: PublicAffairs, 2008.

Duggan, Lisa. *The Twilight of Equality?: Neoliberalism, Cultural Politics, and the Attack on Democracy*. Boston: Beacon Press, 2003.

Easton, Nina J. *Gang of Five: Leaders at the Center of the Conservative Crusade*. New York: Simon and Schuster, 2001.

Edsall, Thomas Byrne, and Mary D. Edsall. *Chain Reaction: The Impact of Race, Rights, and Taxes on American Politics*. New York: Norton, 1991.

Farber, David R, and Jeff Roche, eds. *The Conservative Sixties*. New York: P. Lang, 2003.

Flamm, Michael W. *Law and Order: Street Crime, Civil Unrest, and the Crisis of Liberalism in the 1960s*. New York: Columbia University Press, 2005.

Foner, Eric. *The Story of American Freedom*. New York: Norton, 1999.

Formisano, Ronald P. *Boston against Busing: Race, Class, and Ethnicity in the 1960s and 1970s*. Chapel Hill: University of North Carolina Press, 2004.

Fox Piven, Frances. "Welfare Reform and the Economic and Cultural Reconstruction of Low Wage Labor Markets." *City & Society* 10, no. 1 (1998): 21–36.

Freedman, Samuel G. *The Inheritance: How Three Families and the American Political Majority Moved from Left to Right*. New York: Simon and Schuster, 1998.

Gilman, Nils. *Mandarins of the Future: Modernization Theory in Cold War America*. Baltimore, Md.: Johns Hopkins University Press, 2007.

Grose, Peter. *Continuing the Inquiry: The Council on Foreign Relations from 1921 to 1996*. New York: Council on Foreign Relations Press, 2006.

Hall, Stuart. "The Toad in the Garden: Thatcherism among the Theorists." In *Marxism and the Interpretation of Culture*, edited by Cary Nelson and Lawrence Grossberg, 35–74. Urbana: University of Illinois Press, 1988.

Harvey, David. *A Brief History of Neoliberalism*. Oxford: Oxford University Press, 2009.

Hemmer, Nicole. "Messengers of the Right: Media and the Modern Conservative Movement." Ph.D. diss., Columbia University, 2010.

Herman, Ellen. *The Romance of American Psychology: Political Culture in the Age of Experts*. Berkeley: University of California Press, 1995.

Himmelstein, Jerome L. *To the Right: The Transformation of American Conservatism*. Berkeley: University of California Press, 1992.

Hodgson, Godfrey. *America in Our Time*. New York: Doubleday, 1976.

Judis, John B. *The Paradox of American Democracy: Elites, Special Interests, and the Betrayal of Public Trust*. New York: Pantheon, 2001.

Kalman, Laura. *Right Star Rising: A New Politics, 1974–1980*. New York: Norton, 2010.

Klatch, Rebecca E. *A Generation Divided: The New Left, The New Right, and the 1960s*. Berkeley: University of California Press, 1999.

———. *Women of the New Right*. Philadelphia: Temple University Press, 1986.

Klein, Naomi. *The Shock Doctrine: The Rise of Disaster Capitalism*. New York: Picador, 2008.

May, Elaine Tyler. *Homeward Bound: American Families in the Cold War Era*. New York: Basic Books, 2008.

McAlister, Melani. *Epic Encounters: Culture, Media, and U.S. Interests in the Middle East since 1945*. Berkeley: University of California Press, 2005.

McGirr, Lisa. "A History of the Conservative Movement from the Bottom Up." *Journal of Policy History* 14, no. 3 (2002): 331–39.

———. *Suburban Warriors: The Origins of the New American Right*. Princeton, N.J.: Princeton University Press, 2001.

Medvetz, Thomas. *Think Tanks in America*. Chicago: University of Chicago Press, 2012.

Moore, Leonard Joseph. "Good Old-Fashioned New Social History and the Twentieth-Century American Right." *Reviews in American History* 24, no. 4 (1996): 555–73.

Moreton, Bethany. *To Serve God and Wal-Mart: The Making of Christian Free Enterprise*. Cambridge, Mass.: Harvard University Press, 2009.

Mulloy, D. J. *The World of the John Birch Society: Conspiracy, Conservatism, and the Cold War*. Nashville, Tenn.: Vanderbilt University Press, 2014.

Murphy, Ryan Patrick. "On Our Own : Flight Attendant Labor and the Family Values Economy." Ph.D. diss., University of Minnesota, 2010.

Nash, George. *The Conservative Intellectual Movement in America since 1945*. Wilmington: ISI Books, 2001.

Nickerson, Michelle M. *Mothers of Conservatism: Women and the Postwar Right*. Princeton, N.J.: Princeton University Press, 2012.

O'Connor, Alice. *Poverty Knowledge: Social Science, Social Policy, and the Poor in Twentieth-Century U.S. History*. Princeton, N.J.: Princeton University Press, 2002.

———. *Social Science for What?: Philanthropy and the Social Question in a World Turned Rightside Up*. New York: Russell Sage Foundation, 2007.

Perlstein, Rick. *Before the Storm: Barry Goldwater and the Unmaking of the American Consensus*. New York: Hill and Wang, 2001.

———. *Nixonland: The Rise of a President and the Fracturing of America*. New York: Scribner, 2008.

Phillips-Fein, Kim. "Conservatism: A State of the Field." *Journal of American History* 98, no. 3 (December 2011): 723–43.

———. *Invisible Hands: The Businessmen's Crusade against the New Deal*. New York: Norton, 2010.

Potter, Claire Bond, and Renee C. Romano, eds. *Doing Recent History: On Privacy, Copyright, Video Games, Institutional Review Boards, Activist Scholarship, and History That Talks Back.* Athens: University of Georgia Press, 2012.

Ribuffo, Leo P. "Why Is There So Much Conservatism in the United States and Why Do So Few Historians Know Anything about It?" *American Historical Review* 99, no. 2 (April 1994): 438–49.

Ricci, David M. *The Transformation of American Politics: The New Washington and the Rise of Think Tanks.* New Haven, Conn.: Yale University Press, 1993.

Rich, Andrew. *Think Tanks, Public Policy, and the Politics of Expertise.* Cambridge: Cambridge University Press, 2004.

Robin, Corey. *The Reactionary Mind: Conservatism from Edmund Burke to Sarah Palin.* New York: Oxford University Press, 2011.

Rodgers, Daniel T. *Age of Fracture.* Cambridge, Mass.: Harvard University Press, 2011.

Schneider, Gregory L. *Cadres for Conservatism: Young Americans for Freedom and the Rise of the Contemporary Right.* New York: New York University Press, 1999.

Schoenwald, Jonathan M. *A Time for Choosing: The Rise of Modern American Conservatism.* New York: Oxford University Press, 2002.

Schulman, Bruce J. *The Seventies the Great Shift in American Culture, Society, and Politics.* Cambridge: Da Capo, 2002.

Schulman, Bruce J., and Julian E. Zelizer, eds. *Rightward Bound: Making America Conservative in the 1970s.* Cambridge, Mass.: Harvard University Press, 2008.

Self, Robert O. *All in the Family: The Realignment of American Democracy since the 1960s.* New York: Hill and Wang, 2012.

Shoup, Laurence H., and William Minter. *Imperial Brain Trust: The Council on Foreign Relations and United States Foreign Policy.* New York: Authors Choice Press, 2004.

Skocpol, Theda. *Boomerang: Clinton's Health Security Effort and the Turn against Government in U.S. Politics.* New York: Norton, 1996.

Smith, James Allen. *Brookings at Seventy-Five.* Washington, D.C.: Brookings Institution Press, 1991.

———. *The Idea Brokers: Think Tanks and the Rise of the New Policy Elite.* New York: Free Press, 1993.

Stahl, Jason Michael. "Selling Conservatism: Think Tanks, Conservative Ideology, and the Undermining of Liberalism, 1945–Present." Ph.D. diss., University of Minnesota, 2008.

Stein, Judith. *Pivotal Decade: How the United States Traded Factories for Finance in the Seventies.* New Haven, Conn.: Yale University Press, 2010.

Sugrue, Thomas J. *The Origins of the Urban Crisis: Race and Inequality in Postwar Detroit.* Princeton, N.J.: Princeton University Press, 2005.

Suskind, Ron. *The Price of Loyalty: George W. Bush, the White House, and the Education of Paul O'Neill.* New York: Simon and Schuster, 2004.

Teles, Steven M. *The Rise of the Conservative Legal Movement: The Battle for Control of the Law.* Princeton, N.J.: Princeton University Press, 2012.

Waterhouse, Benjamin Cooper. "A Lobby for Capital: Organized Business and the Pursuit of Pro-Market Politics, 1967–1986." Ph.D. diss., Harvard University, 2009.

Williams, Daniel, and Laura Gifford, eds. *The Right Side of the Sixties.* New York: Palgrave Macmillan, 2012.

Zaretsky, Natasha. *No Direction Home: The American Family and the Fear of National Decline, 1968–1980.* Chapel Hill: University of North Carolina Press, 2007.

Zelizer, Julian E., ed. *The Presidency of George W. Bush: A First Historical Assessment.* Princeton, N.J.: Princeton University Press, 2010.

Index

Academia: balancing liberal, 48, 52, 135; Baroody on balancing, 63; Powell on balancing, 61–62; as primary component of New Class, 93

Adjunct scholars program of AEI, 57

Affordable Care Act (ACA), 199–200

Against All Enemies (Clarke), 190–91

Aid to Families with Dependent Children (AFDC), 164, 170–71

Ailes, Roger, 79

Alfred P. Sloan Foundation, 83

Al Qaeda, 187, 189, 190, 191, 192

Amadae, S. M., 206 (n. 16)

American Economic Association (AEA): concerns regarding, 27–28; early years of, 13, 14; and foundations of modern conservative think tank, 16–20; House Select Committee on Lobbying Activities investigation of, 21–24; incorporation and position of, 14–16; legislative analyses of, 20–21, 26–27; and "nonpartisan" think tank model, 9; Perlstein on, 207 (n. 42); revival of, 24–27; tensions of, 28–34. *See also* American Enterprise Institute (AEI)

American Enterprise Institute (AEI): and alliance with Heritage Foundation, 88; as balance to Brookings Institution, 51–55, 57; Buchanan on, 68–69; complications for Baroody at, 45–46; cultivates moderate image, 110; current position of, 201; decline of, 130–31; Feulner and Weyrich on, 71–73; foreign policy of, 174, 175, 180, 184; versus Free Society Association, 41, 44; growth of, 66–67, 80, 81, 173; Hoover Institution and, 37, 59; ideology of, 1, 66; and introduction of supply-side economics into marketplace of ideas, 96–97; issues addressed by, 78; as key marketer of "neoconservative" identity, 82–83; as media source, 181–82; National Energy Project, 64–66; as premier conservative think tank, 95; promotes deregulation, 83–85; promotes escalation of Iraq War, 197; relationship with Republican Party, 85–86; and repurposing of Powell Memo, 62–63; response to "policy crises," 64–65; shift to foundation support, 55–57; shift toward technocratic consensus, 34–35; use of donations, 57–58; as voice of reasonable conservatism, 81–82; Wanniski's residency at, 101–3; and Wanniski's *The Way the World Works*, 101. *See also* American Economic Association (AEA)

American hegemony, 177–80, 185–86

Americans for Democratic Action (ADA), 29

America Works, 166–67

Analysis and Research Association, 73

Anderson, Jack, 59

Anderson, Martin, 59

Antistatism: of American Economic Association, 15–16, 18–20, 28; of Brookings Institution, 9–10

Antitrust laws, 30, 139

Armitage, Richard, 183

Bacevich, Andrew, 176

Backgrounder, 89

Baker-Hamilton Iraq Study Group report, 196

Balance: American Enterprise Institute and, 48–49, 51–55; and liberal think tanks, 134–35; in marketplace of ideas, 47–48, 76, 174, 198–99; in Powell Memo, 61–63

Ball, Joseph, 20

Baroody, William J. Jr.: and decline of AEI, 130, 131; relationship with Ford, 85; takes over as head of AEI, 95; and Wanniski's *The Way the World Works*, 101

Baroody, William J. Sr.: and AEA as conservative institution, 31–34; and AEI as voice of reasonable conservatism, 81–82; on AEI ideology, 66; and alliance with Heritage Foundation, 88; and American Economic Association, 14; on Brookings Institution, 50–51; Business Council speech, 62–64; and Center for Strategic and International Studies, 175; collaboration with Nixon, 49; on competition, 66; complications at AEI, 45–46; and Free Society Association, 40–42, 44; and fundraising for AEI, 53–54; and Goldwater campaign, 37, 38–40; on grant from Ford Foundation, 56; and growth of AEI, 66–67, 80; on liberal influence on defense policy, 50; positions AEI as balance to Brookings Institution, 51–55; praise of, 27; promotes deregulation, 83–85; resists conservative support, 30, 31; and revival of AEA, 24–26; and shift to marketplace of ideas, 58; shift toward technocratic consensus, 34–35; and Supersonic Transport legislation, 71; and think tank ideology, 1–3; and undermining liberal consensus, 47; under-

standing of newly emergent conservative tropes, 48

Bennett, Bill, 183

Bergen, Peter, 184

Berkowitz, Herb, 109, 156

Bernstein, Michael, 9

"Beyond Repair" (Rothschild), 163–64

Bias: of American Economic Association, 22; of American Enterprise Institute, 54–55; of foundations, 55–56; of William Baroody and Glenn Campbell, 47

Bin Laden, Osama, 187, 188, 189, 190, 192

Bipartisanship: AEA equates nonpartisanship with, 19–20; liberal think tanks strive for, 88

Bjerre-Poulsen, Niels, 213–14 (n. 62)

Blumenthal, Sidney, 204 (n. 4)

Boaz, David, 131

Bolton, John, 183

Bork, Robert H., 102–3

Bozell, L. Brent, 38

Bremer, Paul, 194

Brookings Institution: activities of, seen as nonpartisan, 45–46; AEI as balance to, 51–55, 57; antistatist view of, 9–10; changes in, 127–28; current position of, 201; efforts to be seen as less partisan, 86–88, 137; energy project of, 65; and foreign policy following 9/11, 174, 193–94; and liberal consensus, 11; liberal funding of, 66; as linchpin in institutional liberalism, 49–50; as media source, 181, 197; political usefulness of, 50–51; post-World War II reorientation of, 10–11; as pre-World War II think tank, 7–8; as target of Buchanan's ire, 68

Brown, Lewis H., 15–16, 24

Buchanan, Pat, 67–69

Buckley, William F., Jr., 38

Burns, Arthur, 50

Bush, George H. W., 107, 155–56, 194

Bush, George W.: difficulties of, during second term, 196; foreign policy model for, 186–87; historiography of, 227 (n. 2); PNAC letter to, 189, 191–92

"Bush Doctrine, The," 192–93

Business Council speech, 62–64

Butler, Stuart, 156

Campbell, W. Glenn: and alliance with Heritage Foundation, 88; and Center for Strategic and International Studies, 175; as director of Hoover Institution, 35–37; and growth of Hoover Institution, 81; and revival of AEA, 24, 26; and undermining liberal consensus, 47

Capitalism, Powell on attack on, 60–61

Carter, Jimmy, 85

Cato Institute, 90–92, 124, 131, 181, 201

Center for American Progress, 201

Center for International Studies, 206 (n. 16)

Center for Public Integrity, 191

Center for Strategic and International Studies (CSIS), 175

Center for the Study of Government Regulation, 83–85

Cha, Ariana Eunjung, 195

Chandrasekaran, Rajiv, 195

Checks and balances, 40

Christ, Carl, 118

Civil rights demonstrations, 40

Clarke, Richard, 190–91

Clinton, Bill: DLC's disappointment with, 151–52; on DLC's endorsement of tax progressivity, 143; and health care reform debate, 156–57, 158, 159; and *Mandate for Change*, 150–51; moves toward New Democrat position, 152–53; PNAC letter to, 182–83; presidential campaign of, 148–50; psychological effect of 1994 midterm election on, 160, 161; State of the Union Address

of, 168–69; views on election of, 154–56; and welfare reform, 162–63, 167–72

Coalition Provisional Authority (CPA), 194

Cohen, Benjamin, 103

Cold War, 175–76

Cole, Juan, 184

Cole, Kenneth, 50

Communism, 11

Competitive Enterprise Institute, 191

Congdon, Tim, 120–21

"Congressmen Seek Experts' Advice as Self-Improvement Becomes a Fad" (Harwood and Stern), 50

Conservative think tanks: change in views, 1–3; foundations of modern, 16–20; mid-century, 13–16; postwar, 10–13; prewar, 7–9; scholarship on, 5–6; stages in development of, 3–5; studies on, 204 (n. 4)

Coors, Joseph, 55, 72–73, 79

"Corporate Role in the Decade Ahead, The" (Baroody), 1–2

Council on Foreign Relations, 175, 193, 197

Counter Terrorism Evaluation Group (CTEG), 192

Cove, Peter, 166, 167

Crane, Edward H. III, 91, 92, 94, 124

Critchlow, Donald, 8, 10, 17–18, 87–88, 127–28, 216 (n. 102)

Cuordileone, K. A., 206 (n. 17)

"Current Operations" handbook (AEA), 29

Defense policy and spending, 50, 107. *See also* Militarized foreign policy

"Delighted to be United" speech, 143

DeMint, Jim, 200

Democratic Leadership Council (DLC): and advancement of conservatism, 133, 135, 136; Clinton returns to agenda of, 152–53; and Clinton's presidential campaign,

Democratic Leadership Council
(DLC) (cont.)
    147–50; and defining Mainstream
    Democrat, 139–40; disappointment
    with Clinton, 151–52; disbanding of,
    201; as example of problem of
    demarcation, 221 (n. 2); financing
    of, 140; and foreign policy follow-
    ing 9/11, 176, 192–93; and health
    care reform debate, 156–60;
    influence of, in Democratic Party,
    140–41; and Mainstream Democrat
    and New Democrat identities,
    136–38; and New Democrat
    identity, 143–48; and passage of
    NAFTA, 153–54; policy program of,
    138–39, 141–43; Project for the New
    American Century compared to,
    179; psychological effect of 1994
    midterm election on, 160–61;
    Republican Majority Coalition
    modeled after, 155; and welfare
    reform, 162, 163, 165–67, 169–72
Democratic Party: and advancement of
    conservatism, 135–36; DLC's influence
    in, 140–41; psychological effect of
    1994 midterm election on, 160
DeMuth, Christopher, 131
Deregulation, 83–85
DiIulio, John, 187
Doherty, Brian, 91
Dole, Bob, 158
Dolny, Michael, 229 (n. 37)
Donahue, John, 147
Donnelly, Thomas, 189–90
Double marginalization, 220–21 (n. 1)

Economic Policy Institute (EPI), 151
Economic Recovery Tax Act (1981),
    118–21. See also Kemp-Roth Bill
Economists: at Brookings Institution,
    9–10, 11; at center of "nonpartisan"
    think tank model, 8–9
Edwards, John, 192–93
Edwards, Lee, 213 (n. 48)

Elite, 69
Ellwood, David, 169
Energy Policy Project (EPP), 65
Equilibrium. See Balance
Essays in Supply Side Economics
    (Heritage Foundation), 121–23
Executive Memorandum, 90
Expertise: in policymaking, 114;
    rejection of administrative
    technocratic, 194–96

Fairness and Accuracy in Reporting
    (FAIR), 180–81, 185, 191
Fair Deal program, 10, 20
Family Research Council, 191
Family values economy, 115–17
Federal Aid to Education—Boon or Bane?
    (Freeman), 26
"Federal Child Development: What's
    Developing?" (Heritage Founda-
    tion), 76
Federal Regulation of Lobbying
    Act, 22
Feith, Douglas, 192
Feulner, Edwin J. Jr.: attacks AEI's
    cultivation of neoconservative
    identity, 95; on Bush's defeat, 155;
    on conservatism of Heritage, 110;
    establishes Heritage Action, 200;
    and founding of Heritage Founda-
    tion, 70–73; on Heritage concept,
    75, 126; on Heritage Foundation
    fundraising, 128–29; Heritage's
    success under, 89–90; on Heritage's
    use of report cards, 123–24; and
    historical rewriting of supply-side
    economics, 121–22; on institutional
    role of Heritage, 111; and Mandate
    for Leadership, 108, 109; on NAFTA,
    156; on rise of big-government
    advocacy, 155
Finance Magazine, 82
Financial crisis (2008), 197
Fisher, Antony, 112
Ford, Gerald, 21, 82, 85

Ford Foundation, 36, 52, 56–57, 68
Foreign Affairs, 177
Foreign policy: for Bush administration, 186–87; during Cold War, 175–76; following 9/11 terrorist attacks, 187–95; neoconservative, 177–80; regarding Iraq, 182–84; in 2000s, 174–75; and use of think tanks in media, 180–82. *See also* Defense policy and spending; Militarized foreign policy
For-profit welfare-to-work firms, 165–66
Fox News, 180
Free enterprise, 11
Freeman, Roger, 26
Freeman, S. David, 65
"Free Society, The" address, 40
Free Society Association (FSA), 40–45
Friedman, Milton, 104–5, 156
From, Alvin (Al): and advancement of conservatism, 136; background of, 136; on Clinton and DLC agenda, 152; on Clinton as New Democrat, 171, 172; on Clinton as Old Democrat, 162; on Clinton's presidential campaign, 149–50; on Clinton's State of the Union Address, 168–69; and defining Mainstream Democrat, 139; on DLC sponsors, 140; and formation of DLC, 136–37; on health care reform, 157–58, 159; on Jackson's "Delighted to be United" speech, 143; and Mainstream Democrat and New Democrat identities, 138; on NAFTA and "New" versus "Old," 153; on "New Politics," 145; on 1994 midterm election, 160, 161
Fundraising: for American Economic Association, 25–26, 30–32; for American Enterprise Institute, 48, 53–54, 55–57, 130; for Free Society Association, 44; for Heritage Foundation, 89, 128–29; for Hoover

Institution on War, Revolution, and Peace, 36

Gender roles, Gilder on supply-side economics and, 116–17
Gergen, David, 152–53
Gilder, George, *Wealth and Poverty*, 112–17
Gilman, Nils, 206 (n. 16)
Gold standard, return to, 99, 105, 106, 119, 122
Goldwater, Barry, 27, 37–43, 44, 45, 209 (n. 88)
Greenberg, David, 197, 227 (n. 2)
Greenstein, Bob, 169

Haldeman, H. R., 49–50
Hall, Stuart, 205 (n. 9)
Harwood, Richard, 50
Hazlitt, Henry, 26
Health care reform, 156–60, 162–63, 199–200
Hegemony, American, 177–80, 185–86
Heritage Action, 200
Heritage Foundation: Bjerre-Poulsen on model of, 213–14 (n. 62); and conservative response to 1982 tax increases, 123–25; Coors as funder of, 55; current position of, 201; and decline of AEI, 130; dominance of, in marketplace of ideas, 131–32; espouses traditional conservative position, 117–18; as fast-acting policy shop, 95; financing of, 78–79; at forefront in conservative think tank world, 4–5; foreign policy of, 175, 186–87; founding of, 70–73; as fusionist institution, 214 (n. 70); growth of, 88–89, 128–29, 173; and health care reform, 157, 199–200; and historical rewriting of supply-side economics, 121–23; and identity formation and employment of young activists, 129; ideology and

Longer-range studies, of American Economic Association, 26, 30, 31
Luce, Clare Boothe, 128–29

MacLaury, Bruce K., 86–87, 127
Mainstream Democrat, 136–40
Mainstream Democrat, 142, 145, 146
Maloof, Michael, 192
Mandate for Change (PPI), 150–51, 156, 157
Mandate for Leadership (Heritage Foundation), 108–12, 150
Manhattan Institute for Policy Research, 112
Marketplace of ideas: and AEI as voice of reasonable conservatism, 81–82; AEI's shift toward, 48; balance in, 76, 198–99; challenges facing conservatives in, 67–68; conservative think tanks as integral to, 55; creation and promotion of, 47; effects of, 67; entrenchment of, 198; hegemony of, 134–35; and Heritage's *Mandate for Leadership*, 111; introduction of supply-side economics into, 96–101; promotion of elite conservative involvement in, 62–64; as replacement for liberal technocratic policymaking, 4, 92–95; rightward shift of, 127–28; shift toward, 51, 58, 198; in 2000s, 174
Marshall, Allen D., 24, 25, 28, 29
Marshall, Will, 150, 160, 163, 164–65, 166–67
Martin, Thomas E., 27
McCabe, Edward, 37, 38–39
McCain, John, 184
McConnell, Scott, 180
McCracken, Paul, 131
McCurdy, Dave, 161
McGovern, George, 145
McKenna, James, 77
Media: creation of conservative outlets, 172–73; increase in outlets,

174; as primary component of New Class, 93, 94; use of think tanks in, 180–82, 185, 197
Medvetz, Thomas, 13, 71, 204 (n. 4), 220–21 (nn. 1, 2)
Meese, Edwin, 109
Meyerson, Adam, 124
Mid-century conservative think tanks, 13–16
Midterm election (1994), 160–62
Militarized foreign policy, 175–77, 182–84, 189–95
Miller, James C., 84
Mishel, Lawrence, 169
Moffit, Robert E., 186–87
Moore, Catherine, 145
Moulton, Harold, 10
Moynihan, Daniel Patrick, 143, 170–71
Mundell, Robert, 97, 98–99
"Mundell-Laffer Hypothesis—A New View of the World Economy, The" (Wanniski), 98–99
Murdoch Rupert, 180
Mylroie, Laurie, 183–84, 188

Nash, George, 214 (n. 70)
National Energy Project, 64–66
"National Security Strategy of the United States of America," 192–93
Neal, Steve, 138
Neoconservatism, 66, 82–83, 95, 176, 177–80
New Class, the, 92–94
New Democrat, 146–47. See also *Mainstream Democrat*
New Democrat(s), 143–50; centrality of NAFTA in, 153–54; Clinton returns to agenda of, 152–53, 168; and DLC's disappointment with Clinton, 152; economic and cultural elements of identity, 167; as gendered identity, 161–62; and health care reform debate, 157; and militarized foreign policy, 176; and 1994 midterm election, 160–62;